The Independent Filmmaker's Law and Business Guide

Financing, Shooting, and Distributing
Independent and Digital Films

JON M. GARON

24.95

Library of Congress Cataloging-in-Publication Data

Garon, Jon M.

The independent filmmaker's law and business guide : financing, shooting, and distributing independent and digital films / Jon M. Garon.

p.   cm.

ISBN 1-55652-472-2 (alk. paper)

1. Motion picture industry—United States—Finance. 2. Motion pictures—United States—Distribution. 3. Motion picture industry—Finance—Law and legislation—United States. 4. Motion picture industry—Distribution—Law and legislation—United States. 5. Motion picture industry—Law and legislation—United States. 6. Independent filmmakers. I. Title.

PN1993.5.U6 G34 2002

384'.83'0973—dc21

2002012849

Cover and interior design: Monica Baziuk
Cover photograph: Tim Hall/Getty Images

Published by A Cappella Books
An imprint of Chicago Review Press, Incorporated
814 North Franklin Street
Chicago, Illinois 60610
ISBN 1-55652-472-2
Printed in the United States of America
5 4 3 2 1

Contents

PART ① MAKING A FILM COMPANY TO MAKE A MOVIE

PART (2) FILMING THE MOVIE—PREPRODUCTION AND PRODUCTION

PART ③ SELLING THE MOVIE—POSTPRODUCTION, DISTRIBUTION, AND MARKETING

Acknowledgments

↓

THE TWO PEOPLE whom I most wish to recognize for the completion of this book are unaware that I have written it, yet they were central to both the need for the book and many of its underlying themes. As a young attorney in southern California, I had the opportunity to work with two separate clients, Johnny Solomon and Peter Henry Schroeder, on a number of projects. Johnny is a brilliant comic and a talented producer. Peter Henry is a gifted writer and an electrifying director. Neither is famous, but both are extremely talented and resourceful. Through working with Johnny, Peter Henry, and many other clients, the most central theme of this book was developed early in my legal practice. That theme—*You cannot find opportunities; you must create them*—is central to many of the guiding principles for independent filmmakers. The experience I had working on independent film projects with these two individuals was the primary impetus for writing this book and for teaching hundreds of lawyers the art of trying to serve creative, driven individuals.

There are also a great many people I need to thank for the development and completion of this book, beginning with my longtime editor, critic, and wife, Stacy Blumberg Garon, Esq. Stacy has become an expert in most of the areas where I teach or write, simply because my urge to discuss these issues greatly exceeds her ability to discourage me from doing so. I wish to thank many colleagues at my law firm of Gallagher, Callahan and Gartrell, including Andrea Johnstone, Esq., Celia Wagner, Esq., and Lori

Cyr for their input. Many of my academic colleagues at Franklin Pierce
Law Center, including Susan Richey, Esq., Sophie Sparrow, Esq., Mary
Sheffer, Esq., Bill Hennessey, Esq., and Donna Jakusik, provided me with
helpful advice and ongoing encouragement. Greg Sergienko, Esq., of my
former law school, Western State University College of Law, provided
strong editing direction. Many other friends and colleagues shared their
experience and provided helpful suggestions. Jeremy Williams, Esq.,
deputy general counsel for Warner Bros.; Greg Hartmann (when he could
steal time from his newborn twins, Anna and Rachel); John Farrell, editor of Interface Tech News; Stanley B. Blumberg, Esq.; Wendy Baldinger;
Shimona Pratap Singh; and Deepak Nambier each added helpful comments, ideas, and material that have helped shape the text and encouraged
my completion of it.

    Finally, I must thank my sons, who seldom complained on those nights
I rushed through a goodnight song and knew when to entice me away from
the computer and back to the more important things. As this book is written for new filmmakers and artists, I dedicate it to the artists to come: my
sons, Avery and Noah, and their brother, Alec "Sasha" (*z"l*).

Introduction

↓

TECHNOLOGY IS CHANGING the way the entertainment industry does business. For film distributors, new technologies may change the system of print distribution that has existed since the end of the 19th century. Internet movie sites such as ifilm.com, AtomFilms.com, and inetfilm.com are introducing new distribution opportunities for short films that will only increase as delivery continues to improve.[1] Peer-to-peer services including Morpheus have advanced beyond Napster.com, allowing for file sharing of feature-length films.

Technology is also changing the medium. Film, the standard medium of the feature motion picture since its inception, is starting to be replaced with digital recording devices. Proponents of digital production like *Star Wars* creator George Lucas focus on the greater flexibility and reduced costs associated with state-of-the-art digital image recording. Since today's special effects rely heavily on digital manipulation of the image, capture of the image directly on the digital medium eliminates one step of the process, adding greater speed and flexibility.

Most filmmakers cannot rely on state-of-the-art equipment, however, and instead use rented equipment or less expensive alternatives. This is where the real revolution can take place. Digital equipment is creating a new market for feature length and short films that can be made for thousands rather than hundreds of thousands or millions of dollars. The

Internet and recordable DVDs create a low-cost distribution method for these projects that expand the potential audience well beyond the traditional college campus and film festival circuit. At a minimum, this will create a new opportunity for rookie filmmakers to showcase their skills to the traditional industry.

Despite the newfound access to digital equipment, a host of artistic, business, and legal issues impacts the way movies are made. Some of these traditional "rules" are also changing because of constant change to intellectual property laws, changes in industry standards, and the effect of technology on every other aspect of the movie business.

This book and the associated Web site are designed to provide guidance on the rocky waters for independent motion picture production. The principles are relevant to short films, student projects, and large-scale productions alike.

This book serves as a legal and business guide because making a movie, even a small-budget, backyard production, is a long process of negotiating and signing contracts; complying with labor, health, safety, and revenue codes; recognizing and protecting the rights of artists, writers, musicians, performers, bystanders, and others; and becoming a specialist in dozens of areas of business and law in a matter of weeks.

A. The Role of the Book

This book is a guide, not a blueprint. At some point in the process, the filmmaker must contact an attorney or someone equally experienced. This book is designed to help filmmakers, students, and others interested in filmmaking understand the practical realities of the industry. The book should save the filmmaker a lot of money in legal fees by eliminating the hours an attorney would have to spend explaining the items discussed in the book.

The book may also be of use to attorneys. Very little "entertainment law" has anything to do with the process of making a film. If the filmmaker has a working relationship with a good attorney, particularly a corporate or business attorney, give her the book to highlight those few areas in which filmmaking is different from other business work. This will reduce the amount of time the lawyer will need to spend and may help encourage a reduction in the lawyer's fees.

The book does not constitute the practice of law or provide legal advice that can be relied upon as authoritative. This information is general in nature, and should only be used in conjunction with a licensed attorney, properly familiar with the issues presented in the specific legal matter in question.

This book identifies particular individuals, firms, and companies. Nothing herein constitutes an endorsement of these entities or of their services and cannot be relied upon as the legal basis for engaging such services.

Although many of the companies listed are the largest or most visible in the respective field, the names are used either for illustrative purposes or to provide a starting point for the reader's own research. Conversely, the failure to appear in the book should not be deemed a negative assessment of any particular product, service, or organization.

The book uses some terms that might not seem appropriate. The most striking is to call the digital creation of a motion picture "filmmaking" and the creators "filmmakers." The choice reflects the history of the craft rather than the medium. Historically based terms evolve new meanings. Americans still use the term *album* for a collection of songs recorded and sold together as a compilation, although the cardboard album that held a collection of 78-rpm records has been long abandoned as the distribution mechanism for music. Motion pictures that run longer than an hour will be "feature films" long after the celluloid and optical processes have first assistant directored into distant memory like cardboard albums.

The other language issue is that of gender. Both men and women comprise the legions of writers, directors, producers, actors, and others vital to the creation of an independent film. Gender and racial stereotypes that have historically tended to create barriers for women or minority filmmakers are eliminated when the only issue is whether the buyer of the film likes the final product. Use of both male and female pronouns is important to reinforce this point, but so is clarity. This book will refer to the filmmaker with the masculine pronoun in half the chapters, with the feminine in the others. Hopefully, this balance will achieve both goals.

B. Independent and Guerrilla Filmmaking

Independent movie making is sometimes hard to define. Technically, an independent feature is any film not made at one of the major studios (Sony, Warner Bros., Universal, Disney, Paramount, Fox, and MGM/UA). This would include such films as *American Psycho* distributed by Lions Gate, *Girlfight* distributed by Sony Screen Gems, *Run Lola Run* from Sony Pictures Classics, and many others. Many of these independent film companies are actually owned by the major studios. Miramax, the leading independent film producer, is a division of the Walt Disney Company, New Line Cinema is owned by AOL Time Warner, and Screen Gems is owned by Sony. Despite the increasingly close relationship between the major studios and the independent film companies, the nature of the filmmaking remains much more personal for films made in the independent marketplace.

Guerrilla filmmaking is a special subspecies of independent filmmaking. The guerrilla filmmaker is generally a storyteller with a vision. Sources for guerrilla films come from the stage, from life experience, or from literature that transfixes the filmmaker and makes the production the reason for being. Spike Lee, producer/director/star of *Bamboozled* and *Do the Right Thing*, Jim Jarmusch, producer/director of *Night on Earth*, and John Sayles, producer/director of *Eight Men Out* and *Matewan*, are a few of the more prominent guerrilla artists, but many established filmmakers, including Joel and Ethan Coen, Keenan Ivory Wayans, David Zucker, and Jerry Abrams, among others, created their first films as guerrilla filmmakers.

The essence of the guerrilla filmmaker is twofold. First, the filmmaker must need, desire, and crave to bring *his* movie—not any movie, his movie—to the screen. Second, the filmmaker must have this craving and desire despite the fact that there is no money, social network, business connections, studio interest, or external support available to make this possible.

Another way to describe the guerrilla filmmaker is to characterize him like any other filmmaker—only more so. The guerrilla filmmaker is an entrepreneur with the desire to make a film rather than start a business. Like the typical entrepreneur, the guerrilla filmmaker is an extreme risk taker. By contrast, the traditional independent filmmaker described in this book is a more cautious businessperson than the guerrilla, typically more willing to make reasonable compromises to make his film. Both the traditional independent filmmaker and the guerrilla filmmaker will use loans to make their films, but only the guerrilla would be willing to mortgage his house—or the houses of friends and family. Wherever possible, this book will try to outline the path for the independent filmmaker, but highlight where the traditional filmmaker will choose not to tread. Whenever possible, it will also note those few guideposts available for the guerrilla filmmaker as he cuts his own trail.

Independent filmmaking, whether traditional or guerrilla, is different from traditional studio production because, unlike many commercial films, the film dictates the package. A guerrilla production will not be designed to accommodate stars, investors, or prior contractual commitments. It is less likely to be changed in response to audience response cards. Instead, it may be shaped by opportunities—available locations, actors, situations, or other organic elements—that can enhance or even redirect the story. As a result, many of the steps in the filmmaking process are different from commercial product. Still, when everything works, the resulting films are the best the industry can create.

C. Commercial Web Sites

Although there may seem to be little relationship between guerrilla filmmaking and the streaming of digital media on a small Web site, many of the business and legal issues remain the same. Like any film, the legal ownership in the content of the media must be properly secured. Music will require permissions and licenses separate from the visual elements. The Web site owner—like the film producer or distributor—must be confident that the material does not violate the copyright of any other parties, and that the material included does not defame any living person. If the Web site owner and the copyright holder of the streaming video are not the same, then the same issues will arise regarding the scope of the distribution license in terms of media, territory, length, payment, and accounting. As such, this book will deal with the issues common to Web site streaming video throughout the text. In addition, the creative and business discussions in the book may help the Web site owner to improve the quality of the video and enhance the production values on the site.

D. Who Is the Filmmaker?

Filmmaking is a communal process. The filmmaker becomes parent, artist, instructor, boss, and police to the small army that joins hands to bring the filmmaker's vision to the screen. Each project requires a strong writer, producer, and director to shape the process. Typically, the writer or director takes charge as the filmmaker.

The filmmaker stands at the heart of every production, the individual who serves as the spine and brain of the production. Productions vary, but generally the filmmaker will be the producer or director and perhaps occasionally the writer. It is important that the filmmaker on the team be recognized early. Typically a single individual holds the role, but collaborative teams may share the duty. The writer, director, and producer each have a very different set of responsibilities, and priorities, so there remains a constant tension among the three areas. Ultimately, the filmmaker will dictate how those tensions are resolved.

The filmmaker plays a dual role because he brings together both the creative and business aspects of the film. In independent films, the professional, business, and legal choices serve to improve the creative process. Without the business structure, casts will not be paid, locations will not be available, and the film cannot be exhibited. A coherent business structure that makes organizational sense must exist, be clear to everyone involved in the production, and be utilized throughout the planning and production process. The filmmaker must lead the team and, like a good captain, know how and when to rally the troops.

E. A Chronology—From Idea to Academy Awards

Independent filmmaking generally begins with a single idea, an original concept that will serve as the core of the film project. The owner of that idea may be a writer who can shape the idea into a written script, a director who can visualize how to tell that story, a performer who knows how to portray a character central to the story, or a producer who knows where to find the elements for telling the story. The originator of the idea starts from his strength and shares the idea with the other creative people necessary to translate the idea into a story and the story into a screenplay. At this stage, many of the legal and business choices are already made. One individual becomes the "owner" and others become employees of that owner (or the parties agree to work as partners, or choose more complex legal relationships). The idea is translated from something not protected by copyright into an expressive work that cannot be copied without the owner's consent. Although very early in the process, this is where much of the legal and business planning must take place. Rights to the story must be acquired, the production entity formed, budgets penciled in, and some employment commitments started.

Once the organizational approach has been selected and the script developed, the creative process moves into high gear. A script can be shared with potential investors, shown to actors, entered into contests, and used to introduce the project to the public. The script is protected by copyright from theft (although the ideas and general plot concept will not be protected by copyright). Fundraising can range from simple loans from the filmmaker's family to very sophisticated financial transactions. Financial decisions must be made carefully to protect the growth and success of the project.

A successful script will gain momentum for the project. If the filmmaker is not the director, then a director will be selected. With a working script, the director and producer can agree on a budget for the film that can range from the cost of buying (or even borrowing) the cheapest of cameras to a budget in excess of $100 million for an effects-laden film with well-known stars. The budget may also dictate where filming will take place. Locations are selected or rejected based on the cost of filming in that location, availability, and the location's ability to further the story.

The director, having accepted a working script and projected budget, can begin to make casting choices. Actors are auditioned for roles or interviewed for parts. Since casting is often about chemistry and the interaction of actors with each other, making offers so the right combination of people will accept is a logistical puzzle. At the same time, the director needs to assemble the creative crew behind the camera. A cinematographer and set, lighting, and costume designers are hired to refine the decisions tentatively made by the producer and director.

Throughout this process, money is needed. The director, writer, and producer may require payments during this preproduction process. Expenses begin to mount for the budgeting, casting, and design work. As the money is found, so are the additional people necessary to build the project. Writers, producers, directors, director of photography, designers, and cameramen are hired and added to the team. The script will undergo changes to accommodate the available locations, the assembled cast, and the production team's new insights. With the selection of locations, the rental of equipment, financing, casting, and final revisions underway, the movie production can begin.

Preproduction ends and principal photography begins with the first day of filming. Each day a few more minutes of film footage are captured. Filming is often done out of sequence, based on weather, available locations or sets, cast, or other script requirements. Typically, the day's work is reviewed that night on videotape as dailies or rushes to be sure the production is ready to move on to the next scene. As the footage accumulates, rough editing of the film may be taking place. Finally, after weeks or months of filming, principal photography ends.

With the filming completed, the filmmaker is halfway home. The next stage of the process is postproduction. The footage is edited into a cohesive, linear film that hopefully captures the filmmaker's original idea in a visual story. A composer creates a musical score to highlight the story and enhance the effectiveness of the film. Sound effects, songs, and special effects are added to the film as each edit shapes the project. The finished film, complete with sound, is finally ready for marketing and distribution.

If the film is an independent film, often no prior arrangements exist for the marketing and distribution of the film. Since the filmmaker usually does not do marketing and distribution, the filmmaker shows the film to potential distributors and negotiates for payments based on an advance and a portion of the royalties. Exposure for an independent film often comes from film festivals or film markets, but independent filmmakers can also send videotape copies of their film to potential distributors without waiting for entry into competitions.

At this point the distributor takes over, creating or changing the marketing of the film. If the film runs in movie theaters in the United States, it becomes eligible for a number of award competitions. If the film remains as potent on the screen as the original concept that spawned it, the filmmaker's peers in the industry will vote to nominate the film for an award in the Academy of Motion Picture Arts and Sciences. Following exhibition in movie theaters in the United States, the film will be distributed in movie theaters throughout the rest of the world. After theatrical distribution comes distribution on videotape and through pay-per-view cable television. Approximately a year after the theatrical distribution comes premium cable showings (on HBO or Showtime), then broadcast television, and finally basic cable. If successful, the movie could be shown for decades—or even centuries—to come.

Please remember this book when you thank the Academy for your Oscar.

At each stage in this process, the filmmaker and the team that make up the filmmaking process make hundreds of artistic, business, and legal decisions. Some of those choices are unique to the particular film. Other choices, however, have been faced by many filmmakers before.

Most important, filmmaking is a long, complicated, and complex process, involving thousands of choices, strong personalities, and emotional decisions. Given the pressures of too little time and money, even small mistakes exacerbated by poor communication or haphazard planning can cause disaster. Being proactive, anticipating and planning for future crises, and understanding the consequences of the choices made can really improve the process, resulting in a better movie on the screen and a greater chance of the movie finding its audience. With a more in-depth, sophisticated understanding of the complete filmmaking process, some of the mistakes that impede a filmmaker's success can be avoided or minimized. To assist the filmmaker, each stage in the process will be analyzed in detail to outline the common choices available to the filmmaker and provide a resource for making the most appropriate decision under the circumstances.

Making a Film Company to Make a Movie

The Film Concept

COMIC BOOKS, PLAYS, newspapers, and the imagination of the filmmaker are among the many sources that serve as the basis for new film concepts. Novels, films, comics, and other literary works are protected by copyright, so the filmmaker must acquire permission to make a film using these properties. True stories are free for the filmmaker to exploit, but the subject of these stories may still retain some rights of privacy and the right not to be defamed or injured by the film. By carefully crafting agreements to purchase the rights to make the film, the filmmaker can maximize her flexibility in storytelling while minimizing her risk of future legal problems.

A. Sources

Anything can become a source for a good film idea. From a classic novel to a taxicab,[1] no bad source exists. Most films derive from original ideas, novels, short stories, music, stage plays, and true events. The source material should not limit the creative choices of the filmmaker. From a business and legal perspective, however, each of these sources has certain advantages and certain limitations.

1. Original Ideas

From a legal perspective, original ideas are the easiest source material to develop. No preconditions or limitations exist on ownership of an idea, so there are very few constraints on the filmmaker. As long as the idea is truly conceived by the filmmaker, then the resulting story, which uses only fictional characters and plot points, can be developed without limitation.

Borrowing general ideas from other sources does not violate copyright laws, but such use may run afoul of the filmmaker's preexisting duties under agreements not to use ideas that have been developed by other people. Detailed plots are more than mere ideas, and those are protected by copyright.

The business disadvantage of basing a film on an original idea is that the public has no preexisting awareness of the film project, making it more difficult to market the story. This may also increase the difficulty in raising capital for the production of the film or developing the film's marketing campaign. Despite the ultimate success of the movies, filmmakers and distributors had less difficulty promoting the film *Ali* than earlier boxing films *Rocky* or *On the Waterfront*.

2. True Events

True events are also a tremendous source of material. Whether presented in documentary form or dramatized, true events have a natural resonance. Audiences seem drawn to true stories, which in turn provide excellent marketing opportunities. True stories cannot be "owned" by anyone. The First Amendment grants the filmmaker the right to retell a true story using his own expression.

For the guerrilla filmmaker, many true stories need to be told to promote ideas and impact society. Given these positive attributes, true stories are a natural source for material. A movie such as *Boys Don't Cry*, which highlights rape and murder, is compelling because of the awful truth it reveals. As such, the filmmaker had a story she needed to tell. Nonetheless, there are important legal limitations. Unless the people portrayed in the movie have given their permission or the story's truth can otherwise be established, the filmmaker risks being sued for libel.

Despite the care taken by filmmakers, movies such as *Boys Don't Cry*, *The Perfect Storm*, and *The Insider* are just a few of the many films that resulted in threatened or filed legal actions over unflattering portrayals. While it is often not possible to gain permission from a person to make a film out of a true story—particularly if the story paints the person in an unflattering manner—the filmmaker can limit risk. Careful choices made throughout the writing and filming process, as well as contractual agreements with some of the parties involved in true stories, will allow the filmmaker to reduce exposure to crippling lawsuits or liability that could scare away distributors from otherwise brilliant films.

3. Novels and Short Stories

Novels, novellas, and short stories are a staple of feature filmmaking. Of the various forms of existing literature, the short story is the best dramatic form to transfer to film. Most films tell simple stories in a visual, dramatic form. Time constraints and other limitations on motion pictures tend to oversimplify novels. Still, both books and short stories are often purchased as the basis for films. The business advantage of using literature is that the story is known and may be useful to attract financing and talent. The story can also serve as an introduction to the film's marketing campaign.

The filmmaker will need to purchase the film rights to any book or short story protected by copyright. The author of the story or the author's estate generally holds these rights. The filmmaker may choose to purchase all rights in the story by acquiring the author's copyright ownership, or he may limit the purchase to a limited license granting permission to make and distribute a single film production. If the story is based on true events, then the acquisition of rights must include both the story and any additional rights necessary to fictionalize a true story.

4. Song Titles and Music

Song titles and musical lyrics can also serve as the creative element behind a film. The benefit of a recognized song is increased recognition for the movie title. If the song is famous, then the movie appears famous as well. Songs may be less expensive than other source materials as a method of purchasing instant recognition, particularly if the song has not been heavily licensed for use in commercials or other film production. Neither film titles nor song titles are protected by copyright. Oftentimes, however, the titles are protected as trademarks, so permission is still generally required.

In addition, to include the song in the soundtrack, copyright permission to use the song must be licensed from the songwriter or the songwriter's publisher. If any popular recording of the song is to be used in the film, then the permission of the record producer or record distributor, often called the label, is also required. Permission is generally given in exchange for a licensing fee. Separate permission is required if the filmmaker plans to release a soundtrack album.

5. Stage Plays

Plays are another popular source of film ideas. Legally, plays are treated just like novels and short stories. Unfortunately, because plays tend to use stylized language rather than visual impact for the drama, translating them to film may be much more difficult than one would expect. Some films, such as the Oscar-winning *Driving Miss Daisy*, transfer successfully, but many are financial or artistic disappointments. In the world of guerrilla filmmaking, plays serve as a mixed blessing. The stage history helps to raise funds and draw media attention for marketing, but films based on plays are often treated differently from other films, and this may limit some of the financial potential and turn off distributors. Plays are like film remakes in the sense that the story has been told, and audiences already have experience with the story.

6. Movies

Increasingly, filmmakers turn to the vaults of the studios for interesting stories to retell. Remakes have instant recognition for investors and audiences. Occasionally a remake may be created as a shot-by-shot reproduction, as was done with *Psycho* by Gus Van Sant based on the Alfred Hitchcock classic. More typically, however, a remake takes substantial liberty updating the story and characters.

Remakes may be the most difficult projects to legally acquire. Since the film that is the subject of the remake may itself have involved the acquisition of short story or book rights, all appropriate permissions must be obtained. Further, since film companies often change hands or sell their libraries, researching the chain of title for a film may prove difficult. If, for example, a 1940s film sold the right to distribute the original film on television, then the television rights to the original film must be reacquired if the definition of film in the contract included remakes and sequels.

B. Copyright Limitations on Source Material

If the source material is not original, it is quite likely that someone else owns some or all of the rights[2] to the material. Laws affecting copyright, trademarks, privacy, libel, and contract provide a number of ways to limit the availability of source material, limiting access to the filmmaker. The most important of these legal protections of source material is copyright.[3] A major expansion of copyright law in recent years has turned copyright into a powerful source of protection for authors and artists in all media.

For independent filmmakers, copyright serves as both a blessing and a curse. It provides a source of ownership and protection in the work that is made, but it also creates barriers to the source material that may be used in creating a new film. Filmmakers find themselves on both sides of copyright transactions. They need to acquire source material and need to license their finished products.

1. Exclusive Rights Under Copyright

Copyright provides an author the rights of ownership for his original work. As owner of the copyrighted work, the copyright holder has the exclusive right to reproduce the work, publicly display the work, distribute copies of the work, publicly perform the work, and prepare derivative works.[4]

> A 'derivative work' is a work based upon one or more preexisting works, such as a translation, musical arrangement, dramatization, fictionalization, motion picture version, sound recording, art reproduction, abridgment, condensation, or any other form in which a work may be recast, transformed, or adapted. A work consisting of editorial revisions, annotations, elaborations, or other modifications, which, as a whole, represent an original work of authorship, is a 'derivative work.'[5]

A film based on a preexisting copyrighted work is a derivative work, including a film based on a novel, play, or earlier film. As examples, the Hitchcock thriller *Rear Window* is a derivative work based on the short story "It Had to Be Murder" by Cornell Woolrich.[6] The filmed version of *My Fair Lady* is an adaptation of the Broadway musical of the same name by Lerner and Lowe, which was itself based on the George Bernard Shaw play *Pygmalion*.[7]

The exclusive rights of the copyright holder may be licensed to others. A filmmaker receives permission to use another author's work by obtaining a license from the current copyright holder for the work. The license may be given free of charge, but more typically the copyright holder will require a fee in the form of an immediate payment, the right to receive some percentage of the proceeds from the film, or some combination of immediate payment and future royalties. For example, the author of the short story "The Paleontologist" licensed the first publication of the story in a science fiction magazine, but retained all other rights. As copyright holder, the author may grant permission for the story to be adapted into a stage play while retaining the rights to any filmed version of the story. The author can then choose to sell the movie rights to the short story for a payment such as $5,000 and 1 percent of the gross profits of the film. If the film producer agrees to those terms, the short story author will sign a license agreement that transfers the film rights in exchange for the agreed-upon payment.

If the author is granting exclusive rights to use the copyrighted work, the assignment must be in writing, dated, and signed.[8] Nonexclusive permission may be granted either orally or in writing. As discussed below, the scope of the license depends on the language used in the contract. Since the language is so important, the license should be in writing, with a signature and date, even if it is a nonexclusive assignment. The written form of the agreement creates solid documentation of the transaction. Also, it is important to think ahead. When the time comes to sell the film to a distributor, the distributor wants assurances that others cannot make a film that will compete directly. If the source of the film is based on nonexclusive licenses, then the risk of competition goes up and the value of the film goes down.

The exclusive rights to performance and display allow the filmmaker to control the exhibition of the finished film. As copyright holder, the filmmaker can control who has the power to show the film. This exclusive right may be further limited in any fashion the filmmaker and distributor agree on. The limits may be geographic regions by country, state, or city; they may be limitations on time, so the contract lasts for only a short period; or the limitations may be based on the medium, so one exhibitor is selected for theaters while a second is selected for video and a third for the Internet.

In practice, this means the filmmaker may choose to allow an Internet site a short trial exhibition, limited in writing to a stated period of time, such as one month, as a way to see if there is any interest by distributors of video, broadcast, or even theaters in the United States or throughout the world. The one-month trial, run without publicity, may serve as an inexpensive method of distributing advance copies of the film to possible purchasers. When the trial period ends, the filmmaker can renew the contract or sell the rights to others, depending on the response of purchasers and the public.

2. The Term of the U.S. Copyright and the Public Domain

Copyrights in works created after January 1, 1978, last for 70 years after the author's death, or 95 years if the author is a corporation. For any work created before that date, the time period varies depending on the date the work was first published and the laws applicable. For example, all works more than 95 years old have fallen into the "public domain." Public domain is the term used for anything that has had its copyright expire or was never copyrighted. Anything less than 95 years old must be carefully screened before it is assumed to be in the public domain.[9]

Congress has gradually extended the length of copyright over time. The last extension, known as the Sonny Bono Copyright Term Extension Act, added 20 years to the length of copyrights for works that had not already fallen into the public domain. Before the Sonny Bono Copyright Term Extension Act, the length of copyrights for works created before 1978 had been extended to 75 years. After 1998, the term became 95 years. This means that works 75 years old in 1998 are in the public domain—all works published in or before 1923 are free for use in the United States without copyright protection. Any work that was published beginning in 1924 may still have been protected by copyright when the term was extended, in which case, the work will retain copyright protection until at least 2019.

Because the length of copyright has only recently been increased, extra care must be taken to determine whether a work is covered by copyright. Before substantial investment is made using a public domain work, the history of the copyright should be analyzed.

In addition, copyright protection has been expanded in length and scope in many other countries. As a result, there is no absolute guarantee that a particular work is in the public domain worldwide no matter how old. While famous works such as published novels by Charles Dickens or Cervantes are clearly in the public domain and free for all filmmakers to adapt, most works published in the twentieth century and unpublished materials potentially hundreds of years older may remain protected by copyright in the United States or abroad.

Plays by Shakespeare are in the public domain because they were written before copyright existed. Similarly, a play such as George Bernard Shaw's *Pygmalion* (made into a number of films and adapted for the musical *My Fair Lady*) is now in the public domain because the play's copyright expired in 1988 in both the United States and Great Britain.[10] Copyright provides only limited rights to published works. Once a copyright has expired in the United States and abroad, the filmmaker is free to utilize that material as the source or basis for his film.

3. Copyright as a Barrier to the Film

While copyright is the primary source of protection for filmmakers, it is also a curse. Many potential sources for material are also copyrighted. For the independent filmmaker or Web site publisher, the ability to use public domain material has tremendous advantages. The material is free. There is no need to ask permission to use the material. There are no delays waiting for a response to the request. The material can be altered without the need for any additional consent. There are some rules of thumb regarding which works are freely available in the public domain and can be used as source material and which works must be more carefully scrutinized. Any published materials older than 95 years are in the public domain and can be used freely as source material, at least in the United States. This includes all plays, novels, newspaper stories, and most published music.[11]

In many instances these source materials were never protected by copyright outside the United States. Unpublished materials are more likely to retain some copyright protection because the copyright laws had previously granted unlimited copyright for unpublished works.

For some materials—particularly those of foreign authors or of unpublished works—the reliance on the public domain will always include a significant amount of risk. For example, a novel may have fallen into the public domain in the United States, but may still be protected by copyright in another country, such as Canada or France. Unfortunately, there are no central registries of copyrights, so the status of a novel published in Canada, Europe, or elsewhere in the world must be researched in each country. In Europe, the situation is even more complex because the European Union member countries are required to provide the greatest protection to any European citizen. As a result, copyrights that might otherwise have fallen into the public domain in those countries with shorter copyright terms are now automatically extended to the longer German copyright period of life of the author plus seventy years. As a general rule, therefore, a European work cannot be assumed to be in the public domain unless it was published more than seventy years after the death of the author. For any other work, expensive and time-consuming research is conducted to determine the status of the copyright. To limit this expense somewhat, the filmmaker may wish to limit the research to the most important major foreign film markets, such as Canada, England, France, Spain, Italy, Japan, and Mexico.

Despite their limitations, public domain plays serve as a particularly valuable source for independent filmmaking because the story, dramatic structure, characters, and many other literary elements are provided for the filmmaker. Translating public domain plays into film may serve as an excellent method of learning filmmaking, creating a solid self-education program for the student in filmmaking.

4. Subject Matter of Copyright

Copyright ownership covers, with limited exceptions, "original works of authorship fixed in any tangible medium of expression."[12] Fixation is merely the requirement that the expression be recorded in some manner. The material can be written, recorded, videotaped, filmed, digitized, or otherwise fixed in something entirely new. Screenplays, novels, and all writings are fixed as soon as the words are typed into a computer's memory or written on paper. A stand-up comedian's act is not protected by copyright unless he writes it out or records his performance. A written recording, however, can be in shorthand. An improvisational rehearsal process is not protected unless the stage manager's notes carefully record the session, or the session is videotaped. Sheet music is sufficient to protect a new musical score and a detailed choreographer's notation will be enough to protect a new dance. There is no requirement that the copyrighted work have a copyright symbol © or other notice of copyright.[13]

5. Ideas

Copyright does not protect the underlying idea or concept, however, only the expression of such idea.[14] In practice, this means that basic plots, ideas, or general subjects are not protected by copyright. No one can own "boy meets girl" since the idea is the basis for thousands of plots. The written or filmed story of the boy and girl, including the description of scenes, the dialogue, and the narration, is protected by copyright once it has been fixed on paper or in digital memory. The line between the idea and the expression of an idea is often a difficult one to conceptualize. Dialogue is expression, but copyright covers more than just a film's dialogue. Stopping a runaway bus is an idea. Add well-developed characters, a number of plot twists, and interesting locations and the expression embodied becomes the movie *Speed*. A man-made monster run amok is an idea. Add a struggling scientist, his love interest, and unsolved local murders and it remains an idea. Both *Frankenstein* and *Dr. Jekyll and Mister Hyde* fit the bill. Specific characters and plot twists that are unique to the story and its characters help transform the idea into protectable expression. Dialogue, unless it comes from trial transcripts or other public sources, is invariably expression.

6. Matters Not Protected by Copyright

In addition to ideas, copyright does not cover titles, short phrases such as "I'll be back" or "Hasta la vista, baby," the typeface that may appear in the film's credits, facts, historical information, or works in the public

domain. Any filmmaker is free to use them without fear of copyright violations. The Robert Wise movie *The Hindenburg*, based on the destruction
of the famous German zeppelin, is fair game, even though the facts used
were first published as a rather speculative, conspiracy-based story
instead of the official facts.[15] The same is true of factually-based movies
about the sinking of the *Titanic*, the assassinations of President Kennedy
and Malcolm X, and the many other historical dramas.

C. Other Legal Limitations on Source Material

In addition to the laws of copyright, there are a number of other legal concepts that limit the free use of materials. Most of these limitations can be
overcome if permission is granted from the rights holder. Whether substantial payment is necessary for the permission will depend on the nature
of the rights sought, the size of the film being made, and the relationship
between the rights holder and the filmmaker.

1. Trademarks

Trademarks are words or symbols that identify the goods or services of a
business in commerce. They range from simple product names such as Diet
Coke®, to identifying marks such as the roar of the MGM lion, or the pink
color of Dow Corning roof insulation. Trademarked products are often
licensed for use in films, providing the filmmaker free access to the product in exchange for permission to film. Increasingly, many product man-
ufacturers will pay for the opportunity to have their products featured.

Unauthorized use of another's trademark is a potential problem for
filmmakers but not automatically prohibited. Fair Use and Free Speech
doctrines require that the filmmaker's speech rights be given some flexibility in projecting his message. Both state and federal law, however, protect trademarks from disparagement, meaning that some forms of
embarrassment or criticism are prohibited, so that the trademark holder
could sue for damages or to stop the release of the film. If the unauthorized use of trademarks is to be featured in an independent film, the use
must be made carefully, in consultation with the filmmaker's attorneys.

2. Misappropriation and Idea Protection

Legal protection for "the idea" remains the hottest area in intellectual property law today. Fueled by the high technology fields and trade secret issues, the legal limits of when someone is liable for the use of another's idea have yet to be clearly defined.[16] The safest way to hear new ideas is to be sure a release is signed, clearly stating that, while the filmmaker will not violate the copyright, many similar ideas are often presented, and that the filmmaker cannot guarantee the protection of the ideas. For the writer the safest suggestion is to refrain from sharing ideas until they have been developed sufficiently to have copyright protection.

3. Defamation

A statement is defamatory if "it tends so to harm the reputation of another as to lower him in the estimation of the community or to deter third persons from associating or dealing with him."[17] At common law, a statement was defamatory if it held one out for hatred, ridicule, or contempt. Only a living person may be defamed. A related doctrine known as trade libel applies to businesses. To be defamatory in the United States, the person alleging the defamation must prove that the statement is false as well as that it is harmful, that it pertains to the person suing, and that it has been published to someone other than the person suing.

Once a person has died, his heirs may not pursue the claim. Any publication to a third person, such as through publication in a script, on a Web site, or through sending a letter or e-mail, will give rise to liability if the publication is a false defamatory statement of or concerning the defamed person. Republishing a false defamatory statement will give rise to a new claim for defamation. As a result, a filmmaker is responsible for any defamatory material in the work he creates, licenses, or borrows.

Filmmakers face different legal challenges depending on the nature of the party who objects to the characterization or statements. Public officials, such as the president or state officeholders, and public figures such as O. J. Simpson or Ralph Nader, can only win a lawsuit for defamation against the filmmaker if the filmmaker is found to have published defamatory material intentionally—with knowledge it was false—or recklessly—with reckless disregard toward the truth or falsity of the statement.[18] If the publication is about a private individual involving some mat-

ter of public interest, then the filmmaker can be liable if he is merely negligent in failing to ascertain the truth[19] or in the manner in which the truth
was altered to fit the dramatic needs of the film.[20]

A person will be considered a public official if he or she holds a significant public office, including most elected officials and those who are
in positions of influence on public policy. Merely being a public employee
is not sufficient. The person must have some position of influence, importance, or ongoing scrutiny by the public.

Although the U.S. Supreme Court itself has been somewhat vague, a
series of tests have been developed by other courts. In California, for
example, a four-part test has been used.

> A 'public official' is someone in the government's employ who: (1) has, or
> appears to the public to have, substantial responsibility for or control over the
> conduct of governmental affairs; (2) usually enjoys significantly greater access
> to the mass media and therefore a more realistic opportunity to contradict false
> statements than the private individual; (3) holds a position in government
> which has such apparent importance that the public has an independent inter-
> est in the person's qualifications and performance beyond the general public
> interest in the qualifications and performance of all government employees;
> and (4) holds a position which invites public scrutiny and discussion of the
> person holding it entirely apart from the scrutiny and discussion occasioned
> by the particular controversy.[21]

The purpose of this test is to distinguish the rank-and-file employees
from those government officials who are in the public eye and subject to
public scrutiny. For this reason, the same standards have been extended
to public figures. Famous individuals and those who actively engage in
public discourse on controversial matters have made themselves public
figures, subject to the same legal standards for defamation as those of public officials. As one court explained, "[p]ublic figures are those who command sufficient continuing public interest by their position or their
purposeful activity amounting to a thrusting of their personality into the
'vortex' of an important public policy *and* have a realistic opportunity to
counteract false statements."[22]

Many interesting films are about so-called "little people" who change
the systems or serve as whistleblowers. Many of the characters in films
like *Norma Rae*, *Boys Don't Cry*, *Schindler's List*, and *Erin Brockovich* are

private figures whose stories deeply impact us all. Films such as these often do not involve public figures.

Finally, the person suing the filmmaker for defamation must prove that the statements or depictions are libelous. This requires the person prove the film depicts that person in a manner that is untrue and the depiction is harmful to the reputation of that person. If the jury believes the film is accurate, the filmmaker will not lose the lawsuit. If the film is inaccurate and harmful, the filmmaker will be accountable for the damages to a private person only if the research or depiction was made without reasonable care regarding the facts. For an official or public figure, the research or depiction must be the result of intentional lies or reckless disregard for the truth. A filmmaker should not be held liable for honest mistakes involving public officials or public figures.

One particularly insidious form of libel is to falsely attribute quotes to a person. The Supreme Court has held that otherwise unobjectionable statements can be deemed libelous when they are transformed into quotes.[23] Attributing dialogue to a character in a film can easily achieve this effect. When a film character is based on a living person, the dialogue may include statements that were originally made by critics of that person, but are now portrayed as self-deprecating comments made by the character. This increases the amount of material included in a documentary to which objections may be made.

Fictionalization may also result in the creation of composite characters—fictional characters that embody attributes of a number of live individuals. Because of the requirement that the statement be of or concerning the person claiming defamation, a common practice is to create fictional characters to stand in for unsavory conduct that may have been undertaken by real people. If the fictional character or composite character is identifiable as a real person involved in the situation, then the fictionalization only adds to the potential for liability.[24] This appears to occur most frequently when the fictional character's name bears some resemblance to the living person's name.

Fortunately for filmmakers, courts tend to disfavor defamation awards. This may be a result of the strong respect held by the courts for the First Amendment. It may also reflect respect for the detailed investigative process that major motion picture studios and television networks do for their docudramas and fact-based works. Needless to say the institutional respect for filmmakers will not extend to guerrilla filmmakers and individuals shooting on-the-fly films on shoestring budgets. For this reason, it is vital that, when producing a fact-based story, the filmmaker document every step taken to verify the truth of the story before creating the script and shooting the film. As discussed below, having the people involved in true stories sign agreements reduces the risk that they will sue for defamation, but unless every character depicted in a fact-based story has signed a release, the risk of a defamation claim remains.

4. False Light Privacy Invasion

The common law doctrine of false light creates liability for invasion of privacy by giving a person "unreasonable and highly objectionable publicity that attributes to him characteristics, conduct, or beliefs that are false, and so is placed before the public in a false position."[25] The falsity may be laudatory, but if it is highly objectionable and false, it may be actionable even if not defamatory. A good example would be a story that attributes a heroic self-defense shooting by a police officer. Since shooting in self-defense is not illegal or immoral, it would not be defamatory, but it may still be deemed highly offensive to the officer and a reasonable person, depending on the situation. A docudrama that falsely place a New Jersey firefighter at the World Trade Center rescue effort could result in injury to his career as he struggles to live down the false impression caused by the suggestion. If he suffers financial or other damage as a result, the firefighter would be able to recover against the false accusation.

False light has evolved into a close approximation of defamation for those statements that are injurious but not so contemptuous as to be defamatory. As such, privacy invasions are intentional torts requiring intent or reckless disregard of the truth rather than the negligence standard available for libelous statements made regarding private persons.[26]

5. Intrusion into Seclusion

Not all statements have to be false to be actionable. The right to privacy goes further than defamation or false light to protect a private individual from having unfavorable information published or presented to the public, even if the information is true. The right to privacy is limited in scope.

It will not protect a public figure or a private individual if the information is newsworthy, but the law does offer limited protection "to keep a man's business his own."[27] Unwanted, highly offensive, broadly disseminated publication of one's personal private information remains a common law tort susceptible to Internet abuse.[28] Broad publication of physical or mental health issues, identifying individuals, may result in liability. A well-meaning public service notice, intended to promote social responsibility, that identifies a family in dire financial need could be actionable if published to the public on the Internet.

6. Publicity Rights

The right of publicity is the right to control the exploitation of a person's name or likeness.[29] This has also been extended to protect a person's performance.[30] Publicity differs from privacy because it recognizes that individuals have the right to make money from their good name. New York, California, and many other states protect publicity rights very broadly. The California statute is representative:

> Any person who knowingly uses another's name, voice, signature, photograph, or likeness, in any manner, on or in products, merchandise, or goods, or for purposes of advertising or selling, or soliciting purchases of, products, merchandise, goods or services, without such person's prior consent . . . shall be liable for any damages sustained by the person or persons injured as a result thereof.[31]

The law limits publicity rights to use for sale of goods or services or advertising those goods or services. Film, television, radio, videotapes, literature, newspapers, and magazines are not goods for these purposes. They are forms of communication that are protected by the First Amendment, and the individual's publicity rights do not extend directly to them. That is not true of the ads published in the newspaper or run on television. A newspaper could run an article about Noah Webster illustrated by Webster eating a famous brand of popcorn without his permission.[32] That same picture could not be run in the same newspaper if it were part of an ad paid for by the popcorn manufacturer without Webster's permission.

While a Web site may be analogous to publishing, courts have recognized that a Web site used to promote the goods or services of an organization may be deemed to be a commercial use.[33] Further, most states do not require that the photographs be of famous people.[34] Showing recognizable individuals from corporate events or panels creates the impression of association with a company's products or services and requires the permission of each person who is identifiable in the photographs.

D. Purchasing the Literary Property

To obtain the right to make a movie out of an existing book or play, the filmmaker must license the movie rights from the author or rights holder. Once the proper copyright holder has been identified, a license must be negotiated that awards the filmmaker the right to produce and distribute the motion picture. The nature of the license may vary significantly depending on the type of source material, its commercial value, and its age.

1. Identification of the Copyright Holder

The first step is to determine who properly holds those rights. While it may be preferable to have an attorney experienced in copyright searches, this is an area where some self-help is available. The Copyright Office Circular that provides guidance and information on copyright searches—Circular 22—is included as Appendix B. The filmmaker should find out as much information as he can from the work itself. For example, if the work is a novel, research the name of the author, publisher, location of the first publication, and the first publication date. This may be more difficult for a short story, since it is common for an anthology to carry a single copyright notice for the entire work rather than separate notices for each short story. Nonetheless, the more information provided by the filmmaker, the more efficient the copyright search will be.

Publishers may also provide an excellent source of information. Publishers of books and music often have an ongoing relationship with the copyright holders because the publishers collect the author's royalties. They serve as an excellent starting point for many searches. In addition, the Ransom Center at the University of Texas at Austin has created the WATCH File (Writers, Artists, and Their Copyright Holders), an online database containing contact information for American and English authors, available at http://hemingway.hrc.utexas.edu/watchfiles/search.htm. This ongoing project should prove to be a very useful resource to independent filmmakers.

Having completed a search based on the information provided from the source work, the second step is to check the Catalog of Copyright Entries. This will reflect all the information that was given in the registration of the copyright. The Catalog is available in many public libraries throughout the United States. Unfortunately, it will not further the search much beyond that. The Catalog of Copyright Entries does not include information on assignments and transfers. Since film rights are transferred by assignment, the most critical information will not be in the Catalog of Copyright Entries. Still, the information available will speed up the professional search.

The last step for the copyright investigation is to have a professional search conducted. The Copyright Office can do the cheapest search itself. The Copyright Office charges an hourly fee, so the more information the filmmaker can provide, the cheaper and quicker the search. To improve the search, the Copyright Office suggests the following information be provided:

- the title of the work, with any possible variants
- the names of the authors, including possible pseudonyms
- the name of the probable copyright owner, which may be the publisher or producer
- the approximate year the work was published or registered
- the type of work involved (book, play, musical composition, sound recording, photograph, etc.)
- for a work originally published as a part of a periodical or collection, the title of that publication and any other information, such as the volume or issue number, to help identify it
- the registration number or any other copyright data

Motion pictures are often based on other works such as books, serialized contributions to periodicals, or other composite works. If the filmmaker desires a search for an underlying work or for music from a motion picture, that request must be made specifically. In submitting the search request, the person requesting the search must also identify the underlying works and music and furnish the specific titles, authors, and approximate dates of these works.[35]

If the search shows no assignments, it is time to contact the copyright holder. If the search, however, shows that there has been a transfer, then a lawyer may be necessary. It is important to consult an attorney to understand whether the rights might still be available.

2. Negotiations for the Motion Picture Rights

Having identified the owner of the film rights, the next step is to enter into negotiations for the rights to make the film. If possible, approach the author. It may be preferable to deal directly with the author rather than with an agent because the author may be more flexible on pricing and other terms. Find out if the movie rights are available and what the author wants.

The Literary Property Agreement may be the first contract for the movie. This may mean buying the rights outright or taking out an "option" on the rights. An option agreement provides for all the terms of the purchase of the underlying rights, but the purchaser makes a small down payment in exchange for the exclusive right to complete the transaction during a specified option period. In other words, the filmmaker may pay $100 for the right to purchase the literary property any time during the upcoming year. The filmmaker exercises the option by paying the full purchase price, as is specified in the agreement.

Depending on the specifics of the project, the filmmaker may choose to purchase the literary rights outright or negotiate an option agreement. A common but misguided practice is to negotiate only the option portion of the agreement, leaving the rest of the agreement to be negotiated at a future date. This makes the option much less valuable and may lead to disastrous outcomes at the time the option is going to be exercised. By failing to decide the payment terms and identify the rights acquired, the filmmaker may find that he cannot reach an agreement with the literary rights holder when he has finally raised enough money to exercise the purchase option. Instead, the filmmaker should be sure to negotiate and agree upon all the terms of the purchase contract at the time the option agreement is first negotiated.

The negotiations generally focus on the following terms in literary rights purchase agreements:

- the scope of rights
- the participation of the literary property rights holder
- the risk of noncompletion of the filmmaker's project
- the discretion of the filmmaker
- the amount of money being paid for the rights

The position of an independent filmmaker differs from that of the studio production regarding these negotiations. Typically, the studio production would demand all rights of every kind from the literary property rights holder and absolute discretion on how those rights were exploited. In exchange, the cost of those rights can be expected to be much higher for a studio than for an independent film. For the independent filmmaker, the choices can better reflect the filmmaker's ability to make the film and the rights holder's interest in protecting his work.

a. The Scope of Rights

The filmmaker must acquire the right to use the literary property—whether that is a short story or an unwritten life story—for the film being developed. This is the absolute minimum scope of rights being sought. Despite this, it is better for the filmmaker to acquire rights that are more broadly defined than merely the right to use the story to make the particular film. First, many independent films are produced with poor production quality. If the story is compelling, the filmmaker may have the opportunity in the future to remake the film on a grander scale. The right to make a film does not include the remake rights unless the contract includes that right. Second, the studio film industry is financed by the success of sequels and prequels. Like remakes, the ability to expand the story by making prequels and sequels will increase the opportunities to sell the completed film. Third, the media in which the film is made may not be film. Since the presumption is that the "film" will be photographed digitally, any confusion should be removed early on.

The best clause states that "the filmmaker hereby acquires the exclusive right to exploit the [literary property] in any media now known or hereafter developed, including without limitation the right to make motion pictures, sequels, prequels, remakes, live or episodic versions." In a separate sentence, the contract should also provide that "the filmmaker may produce and distribute the work using any media now known or hereafter developed." The first sentence says that the story can be captured using any technology or media. The second sentence provides that the film, TV show, or Internet broadcast can be sold, broadcast, or packaged in any fashion.

Literary property should also be broadly defined so that it includes any copyrighted work, characters, story, plot, theme, or action embodied in the literary property. In this way, the filmmaker still exclusively owns even elements of the story that are not copyrightable. While this might not stop a third party from creating a similar plot, it will stop the author of the plot from recycling it into a competing project.

As an independent project, it is possible to negotiate these terms to provide more limited rights for the filmmaker. The seller of the literary property may require it if the work is otherwise being used in other media. The greater the grant of rights, however, the better for the filmmaker because it reduces the chances of two or more similar projects competing in the market at the same time and gives the filmmaker a bigger bundle to sell to the distributor.

b. Participation of the Literary Property Rights Holder

In the studio setting, this consideration rarely occurs. Like an uninvited extra cook, the seller of the literary property is often considered a threat to the project and is given very little chance to participate. For the independent filmmaker, however, the owner of the literary property may be a resource rather than a burden. This is particularly true if the film is based on true events. The participation of the rights holder may also provide some marketing and press opportunities. The cost for such access is greater interaction between the filmmaker and the person whose story is being told.

c. The Risk of Noncompletion of the Filmmaker's Project

Although the chance that the rights holder will see his story actually made into a feature film is very low in both the independent and the studio film industry, the fear that the project will not be finished is generally greater with independent films. Presumably, this is—at least in part—based on a second assumption that the studio will pay higher rates for the literary material than the independent production will pay.

To overcome this fear the filmmaker should include specific provisions in the contract that allow the rights holder to reclaim his rights in the event the film is not made. This right—often referred to as the right of "reversion"—allows the rights holder to either reclaim the project or to transfer the project to a new studio. The typical studio conditions regarding reversion include the rights holder's obligation to reimburse the filmmaker for the payments made to the rights holder as well as the new film production company reimbursing the filmmaker for the costs incurred in preparing the film. The right of reversion often does not begin for five years following the sale of the literary rights to the studio.

The studio approach to reversion may meet with a good deal of opposition and may not set the type of tone or relationship the filmmaker is trying to develop. Instead, the filmmaker may elect to vary these terms in a number of ways. The rights can be returned to the rights holder without charge, or a reimbursement payment can be tied to the completion of the project by another company. This allows the rights holder to give the independent filmmaker a chance without making a decision that becomes financially impractical to fix.

The length of the reversion term can also be varied, but so long as some progress is being made, the term should continue to run. Independent films often start and stop for years, so the filmmaker should not promise that the movie will be completed in six months or the project is finished. For example, the rights holder may give the filmmaker the rights to the material for one year, but if an agreed upon amount of money is not raised, then the rights revert. If the money is raised, then the filmmaker has three years to begin principal photography. Once principal photography has begun, the rights are generally irrevocable.

d. The Discretion of the Filmmaker

The biggest advantage an independent filmmaker has over the studios is the ability to earn the trust of the literary rights holder. While the filmmaker generally wants unbridled discretion in telling his story, there are some rights that will only be made available to a sympathetic filmmaker, particularly if the film is based on true events. The filmmaker must negotiate before the work has begun if he is going to limit his control or dis-

cretion in the project by allowing the rights holder to observe, participate, or veto decisions of the filmmaker. The legal power to observe, participate, or veto should be given away very carefully. The filmmaker can
provide the opportunity for the rights holder to observe and participate
without contractually promising access to the rights holder, but if the contract provides for such access, the decision cannot be undone.

Participation can occur in the approval of casting, script, filming, or
finished film. The filmmaker can grant third parties the rights to review
choices at any of these stages of development of the film. This is a valuable commodity of the film, but may allow the filmmaker to acquire rights
to a story for which he otherwise could not outbid a studio.

e. The Amount of Money Being Paid for the Rights

Finally, the payment provisions can be structured in a multitude of ways.
The more obvious arrangements include the following:

- Outright cash payment at time of purchase
- Partial cash payments at each stage of financing, production, and
  distribution
- Deferred cash payment, paid out of financing
- Deferred cash payment, paid out of distribution income
- Percentages of gross distribution income received by the produc-
  tion company
- Percentages of net distribution income received by the production
  company

These different payment schemes may be used singly or in combination. For example, the filmmaker may offer the literary rights holder a payment of $100 for the literary property, with an additional payment of
$4,900 when (and if) the production company secures a specified amount
of financing, as well as 1 percent of the gross income from all distribution
income of the film. The use of a token up-front payment often improves
the trust between the filmmaker and the literary property seller. The use
of deferred compensation allows the filmmaker to reduce the cost of making the film.

If the literary property is the screenplay itself, this technique is particularly attractive. It ties the screenwriter's financial interest to the

completed film, since that is when the primary payments will occur, which may create an additional incentive for the writer's participation in revisions even if the money has run low.

3. Provisions of the Purchase Agreement

The purchase agreement gives the filmmaker the right to use[36] the literary material for any of the stated purposes, including making a film, television show, videotape, or anything the contract writer can think to include. For the filmmaker, the most important provisions for the literary purchase agreement are the following:

1. the grant of rights for the broadest form of license to make movies and related types of shows using any technology
2. the "representations and warranties" or contractually binding promises that the author owns the material being licensed, that no one else has any right to the material, and that no other party has any interest in the transaction
3. the purchase price for the literary rights
4. any royalty or percentage of net profits or gross revenues
5. screen credit

Additional terms. If the seller of the rights is an author, that person may want to add terms such as:

1. the right to write the first (or more) drafts of the screenplay
2. the right or option to write any sequels, prequels, or television versions
3. terms reserving the rights to live stage versions, novelizations, and other writings

4. Option Agreement Provisions

The option agreement gives the filmmaker the power to buy the film rights to a movie in the future and stops the author or publisher from selling the rights to anyone else during the option period. In all other respects, the option agreement is a literary purchase agreement with a few additional provisions. To be enforceable and useable, the option agreement must be more than an agreement to agree. All of the material terms and conditions must be included.

Option agreements can range in length from 2 to 17 pages. The option agreement contains all of the terms of the literary purchase agreement as well as the following additional provisions:

1. the length and starting date of the option period
2. the amount to be paid if the option is exercised and the literary property is purchased
3. the price of renewing the option, the length of the renewal, and the number of times the option can be renewed

In addition, the literary property agreement should include a recital by the author that all the rights are available and have not previously been transferred. This recital will be of some help if the filmmaker cannot afford the copyright search immediately.

In the simplest case, for example, an author has a written a short story entitled "Rosebud, the Sled of Youth." The Author ("Author") published the short story once in a small magazine, retaining all other rights in the work. The contract would state that the filmmaker ("Producer") is acquiring an exclusive option to all rights in the short story entitled "Rosebud, the Sled of Youth" (the "Work"). A different section of the agreement would provide that the Author retains the literary publishing rights to the Work. The option agreement would include a payment of $500 for the exclusive right to develop the Work as a film (or in any other form) for the next year and may be renewed for up to an additional three years by additional payments of $500. The Author would represent and warrant that he has all the rights to the Work and can sell the rights to the Producer.

This option agreement would also include the final sale price for the film. All the fees must be decided in the option agreement. There should be no clause that says that payments will be mutually agreed upon. Invariably, any terms left to future negotiations will grow into problems that can disrupt the filmmaking process. For the filmmaker, the consequences of not reaching an agreement go up dramatically if he is financially committed to the project and has begun filming. The filmmaker should not put off negotiations until a time when he is at a disadvantage in negotiating.

While option agreements are generally preferred over literary purchase agreements because less money must be spent initially, a tremendous amount of money may be saved by purchasing the rights in full up front. Many authors will accept $5,000 in hand rather than the promise of $50,000 if and when the movie is made. Buying rights remains a valuable choice.

5. "Based Upon" Provisions for Treatment Submissions

Another variation on the literary purchase agreement would be a treatment option agreement in which the producer agrees to pay the writer a specified amount or percentage if the finished film was based upon the treatment. This type of arrangement—made famous during the lawsuit between Art Buchwald and Eddie Murphy over the film *Coming to America*—provided payment to Buchwald for his movie treatment and profit participation if the film was made. Although the film was substantially different from the treatment, the evidence was that the treatment was used as the basis for the development of Murphy's independent script. Since John Landis, the movie's producer, used the treatment as part of the development of the story, then Buchwald was entitled to payment.

This was the proper result in the lawsuit, despite the fact that Eddie Murphy had not read the treatment nor used it to write his script. The treatment had been used by Paramount and Landis to keep the production going, and it served as a reference for the producers as Murphy developed his independent screenplay. As a result, the contract that provides for payment if a film is "based upon" a treatment should be interpreted to mean that the treatment author will be paid unless the treatment was wholly unrelated to the subject matter of the finished film.

Because of the vague nature of the "based upon" contract, the producer should try to avoid that term. Instead, the producer can offer a percentage basis to the author of the treatment if the author submits a screenplay, and the screenplay is substantially similar to the final film as provided under copyright law. Since substantial similarity is the copyright test for infringement, this contract essentially provides that if the screenplay uses the copyrighted work, then the screenwriter receives the agreed-upon payment. For a simple arrangement, this provides the easiest contractual framework.

E. Submission Agreements

1. Introduction

The submission agreement is designed to protect the production company from claims by submitting writers of theft of ideas or copyrighted materials. These contracts protect the companies and require that submitting writers waive claims they might otherwise have. The production company's need for such a waiver is reasonable because similar themes, ideas, and characters are often based on cultural influences, and many authors may be developing similar themes.

The basic purpose of a submission agreement is to allow the production company to review treatments and screenplays written by writers who are not employees of the production company. Often, these are "spec scripts"—scripts written as pet projects by writers hoping to break into the motion picture industry or to move up in the industry. Spec scripts are particularly prevalent immediately after a prolonged strike. Given recent labor unrest, there may be a tremendous number of spec scripts in the next few years.

2. Significant Terms of a Submission Agreement

The typical submission agreement serves to limit any contractual claims of the submitting author. Typically these contracts do not limit copyright claims, but focus on claims to ideas, characters, themes, and other materials that do not rise to the level of copyrightable expression. Because it is common for more than one party to develop similar ideas for films, it is important to have a contract that sets out the expectations of the submitting writer and the film company before the production company receives the screenplay or treatment. The production company should insist that no script be accepted unless the submitting writer first signs a submission agreement.

The primary provision of the submission agreement is that no implied contract exists that promises to compensate the submitting writer for use of his idea or an idea similar to his. Although, as noted in Chapter 1, ideas are not protected by copyright, those same ideas and plots may be protected by contract.[37] The producer must be careful to avoid making promises or otherwise creating an oral contract that a submitting writer could rely upon. The written contract must explicitly state that the producer will not pay for submitted ideas, explain that similar ideas may have already been submitted, and condition any submission upon the submitting writer accepting these limitations.

a. This contract represents the only understanding between the parties regarding the submission of any treatment, story, idea, screenplay, or other work (collectively "Work"). This contract supersedes any oral agreement, and it may only be modified in writing when signed by both parties.
b. The production company will accept submission of writer's Work only in exchange for entering into this agreement.
c. Because many writers submit materials, and often similar ideas are submitted or otherwise available, the production company does not pay writers for their ideas.
d. The production company is under no obligation to pay the writer for the idea submitted. The production company is under no obligation to review the Work submitted. The production company is free to use all material not protected by the laws of copyright. The production company is not obligated to keep the materials submitted.

In contrast with the provisions above, a production company should comply with copyright law. A general submission agreement should not be used to force a writer to transfer copyright ownership from the writer to the production company or to give the production company the right to make a screenplay or film from the submission. The submission agreement can state this, in part, as a means to soften the otherwise harsh tone of the agreement.

e. In the event that the writer submits a Work protected by copyright, the writer grants permission to review the Work and make copies of the Work for its evaluation. The writer shall retain all rights to edit or adapt the screenplay and to make a motion picture or audiovisual work based upon the Work unless such rights are transferred to the production company as part of a written agreement.

The submission agreement should also explain that it is the general practice to review all submissions within approximately six months, or such time as is realistic for the producer, but that because of the number of submissions, the production company will contact only those writers with whom it is interested in developing a working relationship. While it is certainly more professional to thank every author, and even to respond with comments if possible, the production company is better off doing so than promising to do so in a contract.

    f. The production company is not obligated to return the materials. The writer will at all times retain an original copy of the materials submitted and hereby releases the production company from any claims that may arise as a result of the production company holding the Work.

The contract might also note that materials will only be returned if the submitting author includes a self-addressed, stamped envelope for the return of materials. Given the low price of copying and the increasing cost of postage, many authors may forgo the return of their materials.

These suggested provisions are similar to the language that a larger production company would use. The submission agreement is designed to protect the production company from claims from authors who send unsolicited materials. Such contracts help courts dismiss frivolous lawsuits before the trial preparation becomes very expensive.

3. Solicited Ideas and the Nondisclosure Agreement

General submission provisions must be modified to fit the particular situation. If the production company wishes to solicit a plot or an idea from an author, then it must be prepared to protect that author's ideas. This arrangement takes on the form of a nondisclosure agreement. Nondisclosure agreements are frequently used in business, and essentially require that both parties agree to share information in exchange for the promise that neither party will use or disclose the other party's confidential information without permission. Indeed, if the previous sentence were written on a napkin and signed by both parties, it would probably be sufficient.

In the solicited idea context, the nondisclosure is slightly different than in the traditional business context. The essential component of the agreement is that the idea, story, plot, characters, or other elements are treated as confidential unless they were already known by the party who receives the material, or they become known in a manner that does not breach the film company's duty of confidentiality. The following contract clauses illustrate the core of the agreement:

a.   Confidentiality. Producer shall not directly or indirectly disclose, disseminate, publish, or use for its business advantage or for any other purpose, at any time during or after the term of this Agreement for a period of seven (7) years, any information received from Writer deemed confidential by the other party ("Confidential Information").

(1.) Definitions. For purposes of this Agreement, Confidential Information shall be defined as any information not generally known in the industry about Writer's story, characters, ideas, themes, plots, writings or expressions, products, trade secrets, services, or any combination thereof, whether or not such information would be recognized as proprietary absent this Agreement, including but not limited to information related to design or product specifications developed by Inventor.

(2.) Limitations. Notwithstanding any other provision of this Agreement, Producer shall not be liable for disclosing, disseminating, publishing or using information which (i) was already known prior to the receipt of the Confidential Information; (ii) is information similar to the Confidential Information of Writer so as to make such Confidential Information no longer unique to Writer; (iii) is now or becomes public information through no wrongful act of the Producer; (iv) is independently developed or acquired by Producer without any use of the Confidential Information in such development; or (v) is required to be disclosed by law. Producer shall, within thirty days of receipt of Confidential Information inform Writer of that material Producer deems not confidential pursuant to this paragraph.

b.   Documents and Materials. The documents and materials of Writer (including but not limited to all data, screenplays, treatments, records, notes, lists, specifications, and designs) are furnished in accordance with the terms of this Agreement and shall remain the sole property of Writer. This information (collectively known as "Evaluation Material") shall, upon the termination of this Agreement, be promptly returned to Writer, including all copies thereof, which are in the possession or control of Producer, its agents, and its representatives.

c.   Term and Renewal. The term of this Agreement shall be one (1) year commencing as of the date hereof; provided however, that Paragraph 1 of this Agreement shall survive termination of this Agreement and shall remain in full force and effect for a period of seven (7) years.

Using these terms, the producer provides significant protection to the writer for his ideas and other materials that are not protected by copyright while still retaining the ability to avoid paying for material that has become public or he already owns.

4. Submissions by Joint Authors

Many of the fiercest fights break out between two people who had been jointly developing a work. A simple contract that explains the duties of each party helps to eliminate these problems. The contract should have a sentence requiring that all ideas developed during the partnership may only be used by mutual consent. If the filmmaker is hiring someone to develop an idea, the contract should require that all ideas become the property of the filmmaker.

F. Boilerplate: Understanding the Rest of the Contract

In almost every contract, the significant terms are followed by a series of similar provisions that control most of the rules for enforcing the contract and operating under the contract. These provisions—often referred to as boilerplate—are quite similar, regardless of the key, negotiated terms of the agreement. Boilerplate provisions are used in every contract, from manufacturing cars to selling cable service, and apply to the thousands of different contracts the filmmaker will enter during the production. The following provides an example of these terms and their meaning.

1. Term and Renewal

The term provision governs the length of the contract. Unless there is another provision allowing for the contract to continue after that date, the contract itself ends, and the future relationships are governed by a new agreement, whether in writing or by oral understanding.

> The term of this Agreement shall commence as of the date hereof and continue for a period of one year; and provided neither party shall not be then in breach of or in default under any term or provision hereof, this Agreement shall automatically renew for additional one (1) year periods thereafter, unless either party gives written notice of its election to terminate this Agreement not less than sixty (60) days prior to the expiration of the term or any renewal thereof.

This provision provides that the contract starts beginning with the date on the top of the page, which is preferable to having two possibly conflicting dates accompanying the signature lines of the parties. Second, the contract has a one-year term, but that term automatically extends each year unless either party decides to terminate the contract. This automatic renewal is quite typical for ongoing relationships. For project work, the event should be specified. For example the contract may terminate upon the completion of principal photography.

Termination provisions can also allow that some provisions of the contracts survive termination. For example, if an agreement provides for financing the film, the contract may automatically terminate if insufficient funds are pledged by a specified date. Notwithstanding the termination of the contract because that date passes, the contract may provide that the provisions relating to nondisclosure of the film idea will survive for an additional period of years.

2. Warranties and Representations of the Parties

The representations and warranties are the basic promises that serve as the basis for the agreement. They generally go to the ability of the parties to enter into the agreement, but may become very specific depending on the nature of the agreement.

Each party to this Agreement hereby represents and warrants that it has the right and authority to enter into this Agreement and that it is not subject to any contract, agreement, judgment, statute, regulation, or disability which might interfere with its full performance of all of the covenants and conditions hereunder.

Because of this, it is common that the representations and warranties for the two parties to the agreement be somewhat different from each other.

An example of the representations and warranties of the author of a story will include the following additional issues:

The Seller [of the novel, screenplay, play, or other literary work] hereby represents and warrants as follows:

The Property has been written solely by and is original with Seller; neither the Property nor any element thereof infringes upon the copyright, publicity rights, trademarks, story rights, or other interests of any other literary property.

The Property is wholly fictional, no portion of the Property has been taken from any other source (other than the public domain), and the Property does not constitute defamation against any person or violate any rights in any person, including without limitation, rights of privacy, publicity, copyright (whether common law or statutory, throughout the universe), trademark, publication or performance rights, or rights in any other property, and any rights to consultation regarding the Property or any element thereof.

The Property has not previously been exploited in any medium except the following [identify what rights have been used], and no rights have been granted to any third party to do so.

In addition, for some projects it is important that nothing interfere with the ability to market the personality involved in the project.

Neither party has committed, and throughout the term of this Agreement neither party shall commit, any act or omission which constitutes a felony or could be deemed an act of moral turpitude. Any breach of this paragraph shall be deemed a material breach.

In such a situation, the representations and warranties need to include a morality clause, guaranteeing good, honorable behavior both before and throughout the term of the contract. The most important aspect of this provision is that it allows the employer to revoke the contract if the misconduct of the employee makes that choice appropriate.

3. Indemnification

Indemnification is the legal obligation to pay for compensation for damage, loss, or injury suffered as a result of a breach of the contract or any duties that arise under it to the other party to the agreement. For example, a screenwriter will be required to indemnify the film producer for any material copied from other sources in violation of copyright law and the representations made by the screenwriter in his contract.

It is not sufficient that each party promises to abide by the promises made in the contract. Each party runs the risk that third parties may make claims against that party as a result of what it has done. For example, the filmmaker wants to be protected from anyone claiming the screenwriter improperly copied that person's story. To provide such protection, the screenwriter must agree to defend the filmmaker, meaning the writer must provide a legal defense for the benefit of the filmmaker. The screenwriter must also indemnify the filmmaker, meaning he must agree to pay any damages if the screenwriter is found to have violated some other person's rights.

> Screenwriter hereby indemnifies and holds harmless the [Film Company] and its employees, independent contractors, agents, and assigns against any loss or damage (including reasonable attorneys' fees) incurred by reason of any claim based upon any breach of the representations and warranties of Seller contained in this Agreement and any documents contemplated hereby. The term "person" as used herein shall mean any person, firm, corporation, or other entity.

In contrast, the filmmaker is generally in the better position to defend the screenwriter for any lawsuits that might arise as a result of the making of the film. Therefore, the filmmaker has a similar obligation to protect the screenwriter from liability.

> [Film Company] hereby indemnifies Screenwriter against any loss or damage (including reasonable attorneys' fees) incurred by reason of any claim based upon its exploitation of the Property which does not involve the acts or omissions of the Screenwriter.

Finally, a general statement that each will protect the other for any actions that it caused serves as a very simple, but effective, provision.

> Each party agrees to indemnify the other and to hold the other harmless from and against any and all claims, action, cause of action, liabilities, damages, judgments, decrees, losses, costs, and expenses, including reasonable attorneys' fees, arising out of any breach or alleged breach of any representations, warranties, or agreements made by it hereunder.

The difficult issue—which of the two actually created the situation that allowed a third party to be able to bring a lawsuit—is often highly contentious, with the result that the two parties to the contract often end up suing each other to determine which has the obligation to pay for the litigation and any damages caused by the lawsuit.

These sample clauses do not include the requirement that the party defend the lawsuit. Defense language is common and can readily be added to these paragraphs merely by inserting the term "and defend" after the word "indemnify" wherever applicable.

4. Resolution of Disputes

Because of the costs and delays involved in litigation, many people prefer to use some alternative, including arbitration or mediation. Mediation provides a person who tries to help the parties to the dispute work out the issues among themselves. Arbitration provides an independent person who acts much like a judge, who will listen to both sides in the dispute and make a determination. Although arbitrators in some jurisdictions may not have quite the discretion of the courts to award injunctions or punitive damages, they have substantial power to craft final remedies. In addition, if the arbitration is binding, then the decision of the arbitrator is as enforceable as that of a judge.

The choice to forgo the right to go to court should be considered carefully. Many protections are given up by waiving the right to use the traditional legal system. On the other hand, the independent filmmaker probably does not have a great deal of money or time to fight the dispute through trial and appeal. As a result, arbitration may be a useful alternative for filmmakers. It is required in most union agreements when disputes arise with union personnel (directors, actors, writers, etc.). Each union will have specific language that it requires be used. Also, the ability to choose the arbitrator allows the parties to use the services of a decision maker familiar with the film industry and the issues involved. These provisions vary greatly, but the following serves as an example.

Any and all disputes hereunder shall be resolved by arbitration in accordance with the American Arbitration Association ("AAA") under the rules then obtaining. Any party hereto electing to commence an action shall give written notice to the other party hereto of such election. The location for such arbitration shall be Los Angeles, California, subject to the convenience of the parties, and any and all rights of discovery available pursuant to such arbitration shall be limited by the applicable arbitration provisions of the California Code of Civil Procedure. The award of such arbitrator may be confirmed or enforced in any court of competent jurisdiction. The costs and expenses of the arbitrator, including the attorneys' fees and costs of each of the parties, may be apportioned between the parties by such arbitrator.

5. Assignment

Most business contracts are freely assignable. In contrast, most contracts calling for a person's individual services are not transferable or assignable. In the filmmaking scenario, both issues are occurring at once. The duties of most of the participants are personal in nature, but the filmmaker may create a company or sell the film company as part of the financing. So long as the filmmaker remains involved in the project, none of these activities should trigger the assignment clause.

The services and obligations under this Agreement are personal in nature and cannot be assigned or delegated. The services of [Film Company] may be assigned upon consent, which consent shall not be unreasonably withheld.

Notwithstanding the foregoing, the transfer of this Agreement to a company owned in whole or part by [Filmmaker], a related company, or to another entity with substantially the same executive and principals of [Film Company], or to a company that employs [Filmmaker] as [producer/director], shall not be deemed an assignment requiring approval under this paragraph.

6. Amendments

Things change. Actors may get sick, locations become unavailable, funding increases and decreases. Nonetheless, when the filmmaker goes to the trouble of creating a written agreement, it is important that any changes be put into writing, so that quick, last-minute promises do not undermine the thoughtful management of the production. As a result, every contract should include a statement that written amendments are required. The requirement is simple. "This Agreement may be modified or amended only in a writing signed by both parties." Even with this language, some jurisdictions will allow for oral modification of the agreements. Further, courts will often find that a party has waived its rights to require a written document as a result of statements made or conduct relating to the transaction. Despite this risk, the provision should be included in the agreement and utilized by the parties throughout the term of their relationship.

7. Severability

In some situations a portion of the contract cannot be enforced. The court (or arbitrator) must then decide whether to throw out the entire contract or just that provision. That choice can be provided for directly in the contract. In most situations, half a contract is better than none, as this provision reflects.

If any provision of this Agreement shall be held to be invalid or unenforceable for any reason, the remaining provisions shall continue to be valid and enforceable. If a court finds that any provision of this Agreement is invalid or unenforceable, but that by limiting such provision it would become valid and enforceable, then such provision shall be deemed to be written, construed, and enforced as so limited.

8. Entire Agreement

To control the issues that may be swirling around the filmmaker, everything should be in writing. A provision that specifies that all the issues have been incorporated into the written agreement may help to overcome claims that side agreements and promises were also made. Even the most well-meaning people hear what they want to hear, so the more exact and structured the contract, the fewer the misunderstandings.

> This Agreement contains the full and complete understanding between the parties hereto with reference to the within subject matter, supersedes all prior agreements and understandings, whether written or oral, pertaining thereto, and cannot be modified except by a written instrument signed by both of the parties hereto. Each of the parties acknowledges that no representation or promise not expressly contained in this Agreement has been made by the other or its agents or representatives.

9. No Obligation

Unfortunately, many films do not get made and opportunities are often lost. The contract purchasing literary properties or services should be sure to protect the filmmaker from claims that he was required to use those properties or services. This will not determine what payments or other obligations the filmmaker must make. The payment terms will specify under what conditions the payments are due. If the payments are due for entering the contract, then the payments are owed, even if the film is not made. Most of the payment obligations are based on using the services, in which case failure to start the film results in no financial obligation.

> Notwithstanding the rights granted herein, [Film Company] is under no obligation to utilize [services/property] in any manner whatsoever, and failure to exercise any rights contained herein shall not constitute a breach of any covenant, express or implied.

10. No Partnership or Joint Venture

The financial and business relationship should also be specified. Courts may ignore these self-serving declarations, but at least they remind the parties how they are supposed to relate to each other, and they may have some effect on courts if any problems do arise.

> [Screenwriter] is an independent contractor with respect to [Film Company] and not an employee. [Film Company] will not provide fringe benefits and [Screenwriter] shall be responsible for all income tax and withholding required which he may bear as a result of this Agreement. Nothing in this Agreement shall be construed as creating a partnership, joint venture, or employment relationship between the parties hereto, and each party is solely and exclusively responsible for its own debts and obligations.

11. Further Documents

Throughout the course of the filmmaking process, a wide variety of financiers, distributors, government agencies, unions, exhibitors, and others are going to request legal documentation regarding the film. Some of those documents will have been created during the production process, but others will not have been necessary or will not be in the form needed. The filmmaker must be able to compel the other participants to continue to sign documents necessary for the production and distribution of the film and the related rights. This provision makes the willingness to sign additional papers an affirmative promise of each party.

> Each of the parties agrees to execute, acknowledge, and deliver any and all further documents which may be required to carry into effect this Agreement and its respective obligations hereunder, all of which further documents shall be in accordance with and consistent with the terms of this Agreement.

12. Notices

The contract should specify the form of delivery allowed. E-mail is typically not included in these provisions, but increasingly it is a useful tool. If it is used, then the sender should confirm that the e-mail has been received. Many notice clauses include the address to which all notices should be sent, and often include the attorney or agent as a second address, entitled to a copy of the correspondence. Often these are left blank, however, so this paragraph provides more flexibility in selecting the applicable address.

All notices, statements, or other documents which either party shall desire to give to the other hereunder shall be in writing and shall be deemed given as when delivered personally or by e-mail (with confirmed receipt), telecopier (with confirmed receipt), or 48 hours after deposit in the U.S. mail, postage prepaid, and addressed to the recipient party at the address set forth in the opening paragraph of this Agreement, or at such address as either party hereto may designate from time to time in accordance with this Paragraph.

13. Governing Law

The parties can also choose which state's law governs the contract, so long as that state is related to the agreement. Assuming one of the parties to the contract is from a particular state, or most of the work will occur in that state, then the selection will usually be respected by the court or arbitrator.

This Agreement shall be governed by and construed in accordance with the laws of the State of California applicable to agreements entered into and wholly performed therein.

The choice of the state selected may depend on the laws of that state. If a state has particularly favorable laws regarding the contract, the filmmaker may wish to choose the law of that state. The choice varies dramatically depending on the state and the issues involved, so the choice should be based on the advice of a lawyer familiar with the issues.

14. Signature Line

The signature should indicate who is signing the agreement and in what capacity. For example, if the filmmaker has formed a film company, then the filmmaker should sign only in his capacity as president of the company, or manager of the LLC, etc. The contract should also identify that the film company, rather than the filmmaker himself, is the party to the agreement. This will limit the personal liability that would otherwise attach to the filmmaker if he signed in his personal capacity rather than as a corporate officer on behalf of the company. Without properly drafting the contract and properly signing the contract, the value of creating the film company will be lost.

G. Literary Tools—Treatments and Screenplays

There are two essential literary tools necessary to develop a film—the treatment and the screenplay. The screenplay and treatment may be written in either order. A good exercise is to use the treatment as a tool in developing the screenplay and then rewriting the treatment to match the screenplay as it progresses.

1. Treatments

The treatment is a short synopsis—typically two to five pages in length—written to highlight the story, plot, and characters as well as to give a feel for the writing style of the film. The treatment serves as a teaser, drafted to pique the curiosity of the reader, tantalizing and creating a hunger for the screenplay.

The treatment will be used to introduce the film to prospective investors, production companies, performers, and crew. The two-page treatment has more impact on the project than anything other than the completed film. Tremendous care must be made not to distribute the treatment too freely or hastily. Filmmakers seldom have a chance to present a film project twice. The early treatment may end the interest of a potential investor because it was drafted too hastily, or because it was written by a producer or other participant who does not possess the ability to capture the essence of the script.

2. Screenplays

The screenplay should be the road map, guide, and final authority for the film. The screenplay must encompass the entire story, including all the dialogue, action, sets, scenery, and characters. A typical screenplay runs between 90 and 120 pages in length, set out in a very stylized and specific format. Stick to the traditional page format. Innovation should be seen on the screen, not on the page layout. A great deal has been written on the format of the screenplay, and there are even a number of computer programs to help write in the correct style.[38] Once a writer learns the basics of screenplay formats, however, any word processor or typewriter can generate a properly formatted screenplay.

A good screenplay must work as literature, as a visual guide, as the film's stopwatch, as a sales tool, and as a calling card. Before any work continues on the filmmaker's project, the screenplay must be substantially completed. While thousands of movies are filmed while the scripts are hastily rewritten on the set, this practice wastes time and increases the editing costs. The guerrilla filmmaker does not have this luxury.

This should not suggest that the finished screenplay will exactly match what appears on the screen. A host of changes, compromises, and new ideas will force the movie to evolve from the original script, but it remains critical that the script be as strong as possible before shooting begins. Even if the choice is made to improvise the story, a script is important to set the dramatic structure, the locations, the emphasis, and the relative timing of scenes. The only obvious exception to this would be a documentary, but even there, many documentaries are well structured and scripted before the film has ever been shot.

A screenplay has many roles, depending on the reader. To illustrate the various roles the screenplay must play, the following should serve as a helpful guide.

Literature
First and foremost, the merit of the story, the characters, and the structure must be strong, powerful, and believable. This is true of even the silliest of parody films. A great screenplay will work as a piece of writing. A literary test will show the weaknesses in all other scripts.

Character List
The screenplay must include enough information about the characters that casting decisions and costume choices can be made. The script should also tell the actors about the character they are portraying and let them know how to develop the character.

Visual Guide

Film is a visual medium. The screenplay should create snapshots of the scenes that can translate directly into storyboards, drawings of the scene on film. Even a film that utilizes storyboards will have the artist draw them from the screenplay. The screenplay creates the visual style that controls all the other visual elements of the filmmaking.

Screen Stopwatch

Scripts are often used as a guide in timing a film. As a rule of thumb, a page in the script equals a minute on the screen. While this may not work page for page, the two-hour, 120-page film is fairly standard and consistent. The stopwatch effect is not an absolute rule, but the principle is sufficiently universal that it should be kept in mind when structuring the screenplay.

Production Clock

Another rule of thumb for the timing of scripts is that a page of script equals half a day's filming for feature films. Television scripts shoot five pages a day. Digital filmmaking does not have any established guides yet. There is much more flexibility in this timing, but once a guide is established, the guide is often followed closely. The writer can use this to his benefit by using more text to describe longer, more difficult shots and utilizing briefer descriptions of shorter, simple setups.

Calling Card

Finally, the script will be used by every actor, investor, production company, or other person in any way connected with the project as the method of evaluation. The script becomes the point of introduction for many of the key participants in the project.

H. Protecting the Filmmaker's Property

As the concept of the film is developed into a screenplay and eventually into the film, the filmmaker must protect the material from theft. For screenplays and treatments, protection will come from the federal copyright law as well as from well-drafted contracts. The Writers Guild of America also provides an evidentiary role.

1. Copyright Protection for the Unpublished Screenplay

As described earlier in Chapter 1, Section B, Item 3, the federal copyright law protects a script or film as soon as it is recorded or put in writing. The various sections of the copyright law differ slightly for works that have not been published rather than those works that have been published. Since the screenplay is generally an unpublished work, it is protected by copyright as soon as it is in writing, whether on paper or on computer drive. An unpublished work does not have to be registered with the Copyright Office. Registration costs only $30, however, and should be filed as soon as there is a hint of difficulty with anyone involved with the project. The $30 copyright filing buys a strong negotiating chip.

Generally speaking it is also a good idea to put the copyright notice on the work. The notice is necessary for a published work to be registered, but may be a good reminder to discourage theft even when used on an unpublished work. A proper notice includes the copyright symbol ©, or the word *copyright*, the year of the copyright, and the name of the copyright holder. For example, the notice on this book reads "© 2002 Jon M. Garon."

Proper registration creates a presumption of a valid copyright. The Copyright Office describes the simple process:

> To register a claim in a dramatic work, submit the following to the Library of Congress, Copyright Office, 101 Independence Avenue, S.E., Washington, D.C. 20599-6000:
>
> (1.) a completed and signed Form PA
>
> (2.) a nonrefundable filing fee of $30 made payable to the Register of Copyrights
>
> (3.) if unpublished, one copy of the work; if published, two complete copies of the best edition of the work
>
> (4.) for a script, the copy may be a manuscript, printed copy, a film video recording, or a phonorecord
>
> (5.) All of the elements must be submitted in the same package or envelope. Registration of the work is normally effective on the day all of the

material is received in the Copyright Office in acceptable form, although your certificate of registration may not be mailed until 6 months after receipt of your submission[39]

Similar rules apply to copyright registration of the completed film. See Appendix B, Circular 45, for a discussion of deposit of the finished film.

2. Writers Guild Registration

The Writers Guild of America (Writers Guild, or WGA) has a depository system that serves as evidence whenever there is a dispute over the authorship of a treatment or screenplay. For $20, any treatment, television script, or screenplay may be registered. The Writers Guild will also accept stage plays and other written ideas prepared for audiovisual works. Registration lasts for five years and may be renewed.

The Writers Guild registration does not replace copyright, but it does serve to create evidentiary proof of the author's work submitted as of the date of the registration. When the submission is received by the Writers Guild, it is sealed in an envelope and the date and time are recorded. The Writers Guild then returns a numbered receipt to the author that serves as the official documentation of registration. Many independent film companies that accept unsolicited submissions insist that the Writers Guild registration number be marked on the script, so that there is documentary proof of the material submitted. The work remains in a sealed envelope which the WGA will forward to the court, unopened, as evidence.

3. Film Titles

The Motion Picture Association of America (MPAA) provides a title registry for its members and contracting film companies. The Writers Guild does not protect titles in any manner. Although the filmmaker and film distributor must abide by the names already taken on the MPAA registry, availability in the system should not be the only review. Motion picture titles are really trademarks and may compete with similar trademarks in other literary works, including novels, songs, albums, and video or computer games. In addition to the MPAA registry, the filmmaker or the distributor should use the service of an attorney or review a trademark search. The best source for such a trademark search is Thomson and Thomson.[40] The company will provide a comprehensive trademark search—including the use in film titles and in other media. Such a search costs between $200 and $500, and it should be conducted by the distributor of the film on the eve of the marketing campaign.

4. Transferring the Filmmaker's Story Rights

In the studio setting, the film studio requires that any script be created as a work for hire so that the motion picture studio becomes the author of the screenplay. Studios also require that the rights to make the film are assigned to the studio and that the rights to create an unlimited number of additional works, which are often known as "sequel rights," are also assigned to the studio. These sequel rights include sequels, prequels, adaptations, spin-offs involving one or more characters or settings, television versions for both episodic (weekly) television and television specials, and every other entertainment imaginable that can be based upon the film.

For the filmmaker who has created an original story, this technique may not be the most advantageous. The independent film company may not be in a position to exploit these works and, as a result, the filmmaker may find his desire to write sequels later in his career are stymied because the rights were assigned to the film company organized for that single production. Retaining these rights gives the filmmaker a measure of leverage to control future opportunities. On the other hand, such reservation of rights must be clearly spelled out so that investors are not misled about the potential for their investment. Similarly, studios financing productions will automatically insist that these rights be transferred to them.

One possible compromise is for the filmmaker to give the option to the film company to exploit these rights, but limit the time period that the film company has such an option. If these sequel rights are exploited within the first three to five years, then the film company should be in a position to participate in them. (The filmmaker should receive some compensation as author, even in this case.) If the rights have not been exploited, then the film company has little direct financial interest, so the rights can reasonably return to the filmmaker. This compromise allows the filmmaker to return to the material later in his career without having to clear the rights from a long-defunct production company.

The Film Company

THE SCOPE OF a digital film project can range dramatically from a single filmmaker walking the countryside with a camera to a massive business involving dozens of employees and potentially millions of dollars in expenses and revenue. The guerrilla filmmaker may be fine without any business planning, but for most filmmakers advance planning will smooth the path for the creation and marketing of the film.

The film company should be organized to anticipate the legal and business issues that will face the filmmaker. A typical, low-budget feature film project will include a payroll involving thousands of dollars, salaried employees, independent contractors, and agreements with trade unions, property owners, lenders, suppliers, and a multitude of support services. The company may be obligated to become licensed by a state, pay federal and state taxes, execute contracts to rent property, license copyrighted works, sell securities, and buy credit. The smallest film remains big business. Because the process requires such great detail, the project will take on the trappings of a "real" business, so the filmmaker should select the business structure best suited to the project and the filmmaker's short-term and long-term goals.

The goal of business planning is to anticipate four primary areas—control, financing, liability, and tax obligations. Control reflects who within the film company has legal authority over decision making. The movie director may have artistic control over the look of the film and the selection of shots, but only the film company can grant that authority. If the director wants to shoot a scene in Hawaii and the film company owner says that the trip to Hawaii is not in the budget, the artistic control of the director will take second place to the financial control of the film company. Even the artistic control described for the director may be revoked if the decisions made are highly unreasonable in the judgment of the film company. Therefore, if the filmmaker wishes to retain absolute control of the film, then she must first retain control of the film company.

Financing issues address the practical problems of funding the filmmaking process. Although digital filmmaking has the potential to greatly reduce certain expenses—camera and lighting rental, film stock purchase, and editing expenses in particular—many of the other expenses remain essentially unchanged. If the filmmaker hopes to use other people's money to finance the film—a position strongly advocated by most lawyers—then the nature of the film company must be designed to reflect that financial participation. Financial participation is closely tied to the issue of control as well. Even in the arts, investors will want some say in the manner in which their money is spent.

Liability is another significant factor the filmmaker must assess to determine the type of business. The business entity responsible for making the film is legally liable for the contractual obligations and any tort liability that may arise while making the film. Contractual obligations include the duty to pay bills, return rental equipment, withhold and pay taxes, and generally deliver on the promises made by the filmmaker. Tort liability generally reflects the duty to pay for any damage or costs associated with accidents (or intentional misconduct) that might arise during the making of the film. If a pedestrian is hit by a car while the filmmaker shoots a car chase scene, then the film company is responsible for paying the injured person and making him whole. Liability may be controlled through the use of insurance, but the responsibility still rests with the film company. The best choice will depend on the objectives the filmmaker has in each of these four areas.

Tax obligations are a specific type of liability that the film company must undertake. Tax obligations, however, need to be planned for separately from other obligations because the choice of business form may change the tax obligations and the amount of taxes owed. To select the most appropriate business form, taxes must be planned for early in the development process. Professional tax planning is beyond the scope of this book, but it is important for the filmmaker to work with an experienced accountant or attorney. Preliminary discussions at the planning stage may save the filmmaker thousands of dollars in taxes later in the process.

Often control, finance, liability, and tax obligations are in conflict. The filmmaker must understand the nature of the project early in its existence because the planning choices may dictate some of the other choices available to the filmmaker. Still, as with everything else in filmmaking, business organizations can change as the situation evolves. If a filmmaker starts out making a small film, but the project suddenly doubles in budget and scope, the filmmaker can revisit the business planning to reflect the new situation. The following sections describe five different structures for organizing a film business, listing their advantages and disadvantages. The final Section F discusses which entities and structures work best for which purposes.

A. Sole Proprietorship

A sole proprietor is a single person who is personally responsible for all aspects of the business. If the filmmaker does not adopt any of the other legal structures described below, then the filmmaker will be treated as a sole proprietor. The business is never separate from its owner. All control stays with the sole proprietor. All liability, including all debts, promises, and obligations, remains the personal responsibility of the business owner. The primary benefit of working as a sole proprietor is that of simplicity. Without any separate legal entity, there are few, if any, formalities needed to conduct the filmmaking business.

A second potential benefit of operating as a sole proprietor is that an individual has a credit history and assets that a new, separate legal entity may not have. Of the independent films financed on credit cards—like Spike Lee's *She's Gotta Have It*—most relied on the personal credit of the filmmaker (as well as the liberal card issuance policies of the credit card companies). If the income and expenses of the film project are relatively small, the choice to remain a sole proprietor may be a very reasonable one.

The legitimate business expenses of a sole proprietorship may be tax-deductible business expenses. The filmmaker must use Schedule C on the 1040 annual tax form and report the expenses and income that she has carefully calculated and itemized during the filmmaking process. Additional rules apply to show that the sole proprietorship is truly a business rather than a hobby. The filmmaker must show that there is positive income in three of every five years or the IRS can treat the filmmaking as nondeductible hobby expenses.

A sole proprietor is not restricted to the name of the filmmaker. The filmmaker can still use a production company name if she wishes by filing a Fictitious Business Name Statement (often known as a "d.b.a." or "doing business as" form). The d.b.a. gives the filmmaker only the right to use a fictional name in a particular state. It confers no limits on liability, nor does it give the filmmaker trademark rights to the name. At the early stages in planning a film project, the filmmaker may elect to file a Fictitious Business Name Statement as the first preliminary step in creating the film company. It may give the filmmaker some priority for use of the name in that state if she later wishes to create a formal business entity, and it also gives her the legal right to conduct business under that name.

The single biggest drawback to operating as a sole proprietor is the personal liability that the filmmaker undertakes. For the digital filmmaker, this issue may be more theoretical than real. Limited liability, protection from personal obligation provided by corporations and limited liability companies, creates a corporate shield for any contractual obligations and for any tort liabilities when the filmmaker is sued as an officer or director of the corporation.

This protection may sometimes be more apparent than real. In the case of contractual obligations it is not uncommon for the creditor to demand a personal guarantee by the filmmaker. This is a legally enforceable promise that the individual will cover the contractual obligations in the event that the film company cannot. The effect of the personal guarantee is to render the corporate protection meaningless.

Tort creditors pose a more difficult problem for the filmmaker. The filmmaker is often the individual conducting the activity or supervising the manner in which the conduct was being done. In the earlier example, the filmmaker shooting the car chase will be personally responsible if she was negligent in allowing the car to be driven in an unsafe manner or for allowing a pedestrian to be too close. If the director is found negligent, then she will be personally liable regardless of the limited liability afforded by the corporation. No legal entity will protect a filmmaker from responsibility for her own actions.

Because there are many instances where personal liability is not shielded by the legal entity, control and fundraising become the more pressing reasons to select a business form. The sole proprietorship provides the maximum level of control desired by a filmmaker, but does not accommodate fundraising. The filmmaker can raise money by taking out personal loans (debt financing), but the sole proprietorship is not suitable for raising capital from third parties. Since the third party cannot receive ownership in the film company and can only receive contractual rights to the film's revenue, most investors will want substantially greater protections. In addition, the payment by the investor to the sole proprietor may transform the relationship into that of a general partnership because the investor has joined with the filmmaker in the business enterprise. This undermines the control sought by the filmmaker without offering any benefits to the investor.

B. General Partnership

A general partnership is any business conducted by two or more people for profit. Like a sole proprietorship, no formalities need be followed for a general partnership to be formed. Also like the sole proprietorship, the partners are each fully and completely responsible for all contractual and tort liabilities of every kind.

The general partnership differs from the sole proprietorship because two or more people share control. Absent any formal contract or business agreement between the general partners, state law governs how that control is shared. In most states, any general partner in a partnership may obligate the partnership. This means that any of the partners can agree that the business will do something, and that contract will be binding on the partnership—even without the other partners being aware of it. On the other hand, decision making is conducted by majority vote. Neither of these situations is healthy for a filmmaking exercise.

The nature of the filmmaking process leads to too many situations where last-minute decisions and ill-informed promises can be made. Granting this contractual power to everyone involved may undermine the management of the film company. For example, it may be that the director—in order to get one last shot at 2:00 A.M.—promises an actor improved billing if only he will do the scene one additional time. That promise will be binding on the film company only if the director has the authority to make such a bargain. If the director is the sole proprietor, then she has only herself to blame if the offer was imprudent. If the director is one of three general partners—with the producer and screenwriter—then the film company will be bound by the hasty bargain.

The rules that govern general partnership can usually be changed by agreement among the partners. Typically, however, general partnerships are used in very informal situations, so no formal partnership agreement is ever drafted or signed. In the absence of an agreement to the contrary, the partners in a general partnership all share equally in the profits and losses. They also share in the responsibility for the partnership's debts and obligations. The obligation to share in the debts does not limit the liability of any individual partner. If only one of three partners has any assets, then that partner will be responsible for all obligations of the film company. That partner can look to the other partners for repayment, but the other partners' duty to her will not reduce her obligation to creditors.

General partnerships are not taxed. Instead, the profits and losses are allocated proportionately to the partners, who then pay personal income tax on the profits or deduct the business losses. The tax rules that allow the partnership not to be taxed are probably the best feature of the general partnership.

Tax benefits aside, it should be clear from the description that a general partnership is not a good business form for operating a film company—no matter how small. A general partnership maximizes risk and minimizes the filmmaker's control. Nonetheless, general partnerships are often formed inadvertently when two people start working together in a profit-making activity, such as a writer and director who plan to split the profits from an independent film. To avoid becoming a general partnership, the filmmaker should formalize her working arrangements early on to avoid accidentally becoming a general partner.

C. Limited Partnerships

Limited partnerships differ dramatically from general partnerships. These are formal, documented, legal entities that provide some of the partners protection from personal liability for debts. It is formed by filing the necessary papers with the state in which it is formed. A limited partnership is managed by the general partner or partners who run the business on behalf of the partnership. There may be one or more general partners. The general partner may even be a corporation.

Except for the managing general partners, all remaining participants are limited partners. Limited partners contribute money or property as capital to the partnership in exchange for ownership in the company and participation in the profits and losses. To remain limited partners, they must have very little to do with the control and operation of the business. They vote on only selected issues that affect the survival of the business or they appoint a new general partner if the existing general partner is dead, unavailable, or unable to act.

Limited partnerships are primarily fundraising vehicles, particularly well suited to sole proprietors who need to raise capital. The limited partners participate by contributing the necessary capital for the business, but they do not interfere with its operations. As the general partner of a limited partnership, the filmmaker retains most of the operational control over the film company. The filmmaker must account to the limited partners on how money was spent, collected, and disbursed, but such obligations are often set at a level of minimal accountability to the investors. While the general partner remains personally liable for all debts and tort liabilities, the obligation is reduced to the extent the limited partners have contributed money to make the movie. The filmmaker can pay the partnership's liabilities with the limited partnership's funds before having to use her own.

Limited partnerships combine some of the better features of the sole proprietorship and the corporation. Although limited liability companies are becoming the preferred business form for certain fundraising activities, the long, successful history of limited partnerships may make that structure an attractive form for the filmmaker seeking to raise funds to make a movie.

Limited partnerships may provide tax benefits as well. Limited partnerships are taxed like general partnerships—or rather, like general partnerships, they are not taxed. The profits and losses are allocated to the partners who pay the taxes or deduct the losses on their individual returns. If the filmmaker has little income to offset the losses, the partnership agreement may allocate losses in a manner that makes the investment more attractive to the investor by allocating a greater portion of losses to the limited partners. Unfortunately for the filmmaker, tax rules have changed over the years so that the benefits of investing in money-losing limited partnerships have been strongly reduced, but there may still be some tax benefits to the investors.

One note of caution—the sale of limited partnership interests, like corporate stock, is the sale of a "security" that is highly regulated under both state and federal law. Many filmmakers violate federal Securities Exchange Commission rules, as well as state and federal laws, by arranging for financing without consulting a qualified attorney. Violating these laws may result in the filmmaker being compelled to return all the funds to the investors, facing significant fines, or even facing criminal penalties. Please see Chapter 4, Section F, for an introduction to securities law and an explanation on how to safely raise funds.

D. Corporations

Corporations are legal entities used to operate the smallest and largest companies in the world. A corporation is managed by a board of directors, operated by its officers, and owned by its shareholders. These may all be different individuals. The corporation provides limited liability for all acts conducted on behalf of the corporation. Still, as described above, the person who acted negligently is still responsible for her own conduct. If the negligence were done on behalf of the corporation, then the corporation would be responsible as well as the employee, so the corporation will provide additional protection for personal liability to the extent that the corporation has assets to pay for the liability.

One of the key features for corporations is the separation of management from control. The investors—the shareholders who have contributed cash or property in exchange for ownership—control the corporation. The shareholders operate by electing a board of directors. The board of directors is made up of professionals who manage the business and hire the employees of the company. The board of directors is bound by operating rules established in the corporation's bylaws. For a digital filmmaker, the formalities of a corporation may seem extreme. Nonetheless, most states allow a corporation to have a single person serve as the board of directors. Unanimous written agreements among the shareholders can bind the shareholders to elect the same person as officer and director of the corporation. Using these techniques, the same corporate form that works for General Motors can be adapted to My Film Company, Inc.

The corporation may be taxed as a separate entity, but if certain rules are followed, then the corporation can choose to be taxed as if it was a partnership. This tax election is known as a Subchapter S Corporation election. To elect to be taxed as a partnership, the company must limit the number of shareholders to 75 and limit the types of stock sold. For the small film company, these and the other restrictions often do not pose significant burdens.

There are no significant downsides to operating as a corporation. Corporations can range from an entity owned by a single person to one owned by millions of investors. Corporations require a certain amount of formality, but these are relatively easy steps to remember, and there are thousands of books and software programs to assist with these steps. Perhaps the greatest danger of adopting the corporate formation is trying to over-simplify the task. Many authors create standard documents for corporations, but these one-size-fits-all materials often create problems for their users. Filmmakers should be cautious to avoid the corporate form book, but may readily embrace the corporate form.

E. Limited Liability Companies

The limited liability company, or LLC, is a relatively new form of business entity, only gaining popularity in the past decade. The unique feature of the LLC is the flexibility it provides to the owners. The owners of the LLC, typically called members under most state statutes, have limited liability like shareholders in a corporation as well as the ability to elect to be treated as a partnership for tax purposes.[1] The LLC has become a favorite vehicle for small business planners because it gives the owners maximum flexibility regarding the structuring of control and financing while reducing liability and tax obligations.

The Internal Revenue Service adopted rules in 1997 that allow the LLC to elect whether to be taxed as a corporation or as a partnership. By adopting this rule, the LLC has the greatest flexibility of any business form. To be classified as a corporation for tax purposes, however, the LLC must have two or more members. So if a sole proprietor wishes to have the business taxed separately as an entity, the only option is a Subchapter C Corporation rather than a limited liability company.[2]

As described by most state statutes, the LLC is owned by its members and operated through its managers. The required filings—the Articles of Organization—are often one-page, fill-in-the-blank forms that must be filed with the secretary of state in the state in which the film company will be located.

In addition to the Articles of Organization, the filmmaker should—but is not legally obligated to—create an Operating Agreement for the LLC. The Operating Agreement establishes the rules for managing and operating the business. In many states, the Operating Agreement may simply state that the manager—the filmmaker—has sole management authority, that there will be no meetings, and that the profits and losses will be shared in a specified manner between the manager and the other members of the LLC.

In most states, the creation of the LLC simply requires that a one-page form be completed and submitted to the secretary of state along with a tax payment. In addition to the filing of this certificate, a film company LLC must have a written, signed Operating Agreement that serves as the articles and bylaws of the organization to set out the rules for operations, governance, and payments.

Many of these provisions are common to every LLC, and these provisions will be found in virtually every formbook. These include the name of the LLC, the admission and removal of participants, place of business, maintenance of capital accounts, terminations, and transfers of interest. Nonetheless, there are a few particular issues of concern to the filmmaker.

For example, investors in the film company may not wish to give such unbridled discretion to the filmmaker, particularly over the raising of capital or other financial decisions. One of the primary benefits of the LLC is the opportunity to shape the business entity to reflect the nature of the investors' interests and the filmmaker's needs.

The only real drawback to the use of the LLC is the limited experience that the business and investment community has had in using the form. Investors sometimes want to purchase shares of a corporation because they are used to financing businesses using that traditional form.

F. Choosing the Best Structure

For many independent filmmakers the limited liability company is the best choice for forming a film production company. The Operating Agreement is more flexible than corporate bylaws for structuring the film company operations. It provides as effective a limitation from personal liability as does the corporation.

For films financed with outside investors, the traditional corporate structure may serve as the best vehicle. The use of multiple classes of stock and shareholders' agreements can be drafted to achieve the same results as those sought under the Operating Agreement. The tax advantages of a partnership may have little value for the film company, since the investors are more interested in the long-term growth of the investment than short-term losses for tax purposes. As a result the preferred form of structure depends on the particular makeup of filmmakers and investors.

For guerrilla filmmakers as well as many independents, there may not be any benefit to forming a separate entity unless the filmmaker is seeking investment financing. Most debt will come from personal loans or unsecured personal credit cards. These obligations will not be changed by using a corporate or limited liability form. Most tort liability—liability for accidents—will arise from activities in which the filmmaker is personally involved. Since the limited liability only shields the filmmaker from liability as an officer or director of the business, it will be of little value to shield the filmmaker from liability for accidents she caused or for her failure to supervise the cast and crew.

If the filmmaker is shooting a short project with a small cast and crew, then the filmmaker may be best advised to remain a sole proprietor. On the other hand, if the size of the project increases or if investor financing becomes a part of the organization, then it is very important that the filmmaker work through the corporation or the limited liability company. The worst choice is to ignore the problem and have the law treat the project as a general partnership.

The decision to switch to a business entity from a sole proprietorship need not be made immediately. The tax laws allow for the sole proprietor to exchange her business for the assets[3] of a new entity without paying a tax penalty. From the outset of the film project, the filmmaker should have the business management in mind and should work with a lawyer and accountant as early as possible to create the necessary business entity when the filmmaker is ready.

Duties of the Film Company

As MENTIONED IN Chapter 2, a typical film company of even modest size quickly undertakes all the attributes of a well-established business. The company, however legally structured, will need to engage employees, rent equipment, pay taxes, raise working capital, and sign contracts with landlords, insurance companies, lenders, and many others. If at all possible, the duties of filmmaking should be separated from the duties of operating the film company. While many filmmakers serve as chief cook and bottle washer, team efforts are often more successful. In this way, the filmmaker working with an actor regarding character does not have to be discussing her payroll and tax forms at the same time. The separation of the business from the artistic functions improves both professionalism and focus.

While a film company has all the same legal and business obligations of any service company, certain obligations are most important for the successful completion of the film. The following introduces the most basic of these areas.

A. Financial Accounting and Responsibility

The financial accounting of a motion picture is extremely detailed, complex, and vital. It is not a coincidence that Michael Eisner became the CEO of Disney by learning the business in the accounting department. Many other studio heads were lawyers earlier in their careers. Good accounting increases the odds that the film company will have the funds necessary to pay salaries, rent equipment when needed, and still edit the film.

1. Planning

Often, participants in independent filmmaking agree to be paid from the profits made by the film company on the film. This requires that the costs be carefully itemized and reported so that all participants are treated fairly and the profit participants develop confidence that there will be profit generated if the film becomes a success.

The most critical phase in filmmaking accounting is the first step—budgeting. Chapter 5 provides a detailed analysis of the film budget process and the items that go into that budget. The budget provides a blueprint for the structure of the film company and the film project. The production budget detailed in Chapter 5 focuses on the expenses of making the film, but the budgetary process is primarily a planning tool. The budget allows the filmmaker to identify the scope of the project, the magnitude of the financial resources needed, the scheduling of receipts and payments, and the long-term obligations that might exist if the film is not a financial success.

A well-organized film company will create a business plan to serve as sounding board and map, anticipating each phase of the film project. That business plan will help communicate the corporate planning to potential investors and more cautious creative participants who demand a realistic chance of success before they commit to a project.

2. Record Keeping

Equally important is the record keeping required for the film company. Record keeping serves two distinct goals. First, it provides the documentary proof of the production expenses, essential documentation for tax payments, and the calculation of the company's expenses. Since many participants' payments are calculated based on the profit of the film company, failure to document expenses will lower the break-even point for the profit participants. It also serves as proof that the expenses were made, which may be required for some financing options.

Second, record keeping allows the filmmaker to monitor the costs of set construction. If 14 days into a 21-day shoot the film company has already spent 90 percent of its set construction budget, the filmmaker will have to make some choices. Perhaps most of the money was spent on a single set that has been used throughout filming. Then the remaining 10 percent of the budget should be satisfactory. If, however, the set construction costs are generally the same for each day of filming, then the filmmaker can expect to run as much as 40 percent over budget on set construction. Knowing this, the filmmaker can choose to scale back on set construction, increase the set construction budget by reducing other costs, or plan to increase the production expense. Without the advance knowledge, the filmmaker could find himself without funds in a checking account, suddenly shut down in the middle of production. A good accountant may not improve the film but she certainly will improve the chances of completing the film.

3. Accountability

Carefully accounting for all expenditures along the way is the best way to ensure that funds raised will be available throughout the filming and editing process. The budget is the road map for which the accountant must serve as vigilant navigator.

When money begins to flow, the danger always exists that it may be misspent. The accounting process provides accountability. Independent films can range in budget from a few dollars to hundreds of millions of dollars on the scale of George Lucas's *Star Wars* films. For accounting purposes, misspent resources do not include failed creative choices, such as purchasing a wedding dress for a scene that is later redrafted to take place in a dance club. While that may be a regrettable expenditure, the money purchased the intended costume and the balance sheet reflects the value of the dress even if the film does not. Instead, misspent funds refers to personal purchases improperly attributed to the production company, money stolen, and expenses attributed to the wrong budget line.

Whenever someone other than a sole propietor is handling the film company's payments, a system of accountability must be established. The nature of the system depends on the size of the project and the number of individuals authorized to spend company money. The key is that for every expenditure there is a receipt, and every receipt is attributed to a particular budget line. A film company can authorize its scene designer to buy materials as necessary, so long as the expense remains within the agreed budget. As payments are made, the receipts are tabulated. This helps to guarantee that the designer has spent the money on set materials while allowing the business manager to compare the expenditures to the approved budget.

The need for careful accounting becomes most difficult near the end of principal photography. As the tension mounts to finish the filming on schedule, the frenetic pace often encourages frenzied choices. Late hours result in crumpled receipts piling up in ashtrays. After the frenzy, the receipts are flattened and submitted for reimbursement. The delay in submission allows the expenses to balloon, possibly eliminating the funds left for postproduction. Particularly on low-budget films, money is tight. Even a few bad choices at the end of principal photography can derail the project.

A film company should plan to assign the accounting and internal auditing function to someone early in the development of the film company. While not glamorous, a good production accountant can help ensure the film is made.

4. Reporting

The final aspect of accounting relates to the obligations to report income and pay taxes. Unless the filmmaker operates a sole proprietorship, the film company must report income or losses. That information is used to pay taxes—either directly by the corporation or indirectly by the participants in limited partnerships and limited liability companies. Movies are unique assets subject to illogical and highly manipulatable generally accepted accounting practices. These accounting rules allow the film company either to speed up the depreciation of the film to generate business losses and reduce tax liability or to slow the depreciation down by predicting long-lasting revenue from the movie that increases the film as an asset on the books of the company.[1]

Although the guerrilla filmmaker may pay little heed to the accounting consequences of the film, investors and financiers will. The successful film company should engage the services of a qualified accountant who can help the company establish a strategy to deal with the tax and reporting obligations for the project.

One additional note of caution: the tax reporting for a marginally successful film may continue for years—in some cases, the tax forms outlast the prints of the film itself. The filmmaker must be prepared to accept this obligation to continue to collect fees and provide tax reports when creating the film company.

B. Employer Obligations

Employment and labor obligations are perhaps the most detailed and least followed aspect of independent filmmaking. The myriad federal and state laws are poorly crafted to address the filmmaking industry. Production typically ends and the employees are dismissed before regulators have an opportunity to object to the business practices, and, luckily for independent filmmakers, the employees themselves are typically young and disinterested in their legal rights.

Nonetheless, the employer's duties are significant legal obligations that can create headaches for the successful filmmaker. A crew member paid a small stipend may successfully claim she was supposed to be protected by minimum wage laws as well as overtime for all time worked in excess of a 40-hour week—or even an eight-hour day in California. Filmmakers may not choose to label everyone an independent contractor if the individuals are working under the direction and control of the film company for an extended period of time. Employers must pay particular attention to the hiring practices, wage and hour laws, and antidiscrimination policies when managing the significant labor force involved with even the most modest of film projects.

1. Hiring

Hiring decisions for a motion picture include both very subjective decisions regarding casting as well as much more routine hiring decisions for support staff and technical personnel. Although casting is a form of hiring, it is treated separately as part of the process in developing talent.

For the remaining employees, a broad range of rules and legal limitations are designed to ensure that job applicants are treated fairly. An employer may not discriminate on the basis of categories such as race, national origin, gender, sexual preference, age, or disability. In particular, the Americans with Disabilities Act requires that the employer make reasonable accommodations for an employee's disability unless that disability affects an essential job function. So, for example, a deaf candidate would be precluded from the job of sound engineer because of the essential function necessary to hear and judge the sound quality, while that same person—if qualified—could become a stunt person.

To deny a job on the basis of a disability, that disability must affect an essential job requirement. In the previous example, the deaf stunt person could not properly be passed over for a less qualified applicant who is not hearing impaired merely because the person might be given a few lines of conversation later in the film. Similarly, the company must make reasonable accommodation, so the company would be required to find a method to provide visual rather than auditory cues to begin and end action during filming.

Because discrimination is illegal, the film company must take steps to avoid asking interview questions that would trigger discriminatory possibilities. The Equal Employment Opportunity Commission treats questions unrelated to the position's skills and experience as discriminatory. On both written questionnaires and in oral interviews, the interviewer should focus on issues related to the applicant's skills, availability, and ability to fulfill the position. Often interviewers make small talk to begin to break the ice during an interview, but questions regarding marital status, religion, or other personal issues that might be used to discriminate are inappropriate and impermissible. The rules do not change whether the person being hired is the film's director or the assistant script supervisor.

The hiring process also involves a significant amount of selling by the film company. Often, with independent film production, the company must convince the applicant to work for a deferred salary or minimum wage in exchange for a chance to participate in the windfall when the movie hits it big. While such projections serve to fuel the optimistic vision of the filmmaker, the film company must take care not to falsify the status of the project or the experience of the participants. Lies regarding the financing status or professional expertise of the filmmaker are commonplace, yet such misrepresentations are unfair trade practices under the Federal Trade Protection Act and grounds for lawsuits if the project fails to meet the employee's aspirations.

Once the applicant has been hired, the film company must also verify the person's eligibility to work in the United States. This can be done by following the instructions on Form I-9 from the Immigration and Naturalization Service. Employees must complete this form within three days of beginning work and provide documentation within three weeks. The company must then retain the I-9 for one year following the termination of the employee or a maximum of three years from the date of hire. In addition, all employment applications and resumes must be retained for one year, even if the person was not hired.

2. Employment Status—Independent Contractors and Employees

One of the common techniques to avoid dealing with employment situations in the independent film production community is to treat everyone as an independent contractor. This approach is only appropriate occasionally and can lead to significant problems for the film company.

An independent contractor is a person who is self-employed and provides service to the hiring party as a client. For example, craft services (the catering person) would typically be an independent contractor, providing craft services for a number of clients including the film company. Since the film company is engaging personnel to make the film under its direction and control, the film company should expect that most of the personnel hired are employees rather than independent contractors.

Unfortunately there is no steadfast definition of an independent contractor, despite the significant tax and insurance liability that can accrue for overusing the independent contractor status. The IRS and courts first look to the company's ability to control the activities of the person. If the hiring party dictates the location where the work will be done, the hours, and the manner of the work, that will generally infer an employee. If the person hired controls those factors, that suggests the person is an independent contractor.

Another significant factor is the ability to provide services for multiple clients. In the catering situation, the film will probably be one of many clients handled simultaneously, strongly suggesting the independent status of the person. Similarly, ownership of one's tools and equipment suggests an independent contractor.

Given these general parameters, most participants on a film project are not independent contractors. The cast, director, and designers work under the direction of the film company using equipment rented by the film company. Costumers, craft services, sound engineers, and special effects teams tend to be on a shoot part-time, bringing their own tools and servicing multiple clients when the work is available. For these individuals, independent contractor status may be more appropriate. Form I-9 documentation need not be completed by independent contractors.

The difference between the two categories is significant. The employer must pay social security taxes for employees and withhold employment taxes on behalf of the employees. These costs and duties do not extend to independent contractors. Independent contractors have no deductions taken from their paychecks and retain responsibility for all taxes. To discourage treating employees as independent contractors, the IRS provides that an employer that improperly treats an employee as an independent contractor will face significant tax liability, including payment of back taxes, interest, and penalties.

In many states, a company must also pay additional state taxes to cover state workers' compensation funds. In exchange, the laws require that an employee grievance process be followed for any work-related injuries. Costs are covered by the workers' compensation insurance, and the injured employee may not sue for negligence by the employer. An independent contractor does not have the benefit of the state workers' compensation insurance and has no restrictions on suing the film company in the event of a personal injury on the set of a production.

In addition to the traditional dichotomy of employees and independent contractors, a film project often has unpaid assistants. Depending on the state laws, these assistants may or may not be covered by workers' compensation insurance. Unfortunately, due to long hours, dangerous equipment, and crew inexperience, independent film productions have a high rate of accidents. A company may find it is cheaper to pay volunteers a minimum wage than to purchase liability insurance to cover their participation.

3. Employment Status—Exempt or Salaried Employees

Like the dichotomy between independent contractors and employees, the distinction between exempt and salaried employees affects the obligations the employer has toward the employee. The exemption is from wage and hour laws, providing that an exempt employee can be paid for the scope of the project rather than the hours worked. Minimum wage laws protect salaried employees, providing overtime for work in excess of 40 hours per week, or even eight hours per day in some states.

Exempt employees are categorized as executives, administrators, professionals, and salespeople. Professionals must earn at least $170 per week and utilize originality, creativity, or specialized knowledge in the position, generally from advanced training. If the salary minimum is met, then many of the employees working in specialized positions on a film would qualify as exempt. The executive category requires supervision of at least two individuals. Generally, anyone with supervisory duties on a film will be working in a professional capacity.

Administrators must exercise independent judgment in their administrative duties. This category sounds unnecessarily vague since, hopefully, every employee exercises independent judgment throughout the day. Maybe this is less true outside of the film industry. Executives and administrators need only be paid $155 per week to meet the statutory minimum, so these categorizations may be relevant.

Although the distinction between salaried and exempt employees does not run the same magnitude of risk as does the distinction between that of independent contractor and employee, a film company should make every effort to comply with the law, if possible. Admittedly, at some point the filmmaker may be required to take legal risks to continue the production. If there is no money left in the production account and there are 12 pages of script left to shoot, then the film may be completed by volunteers— since everyone was technically laid off when the funds gave out.

4. Tax and Withholding Status

The film company has a number of obligations regarding employee tax payments. Immediately upon hiring, the employee should complete Form W-4 to determine the amount of taxes that are to be withheld from the payroll for the purposes of paying federal, state, and local taxes. The W-4 must be kept for four years following termination of the employee. The employer must deduct the appropriate amount of money from each employee paycheck and deposit this money in a separate account. Severe fines and even potential criminal liability can be incurred for withholding an employee's tax payments and failing to submit those payments to the government.

The withheld payroll tax is submitted monthly for companies with a payroll not greater than $50,000 and twice monthly for payroll deductions greater than $50,000. Additional rules apply if the deductions are significantly smaller or larger than these amounts.

Following the end of each calendar year, the film company must submit a statement reflecting the annual payment and taxes submitted for each employee. The employee must receive Form W-2 by the first of February each year, and the IRS must receive Form W-3 by the first of March. Failure to file these forms can result in fines. More important, the former cast and crew need these forms to complete their own taxes, and the film company has an obligation to provide this information. The film company should do whatever it can to maintain goodwill with former employees, so that frustrations do not arise and the former employees do not start to investigate the myriad employment and labor violations that regularly occur in independent film companies.

The purpose of this section is to ensure that the filmmaker can make well-informed choices and choose pragmatic solutions based on the associated risks. For example, a filmmaker should never fail to submit payroll taxes, even if that payment were to require that he treat three employees as exempt rather than salaried. Most accountants and attorneys would also recommend that a filmmaker forgo a scene involving an expensive wind machine to solve both employment problems—which reflects why accountants and attorneys rarely become guerrilla filmmakers.

5. Loan-Out Employment Services

The best solution for many of the employment obligations for an independent film company is to service the personnel functions through a loan-out employment service. These companies become the employer of record for the employees. Legally obligated to handle the tax forms, they ensure proper withholding and collect funds needed for payments to the Screen Actors Guild (SAG), other unions and guilds, and talent agents as required. For some production companies, this cost may be an extreme luxury, but for productions of even modest budgets, having a loan-out employment service may become a very sound investment in the longevity of the film company.

Payroll services handle the administration but do not serve as the employer. These services cost less because the primary duties do not shift from the production company to the payroll service. Payroll services are useful for handling the details of bimonthly check writing, but they do not solve the longer-term issues of record keeping.

Increasingly, for small production companies, these basic payroll services can be obtained equally well using commercial software. Software requires that someone remember to operate it and provide the checks, but the software provides sufficient information and support for the small filmmaker. Armed with a checklist of the proper forms to submit and a schedule of submission, a software package will often provide most of the benefits of a payroll service for a fraction of the cost.

6. Profit Participants

Particularly for guerrilla filmmaking, the notion that minimum wage will be paid—or even that basic employment records will be filed—stands as little more than wishful thinking. While these fundamental steps should be taken, practical guidance should be related to the art of the possible. For those companies that will not otherwise attempt to meet their hiring obligations, another approach may be to include all the participants in the risks and rewards of the film.

Unlike employees, the owners of an enterprise are not generally covered by hour and wage laws, nor are they included in workers' compensation insurance. The owners—general partners, members, or shareholders—assume the risk and participate actively in the enterprise, so the legal protections are less necessary. Using an LLC structure, an operating agreement that treats all participants as managing members of the LLC may avoid many of the state and federal employment obligations. If the film company truly consists of the cast, the director, and the producer, it may be appropriate to allow everyone to share in the risks, minimized to the extent possible using the LLC, and share in the rewards. The portions need not be equal. The filmmaker can retain a larger share, reflecting his broader role in the film.

This technique should not be abused. As the scope and budget of a project increases, the reasonability of this approach diminishes. Nonetheless, for guerrilla filmmaking this practical structure may at least serve to rationalize the practice adopted.

C. Decision Making

Good decision making includes both effective communication and clear lines of responsibility. If the filmmaker, business manager, and production company leadership know what is happening with the production, they all have a common basis for decision making. Delegation of responsibility will allow the filmmaker to share the load. The decision-making model within the film company provides the structure for planning all aspects of the film production. Many of the plans include artistic choices involving locations, cast, and story. Other decisions may be less important but still essential to the success—or even completion—of the film. These include equipment rentals, location negotiations, film permits, and service agreements.

The film company serves as the party with which every contract and negotiation must take place. The filmmaker must be very careful to allow the film company to be the responsible party rather than entering transactions personally. This distinction does not matter if the film company is a sole proprietorship or general partnership, but the benefits of forming a corporation or LLC will be lost if the filmmaker disregards the role of the company and puts his own name on contracts rather than signing on behalf of the company.

Planning becomes the purview of the film company as a whole. Both artistic and business concerns must be balanced during the initial planning and throughout the ongoing production. This requires that the filmmaker work closely with the business manager and other senior staff to explore the impact of significant decisions on an ongoing basis. As the production grows, responsibility for some decisions is delegated, so it becomes critical that information is shared among the affected parties.

If possible, production meetings of the senior management should be held regularly so that as much as possible is coordinated. Francis Ford Coppola tells the story of a very expensive scene from *Apocalypse Now* in which he initially ordered an extravagant set, including perfectly authentic food, wine, and costumes. Later, as the budget spiraled out of control, he ordered the budget cut. Casting greatly reduced the expense of the cast hired for this scene, but the other departments never got the message. Out of utter frustration, Coppola stopped filming and refused to use the scene.[2]

On a lesser level, this type of expensive mistake happens frequently. A delay in notifying the costume designer of a change of cast may result in wasted effort and money. Location changes can cascade throughout t he production. If everyone knows of a cash shortage, then every department can look to find the least harmful areas to cut expenses and defer payments.

Equally important, the decision-making process must allow for delegation of some authority. Below a certain dollar amount, for example, designers should be able to approve expenses directly. So long as the designers then promptly report the expenses, the film company can track the purchases and the impact on the finances. Together, communication and delegation allow the production company to improve the chances of successfully completing the film and free the filmmaker to focus on the important artistic issues.

D. Business Continuity

The film company provides the continuity for the film as it moves from theatrical exhibition to video, foreign distribution, television, and Internet broadcasting. A successful film might continue to earn revenue for decades. The film company must be organized to anticipate this long-term commitment.

The film company provides the continuity for the employment and tax record keeping, the regular distribution of profits, if successful, the distribution of revenue for unions or other gross income participants, and the legal ownership of the film. If new markets open for film distribution or the film becomes very popular, then the licensing opportunities and obligations of the film can continue for many years. Again, delegation may become critical. A successful film often propels many of the production team into increasingly larger projects. This makes it difficult to manage the often more modest revenue from the independent films. Delegation to a professional involved with the project—such as the accountant or attorney—may allow the film company to continue to meet its obligations while allowing the filmmaker to grow his career.

Financing the Film Project

FILM FINANCING IS the most difficult aspect of independent filmmaking—both raising the money and complying with the applicable state and federal laws. As the amount of money raised increases, so does the importance of working with an experienced attorney. When raising money, even small mistakes can result in the end of the production, fines, and criminal liability. Extreme care and attention to detail must be used when raising capital for a film.

No matter how small the project, funds are going to be required to make the motion picture. This may range from a few dollars for out-of-pocket expenses to hundreds of millions of dollars for top-name stars, special effects, and postproduction effects and editing. The more typical amount for guerrilla and independent filmmaking ranges from a few thousand dollars for digital cameras, computers, and software to a few million dollars for a union cast film shot on 35mm film.

There is no "correct" way to choose to make the film, but these choices are often dictated by the cash available more than any aesthetic sensibilities. If the film company has been able to pre-sell some of the distribution rights, then making the film directly on 35mm film enhances the production quality and promotes the professionalism of the project. If the film is being financed through a network of the filmmaker's family and friends, then a choice to defer the costs of 35mm until the film is successfully completed may be more realistic and responsible. A super-low-budget digital

film may find a large audience, sell DVDs and videotapes, and be distributed on cable and television without ever needing the expense of a 35mm
version. A modestly successful digital film produced for $25,000 that
returns $75,000 in videotape and cable revenue will greatly exceed the
return of any studio film and serve as an excellent credit, helping the filmmaker and cast promote their careers. Ironically, by shooting low, the filmmaker might also have the opportunity to remake the film later in her
career with the luxury of studio financing.

A. Introduction—Survey of Financing Tools

There are a number of distinct sources of money for film financing, and
every film uses some combination of these sources to finance the project.
First, equity investment may come from outsiders funding the film company or in exchange for financial participation in the particular film. Second, the filmmaker may raise production funds by selling the right to
distribute and exhibit the film prior to the film's creation. Third, the filmmaker may use loans to make cash available for the production. This third
category is known as debt financing. Funding is first distinguished
between debt financing in the form of loans or credit, and equity financing in the form of sales of property.

In debt financing, a lender such as a bank gives the borrower money
in exchange for a promise to repay that loan on time. The bank makes
profit by charging interest on the loan. Loans place the risk of failure on
the borrower because the lender expects to be repaid whether the film is
a success or a failure. On the other hand, although the borrower must pay
back the principal and interest regardless of the outcome of the film, the
lender does not participate in any profits above the interest. As a result,
the borrower stands to make significantly more profit if a successful film
is debt financed rather than equity financed.

Equity financing requires the filmmaker to sell interests in either the
film or the film company in exchange for the funding. This serves to distribute the risk of the project because the investor only receives his money
back if the film shows a return. If a filmmaker sells 50 percent of the corporate interest to an investor, for example, then the investor will lose his

entire investment if the film is a complete failure. If the film is a tremendous success, the investor will receive 50 percent of every dollar of profit—far more than the lender would have received.

Assume that a particular digital film can be successfully shot and completed for $100,000. Of this amount, half came from outside sources. The following reflects the difference to the filmmaker. First, assume the film makes a total revenue of $400,000.

	Lender	Equity Purchaser	Filmmaker's Own $$
Terms	10% Interest	50% Purchase	None
Contribution	$50,000	$50,000	——
Interest	$5,000	——	——
Cost of Film	$105,000	$100,000	$100,000
Gross Revenue	$400,000	$400,000	$400,000
Net Income to Film Company	$295,000	$300,000	$300,000
Profit to Filmmaker	$295,000	$150,000	$300,000

Next, assume the film generates a total revenue of only $50,000:

	Lender	Equity Purchaser	Filmmaker's Own $$
Terms	10% Interest	50% Purchase	None
Contribution	$50,000	$50,000	——
Interest	$5,000	——	——
Cost of Film	$105,000	$100,000	$100,000
Gross Revenue	$50,000	$50,000	$50,000
Net Income to Film Company	−$55,000	−$25,000	−$50,000
Profit to Filmmaker	−$55,000	−$25,000	−$50,000

From the chart, it becomes clear that equity financing serves to soften the losses of the film project, but it also reduces the profits. Debt financing maximizes the profits but places the entire cost of loss on the filmmaker—and adds the cost of interest to boot.

The most beneficial situation for the filmmaker would be to receive 100 percent of the film costs from an equity sale in exchange for substantially less than 100 percent of the income—in the range of 25 to 50 percent. In this way the filmmaker shares in a portion of the profits but undertakes no cash risk of loss. Nonetheless, many independent filmmakers—including successful directors such as Spike Lee and Francis Ford Coppola—have used their personal funds to finance all or part of their films. There are no legal limits or restrictions on this practice. Despite the adage that a filmmaker should only spend other people's money, personal funds are invariably part of the film financing mix.

B. Financing Based on Distribution Deals and Presale Arrangements

Unlike other industries, there are two discrete types of equity sales in the motion picture industry. The first is sale of securities in the film company. By selling stock in a corporation or membership interests in an LLC, the company raises funds by increasing the amount of equity owned by people other than the filmmaker. This is the typical model of equity financing.

The second form of equity financing involves selling the film's distribution rights. In this form of equity financing, the company sells its assets in exchange for a present or guaranteed payment. For example, if the film company sells its rights to Canadian distribution in exchange for $50,000, then the future revenue will exclude Canada whether the Canadian markets generate $5,000, $50,000, or $500,000. In terms of the leverage discussion above, this form of presale agreement serves to reduce the potential for future income, but also serves to reduce the risk of loss. Unfortunately the business realities for pre-sell agreements often require that the completed film be delivered prior to any payment. This, in turn, requires the filmmaker to borrow from a lender, using the pre-sell agreement as collateral for the loan. Under this structure, the interest costs are not avoided, and the filmmaker may still shoulder the residual risk of the presale fees not materializing. Nonetheless, since pre-sell agreements allow the filmmaker to finance a project without personal funds at stake, they remain very attractive to the filmmaker. The pre-sell and distribution deals vary significantly. Some of the more common structures are described briefly.

1. Cash Deals

In all but the rarest situations or lowest of budgets, a filmmaker will not be able to earn a cash advance to fund the production based on a guaranteed distribution. There was a time when companies such as Cannon Films would create one-sheets (theatrical advertising posters) that the company would exhibit at the international film markets. If it was successful selling enough territories based on the poster, then Cannon would contact the named talent and begin the process of producing the film. The remaining posters would be discarded and those projects never started.

From the filmmaker's standpoint, cash for the production is the most critical requirement of any financing structure. No amount of future promises will cover rental fees or payroll. Modest cash advances may sometimes be available, but this is the exception to the rule.

2. Negative Pick-Up

Although the details can vary greatly, the term *negative pick-up* means that the film studio or distributor pays for the cost of the film to be finished to the point that a completed negative is ready to use. Generally, the filmmaker using negative pick-up financing sells the film to a film studio in exchange for reimbursement of production costs and some form of profit sharing from the proceeds of the film. For example, if a filmmaker has a budget of $1,000,000 for a film project, the filmmaker would "sell" the film by promising to deliver a completed motion picture substantially the same as described in the screenplay in exchange for a payment of $1,000,000 by the film studio. The film studio would then have the obligation to finish the prints for the film, pay for the marketing and distribution of the film, and split profits, if any, with the filmmaker on an agreed-upon percentage basis.

The negative pick-up is the filmmaker's "field of dreams"—if the filmmaker shoots it, the money will come. Making the movie requires that the script be followed, the agreed-upon casting not be changed, the length of the film be acceptable, and the film be eligible for the MPAA rating desired by the distributor, typically a PG-13 or R. The amount paid for a negative pick-up transaction need not be the same as the production cost of the film, although the studio will often seek to cap the payment at this amount. If so, the filmmaker must be sure to include budget items for herself, the business manager, and others who have invested sweat equity in the budget being used as the basis for negotiations with the studio. To add these items late in the negotiations will result in little or no personal payments.

The negative pick-up does not eliminate the risks to the filmmaker, because the funds are generally not made available until she has completed the film. Nonetheless, the risk is much lower than almost any other form of filmmaking. Unlike the studio deal, described below, the purchaser has few rights to watch the filmmaking process or interfere in the making of the film. Of course, the filmmaker has two primary risks. First, she risks that the film does not get finished, meaning that none of the expenses are paid for by the distributor, leaving the filmmaker holding the bag for all costs. Second, she risks that the film goes over budget, requiring the filmmaker to use unreimbursed personal funds to complete the film. Both situations doom would-be filmmakers regularly.

3. Distribution Guarantee

Since the negative pick-up does not immediately result in cash to the filmmaker, she must use the negative pick-up agreement as a form of collateral against which the film company can borrow money from a bank or other lender. If the purchaser is a stable, well-established company, lenders are generally willing to finance this type of arrangement. The distribution guarantee agreement provides that the film's distributor serve as guarantor of the loan. Since the lender is entitled to repayment regardless of the film's revenue, the distributor's guarantee of the loan puts the lender in a position of much greater security than if the filmmaker is solely responsible for the loan.

Invariably, the lender will also require that the film company furnish a completion bond that serves as a form of insurance against the film not being completed as required by the purchasing distributor. Together, the loan interest and the premium cost of the completion bond will add at least

20 percent to the cost of completing the film. Short-term financing may increase this cost substantially.

The distribution guarantee and negative pick-up arrangement fueled the independent film boom of the 1980s as companies exploited the new distribution channels of cable and home videotape. While this form of financing continues to provide a primary source of revenue for independent films, most of the large independent film companies have merged into studio-driven conglomerates (such as Miramax, Castle Rock, Orion, and New Line Films) or gone out of business (Carolco, Nelson Entertainment, Cannon Pictures, Cinecom). Nonetheless, many small film companies continue to purchase films on a negative pick-up basis.

4. Foreign Distributors, Markets, and Territories

Foreign distribution has grown to become the single largest category of film distribution income, exceeding both domestic theatrical exhibition and video sales for revenue. Despite its importance, however, foreign distribution provides risky territory for independent films because the language, currency, and legal enforcement barriers often make it difficult for the filmmaker to collect royalties or enforce contract rights. For foreign territories, the filmmaker is best served by selling the rights to a territory outright, rather than seeking an advance and a royalty payment. This structure, if possible, avoids the vagaries of currency exchange and the unfortunate but all-too-common practice of foreign distributors' refusals to distribute royalty income.

The cost of collecting small royalties from a foreign distributor in a small territory can be larger than the amount of payment being sought. Even if payments are forthcoming, the difficulties of auditing the foreign receipts and dealing with clever accounting practices make this income source highly volatile for independent film companies. More modest prepayments will result in greater cash in hand for the filmmaker and should be the preferred strategy for all but the most reputable of distributors.

Nonetheless, independent filmmakers have occasionally been successful selling the rights to foreign territories in exchange for advance payments and using these payments to finance all or most of the film's budget. These transactions can be directly through cash payments or through letters of credit that are deemed sufficiently sound by the U.S. lenders.

Often the strategy in these sales follows that of Cannon Films—invest early in the poster art, so that the purchaser knows what it is marketing. Few people have the skill necessary to read a screenplay (or even view a rough cut) and successfully visualize the final film. On the other hand, most of us have attended at least one film solely on the basis of the poster. Perhaps this form of financing seems artistically impure, but commercial success for a film requires commercial techniques.

During the independent film boom of the 1980s, the combination of new marketing opportunities and healthy tax regulations led to an infusion of foreign financing capital. This financial resource, if it ever truly existed, has disappeared as a result of changing economic conditions and substantially more restrictive tax regulations.

A new international era may be developing, however, as the Internet and improved international distribution are reawakening local production in countries throughout the world. Independent U.S. filmmakers may find opportunities to collaborate or coproduce with production companies outside of the United States. Occasionally these coproductions will provide financing to the U.S. company, but more often the foreign company has subsidies for its local production and will provide services in exchange for the co-ownership of the project. While such an arrangement entails a number of unique risks, it may also provide some attractive side benefits to the independent filmmaker in terms of expertise and travel.

5. Studios

The traditional Hollywood studio manufactured motion pictures. They purchased the raw materials—stories and talent—and produced finished films that they exhibited in theaters throughout the world. Over time, the production activities separated from the distribution activities, so that the studio would distribute and promote films produced by other film companies, reducing the studio's risk that the film would not be made.

Today, the major motion picture studios are primarily distributors rather than film production companies. Instead of directly purchasing stories or scripts, the studios work through existing relationships with established production companies. Those production companies serve to package the script, develop the budget, and manage the production. The budget will include a negotiated fee for the producer's own expenses and income. The agreement between the producer and studio will also deter-mine the participation in the film's revenue that will be paid to the pro-ducer. The studio will finance the project on an incremental basis, providing the necessary funding for each step of the process. In exchange, the studio has primary control over the project and the ability to termi-nate it throughout its development.

The incremental approach, known as a production and distribution deal, allows the studio to maximize its control while minimizing its cost. The producer will typically receive a small fee for early preproduction activities. Although the costs of script and budget preparation often exceed this payment, the producer covers this risk rather than the studio. If the studio is interested in further development of the project, it will release funds to the producer to pay for selected key aspects of the pre-production. Locations will be scouted, the script rewritten or polished, and key personnel identified. Throughout this process, the producer will receive little or no additional pay.

Eventually, however, the studio may commit to the project. For some directors and actors, the studio will be obligated to pay them whether or not the production is ever filmed. Prior to making this commitment, the studio will "green light" the film and commit to principal actors, director, and designers. During this phase of preproduction, the studio will typi-cally distribute a small portion of the producer's fee. The bulk of the pro-ducer's fee will be paid during the principal photography, with small payments withheld until the delivery of the first rough cut of the picture and the delivery of the final picture.[1]

For the independent filmmaker, the choice to make a picture under a studio-financed production deal represents a blessing and a curse. The potential success that a well-made studio film has greatly exceeds that of any independent film. The studio's marketing budgets and promotional savvy can make a household name out of anyone, opening the door for tre-mendous professional control on subsequent projects.

The curse is that the independent filmmaker gives up control immedi-ately. Rarely do studio screenplays resemble the writer's first drafts, and novice directors will be second-guessed at every turn—if the filmmaker is allowed to remain attached to the picture at all. Still, that is where the money is. For most artists it is commercial success that buys them the lux-ury of later artistic control.

C. Cash Management of Sales Financing

In each of the various funding scenarios, other than an outright sale to a motion picture studio, the film producer must still bear the burden of both controlling the costs and paying the bills as they accrue. Although the filmmaker may have sold the right to distribute the film (or assigned the copyright) in the completed film, these are future transactions that do not translate into production funds. Instead, the filmmaker must apply to a lender to provide the cash to make the movie.

Although they are rare, some commercial banks do provide this form of independent film lending. Two of the more successful are the Lewis Horowitz Organization (a division of Southern Pacific Bank) and Comerica Entertainment Industries (a part of Comerica Bank). The experience and knowledge of these banks allow them to assess the credit risk of the independent production and lend funds on the basis of the production's collateral.

To receive a commercial loan for creation of an independently financed film, the film company must credibly present evidence it will be able to repay the loan and that it has sufficient collateral to cover the principal amount borrowed. Just as a home purchaser must show the intended property is worth at least as much as the loan, the filmmaker must demonstrate the value of the financed project exceeds the loan requested.

To serve as proof of value and collateral of the loan, the film package must demonstrate the value of the project to the lender. Since filming has not yet begun, the collateral includes the screenplay and story rights; legally binding commitments by the key personnel to participate in the film; the production budget, including a draw-down schedule for the use of the proceeds as they are paid to the filmmaker throughout production; and, most important, legally binding guarantees for the territory sales, negative pick-up, or other financing arrangement. These contracts must specify the guaranteed minimum the filmmaker will be paid, and that amount can be used as collateral to be pledged against the value of the loan.

For distribution agreements, negative pick-up contracts, or presales involving non-U.S. territories, the financing becomes a bit more complex. Issues involving fluctuating exchange rates, governmental stability, and creditworthiness further frustrate the lending process. Fortunately, to assist with these issues, the Export-Import Bank of the United States has entered into a program with U.S. lenders to guarantee those loans made on the foreign agreements. Under the Film Production Guarantee Program, a participating bank such as Comerica or the Lewis Horowitz Organization can provide a loan based on as much as 90 percent of the value of the collateral, depending on the stability of the purchaser's home government and currency. Collateral coming from somewhat higher-risk countries can be counted at 60 percent of the face value.

Of course, the discounts involved in the Film Production Guarantee still require that at least 10 percent of the financing come from the filmmaker or producer. In addition, the funds are not available based on the nonguaranteed expectations of the film. This will require the filmmaker to use the bank financing and Production Guarantee Program in conjunction with a secondary funding source, whether that be the personal assets of the filmmaker or other sources.

Finally, to get the collateral ready for the bank, there may be significant expenses, particularly with regard to key personnel—cast and crew who require an advance payment to legally bind themselves to the project. This short-term bridge financing may be substantially more expensive than other financing sources, and the cost of the interest payments must be included in the budget for the project.

D. Self-Financing the Production

The simplest form of self-financing is for the filmmaker to take cash from her savings account and transfer it to her business account. While this certainly works, few filmmakers have sufficient savings to use this system. In addition to personal cash, filmmakers can seek nonprofit grants, personal loans, and other avenues to help complete film projects.

1. Nonprofit Productions Business Financing

For guerrilla and digital filmmakers, nonprofit grants often go unnoticed. Many nonprofit organizations are willing to participate in independent film projects. Some invest in projects because they are interested in promoting the particular message of the filmmaker—this is particularly true for doc-umentary filmmakers. In addition, arts organizations will promote inde-pendent filmmaking as an art form through grants and scholarships.

Such organizations include the Soros Documentary Fund, assisting the development of documentaries on social issues; the Fund for Jewish Doc-umentary Filmmaking, focusing on Jewish history and culture; the National Black Programming Consortium, focusing on films emanating from African American communities; Astraea National Lesbian Action Foundation, addressing issues in the lesbian community; and many geo-graphic programs such as the New York State Council on the Arts, the Minnesota Independent Film Fund, the Pacific Pioneer Film Fund, and the Texas Filmmakers Production Fund.[2]

The Paul Robeson Fund is typical of the documentary funding model. Grants ranging from $2,000 to $15,000 are provided for documentaries dealing with relevant social issues. Filmmakers must complete grant appli-cations that detail the project and provide samples of their prior work.

For many other nonprofit opportunities, the sponsoring organization may not specifically be looking to finance a film project, but rather pro-vides funds for community outreach, training, or other goals. If the film being developed achieves those goals, the film project may become a valu-able opportunity for the organization.

A limitation on nonprofit fundraising is that the money is often quite modest. The donors may also lack any sophistication regarding the proj-ect. When funds become available from a source connected with the film industry, those funds may often lead to other opportunities to promote the film or obtain valuable connections essential for casting or production of the project.

Another benefit of the nonprofit funding model is the respect given to the filmmaker. Nonprofits often recognize that most of the work done by the filmmaker is essentially volunteer time, donated to complete a worth-while project. As a result, the filmmaker may be granted wide latitude and offered a great deal of respect by the funding organization.

A nonprofit may also serve as a conduit for additional funds donated by supporters of the film project. For example, if a church were willing to sponsor a production based on the life of one of its former pastors, the church would probably provide a modest grant toward the production costs (and may provide the use of the church without charge as a shooting location). In addition, the church could collect funds for the film project from other donors.

The donations would be tax deductible to the donors so long as the film remained a charitable activity on behalf of the church. The supporters of the film would receive a charitable tax deduction rather than any hope of receiving proceeds from the film, but, given the typical return on investment, such a model may be financially sounder than many of the commercial models attempted by independent filmmakers.

2. Guerrilla Financing: Personal Debt—Credit Cards and Home Loans

When self-financing without cash in hand, the filmmaker often turns to available sources of debt financing. Personal credit cards and personal collateral often serve as emergency money for filmmakers. These sources are generally expensive because they have high interest rates. They are also highly risky because the debt becomes due whether or not the film is completed.

For the true guerrilla film, pre-sell arrangements and studio financing—with its attendant studio control—will simply not work. A guerrilla film is not fully conceived until finished. If the guerrilla filmmaker is well financed, the spontaneity and hunger that should inform the work can quickly turn into bloated excess. Many second pictures suffer from the sudden affluence of full financing. The guerrilla filmmaker tempers the urge to explore "what if" with the painfully limited resources available. When the resources become plentiful, the line between creativity and self-indulgence blurs. A disciplined independent or guerrilla filmmaker can make the transition into a studio director, but only by substituting other restraining forces for the financial restraints of the independent filmmaker. Whether those restraints are scheduling, financing (again), or artistic vision, something must serve to challenge the filmmaker, forcing her to make only the best choices for the story rather than exploring the limitless possibilities that the question "what if" can bring.

As a guerrilla filmmaker, the primary source of personal financing comes from discretionary income and loans. A guerrilla filmmaker who can finance a film exclusively from discretionary income—savings that will not be missed—needs little advice regarding the financing of the film.

Tell your story, make your movie, and suck as much of the marrow from the production's bones as you can.

Most guerrilla filmmakers, however, do not have the luxury of sufficient discretionary income. Instead the financing comes from the ability to obtain personal loans on credit cards or through home equity lines of credit. In home equity lending the filmmaker borrows money from the bank by securing her primary residence as collateral. Historically, a bank would only lend to someone who maintained at least 20 percent equity in the property. In today's competitive lending market, banks often lend even if the homeowner has little or no equity in the property.

If the filmmaker is married, her husband will typically be a co-owner of the property. The bank will require that all parties who own the property sign the loans. This makes both the filmmaker and the nonfilmmaking spouse personally responsible for the loan. In most states, the loan must be repaid even if the house is worth less than the value of the loan.[3] The danger of borrowing against one's home is that the risk of the film not selling jeopardizes the house of the filmmaker. This is a significant burden for the filmmaker to impose on the nonfilmmaking spouse, particularly when added to the time commitment and personal sacrifice that the guerrilla filmmaker's work extracts from her family.

The filmmaker should carefully consider the expenses for the interest and principal payments required. If the only way the filmmaker can cover the payments from the loan is to successfully sell the film, then the filmmaker should restructure the budget or take other steps to avoid this risk. I have never given different advice to any student or client. Change the budget, change the project, or find another way to tell the story. I have never heard of anyone who has gambled her house on a film and won. If the filmmaker can cover the interest and principal payments, then using her home as collateral is merely an unwise, highly risky choice that should be avoided if possible.

The other personal source of funds for financing the film is revolving credit—credit card debt. Because of questionable lending practices, a moderately successful individual with a reasonable amount of personal debt can be offered up to hundreds of thousands of dollars' worth of credit cards. Credit cards are unsecured and generally offered for personal rather than commercial use. The cards are generally in the filmmaker's name rather than in the name of the film company. The filmmaker should carefully consider the consequences before committing her personal assets by financing the film through the short-term, high-interest loans available from credit cards. While the attraction is obvious, and filmmaker Spike Lee built his early success on credit cards, the downside can be financial ruin.

If used at all, credit cards should be left for last. Having a credit card available can serve as a rainy-day fund to cover the final costs of editing when the investments and production expenses go slightly over budget. They should also be paid off first to avoid the high costs of the loans.

Finally, some guerrilla filmmakers convince the cast and crew to "lend" the production their credit cards. This practice is unethical and should not be used. No matter how tempting this offer, the filmmaker should avoid this last temptation. The named party on the card is the person responsible for the debt. Even a promise—or written agreement—by the filmmaker to cover the costs on the card will have no effect against the bank issuing the card. Since a crew member's credit card would not be used unless the production had no assets, the effect is to make the other participants in the film financially obligated for the debts of the production. If members of the cast or crew have the financial ability to become investors, then they should be properly informed and rewarded as investors. The so-called borrowing of their credit cards provides these crew members no protection while exposing them to significant financial risk.

E. Financing the Production Company—the Limited Liability Company

Financing the film based on presales or production financing, discussed earlier, focuses on sales of the finished film. Each of those methods essentially sells the future profits of the film in exchange for present funds to make the film. The two self-financing techniques provide funds for the filmmaking but do not require any return based on the success or failure of the film.

When financing the production company itself, rather than the film, the filmmaker is selling interests in the business entity that is making the motion picture. This is a sophisticated transaction involving securities laws, federal disclosure requirements, and complex tax and reporting obligations. Although quite common, selling interests in a film company is a complicated transaction no different from forming any other sophisticated business.

Production company financing is generally accomplished by selling interests in the film company created for the production of the movie. The basic rules discussed below apply to all business forms, corporations, limited partnerships (LPs), and limited liability companies (LLCs). Because the LLCs are the most flexible of the three as planning devices, the book assumes that the business is formed as an LLC.

1. Basic Requirements and the Meaning of "Disclosure"— Making a Federal Case Out of Film Financing

The investor, any person investing money into the film project, expects a return of the investment or capital and profit on the money if the LLC has made a profit. Under both state and federal law, the first obligation a business has when raising capital is to provide full disclosure of all the material facts regarding the investment and its risks. This simple rule—that the filmmaker must fully disclose all the terms of the investment—is often overlooked, but at the filmmaker's peril. Failure to fully disclose all the material terms can result in the investor being entitled to a complete return of his investment directly from either the filmmaker or the film company, depending on which of the parties has assets. The filmmaker could also be held criminally liable for knowingly misrepresenting the risks involved in the investment. All the other planning done by the accountants and lawyers will be worth nothing if the filmmaker hides information or misrepresents the facts regarding the production.

All information provided to investors must be accurate when made and kept updated. The harder aspect of understanding the obligation of full disclosure is identifying what facts and issues are material. At its heart, material means information that is important to the investor, information a reasonable person would consider important in deciding whether or not to invest.[4] Put another way, the information is material if there is a substantial likelihood that the information would be considered as having significantly altered the "total mix" of information made available. This includes the terms of any investment deal, but it also includes information regarding the film, the production, the competition, and anything else the filmmaker thought was important to say when promoting the project to the investor.

2. Structures

The basic structure of the film business entity must provide the core ownership and management for the filmmaker with limited protections for the investor. Depending on the form of the business, organizational papers must be filed and submitted to the secretary of state along with a tax payment. In addition to this filing, a film company must have written and signed articles and bylaws or an Operating Agreement that sets out the rules for operations, governance, and payments.

a. Business of the Company

The first question to answer is whether the film company is being created for the purposes of the particular film project or whether it may be used for multiple projects—sequels, unrelated films, or other projects entirely. Today's typical corporation's bylaws state that it can conduct "any lawful business," meaning any business that exists. For Disney, that makes sense. To protect small investors, however, the better choice is to limit the investment to a single film project. The filmmaker can always try to amend this decision at a later time, but of course, the investors will then have a voice and a vote in such a modification. If the purpose of the company is not limited, the filmmaker can continue making movies until the money runs out, so that even if the first film returns a nice profit, the income is retained for future films. In such a case, the investor may still receive nothing. Given the risks involved in motion picture investing, the more equitable approach is to limit the investment to the production or productions agreed upon at the time of investment.

b. Control

The filmmaker must retain management control, at least throughout the initial production and distribution of the project. The Operating Agreement of the LLC should be drafted to guarantee that the filmmaker retains control of the film company's management, to the greatest extent permitted by law. Even here, this cannot be absolute. The filmmaker will eventually die[5] or become unwilling or unable to manage the operations of the film company.

c. Personal Obligation of the Filmmaker

The nature of an independent film is a highly personal undertaking. As a result, the Operating Agreement should reflect the importance of the filmmaker's role and include specific provisions in the event the filmmaker becomes disassociated with the project. In many ways this serves as a form of protection for the investor, but it also recognizes that this film project is a personal endeavor. For example, the death or incapacity of the film-maker may terminate the project. Similarly, the professional unavailabil-ity of the filmmaker—whether because the person has become too famous or too frustrated—is irrelevant; the project should end.

d. Project Milestones

Like the personal nature of the filmmaker, films can languish for years as money is found to complete them. The Operating Agreement must be very clear regarding the rules about the availability of the investor's money. The investor should be obligated to pay immediately, and should receive no interest in the company until payment is received. If the budget calls for a minimum amount of $150,000 cash available, the investor must agree that his funds can be spent prior to the company raising the entire $150,000. If not, the investor's purchase payment should be put in escrow and held until the film company has sufficient funds. Most typically, the investors' funds are released under the terms of the Operating Agreement when there is enough to make meaningful progress. Here, for example, if the film can be made for $150,000, then the agreement may provide that the funds will be released when $100,000 is received, because that is enough to get through preproduction and principal photography.

e. Management Fees

The filmmaker, as manager of the LLC, may choose to receive some portion of the revenue as payment for services provided. The choice to pay oneself is neither a good or bad choice. So long as the payment structure is fully disclosed, rather than hidden in fine print or unstated, the investors can have no legitimate complaints. Such payment is akin to the producer's fees charged to the studio. On the other hand, if all participants in the project worked without pay, and the investors assumed a very high risk, then it may be appropriate to forgo any producer's payment. Both approaches have been used. The key is to explain specifically the basis for the investors' return on capital and participation in net revenue.

f. Wrap-Up of Ownership

The structure should also provide for a mandatory repurchase of the investor's interests at some point in the future. For example, this may be triggered by a lack of production company revenues for a three-year period. Such a clause would provide that if the production company has not more than a minor amount of income (say $5,000), then the manager can repurchase the interests of the investors by paying a preset fee, or by providing for mandatory arbitration if the parties cannot voluntarily agree on a price.

g. Deferred Compensation for Some Participants

Most independent film companies are unable to pay all their expenses. Instead, they rely on locations, cast, crew, and service providers to work on credit. To balance the risk of nonpayment, filmmakers often promise revenue or profit participation to those parties as well. The company must plan carefully regarding these contingent payment obligations. They must be incorporated into the budgeting process and clearly identified in defining the revenue returns to which the investors are entitled.

For example, it is common to grant the investors a return of capital before the producer takes her portion of gross revenues. Often investors are entitled to as much as 125 percent of their initial investment before the producer receives payment. The Operating Agreement must specify whether the deferred compensation due to the cast, crew, and other service providers are entitled to payments prior to the investor's payment. If the motion picture has a cost of $150,000, an investor may think the film has a reasonable chance to return the majority of the investment and the potential to return far more. If instead, the picture has a "cost" of $150,000 reflecting the expenses that could not be deferred and an additional $250,000 in deferred compensation, then the investor may not receive his first dollar until after $400,000 in revenue has been earned. This dramatically changes the risk and is therefore highly material to the structure.

The Operating Agreement can provide that the deferred compensation is paid first, the investors are paid first, or both paid proportionately at the same time.[6]

3. Limitations

As legally recognized businesses, filmmakers undertake business and professional obligations toward their investors as well as the employees and other participants of the project. If the filmmaker uses other individuals to serve as managers of the LLC or directors of the corporation, those individuals have a similar duty to act in the best interests of the business.

Further, the law does not like to vest unbridled discretion in a single businessperson's hands. State laws will protect the investors in some situations, requiring that the filmmaker provide the investors with information and an opportunity to vote on the suggested change. For example, if the company has insufficient funds to start its movie and another film company has insufficient funds to complete an unrelated picture, the filmmaker might wish to merge the two companies in order to receive producer credit and associate director credit on the second picture. Nonetheless, the merger can take place only if the shareholders or members of the LLC agree. Similarly, the filmmaker could not take the money invested in the first film to the second film, because that would breach her duty of good faith to the investors and the film company.

4. Commercial Loans

In addition to the sale of company interests or equity financing, the film company can also seek to obtain commercial loans. Since the only significant asset of the production company is the uncompleted film, the lending practices are essentially those of the negative pick-up financing and distribution deal. The lender will require the following elements be in place before it will agree to finance the film:

1. A reputable distributor that has entered into an agreement to distribute the finished film;
2. A completion bond company guarantee that the film will be completed for the agreed-upon budget;

3. A budget that accurately reflects the anticipated costs of the film's production;
4. Sufficient general liability, and other insurance;
5. Adequate security agreements between the lender and the production company so that the lender holds a perfected security interest in both the physical and intangible property of the production company; and
6. Written, enforceable contracts committing the principal cast members to appear in the production.

When the filmmaker can package these elements, certain lenders may be willing to provide credit to the film company. Payments by the lenders are typically made weekly, upon proof of satisfactory progress during the prior week's shooting. Finally, the bank will require a security agreement that puts a lien against the developed (and the exposed) film stock and the copyright in the film, so that the lender can foreclose on the assets in the case of nonpayment.

For a company that has received significant cash investments, there are some lenders willing to provide small lines of credit to filmmakers. In these cases, the bank or lender may not ask for the completion bond or the weekly updates because the risk to the bank is minimized by the investor's participation. The creditor will have priority for repayment over the investors so, in the event of default, the bank will be repaid in full before the investors receive any of their funds. The company's assets, including the copyright to the film and its cash reserves, provide sufficient security for the lender to accept the risk of providing the modest loan.

F. Limits on Financing

Because the sale of interest in the film or film company is governed by state and federal securities law, there are a number of important limitations on the way a filmmaker can raise investment funds. These limitations do not typically apply to presale arrangements and other distribution-based financing, which is yet another reason such financing is preferable to soliciting investor funds. Still, if Aunt Betty's investment is the only way the film can get made, this section will identify when it is fair to ask Aunt Betty for funds and when it violates the law to even ask.

The offers to sell and sales of securities are governed by the Securities Act of 1933 and the Securities and Exchange Act of 1934. Unless exempt from the federal rules, the offer to sell the securities must be accompanied by a detailed disclosure document called a prospectus. In addition, every state but Nevada has its own law governing the offers to sell and sales of securities. The state laws set forth specific rules for the offers to sell securities and often allow the state to judge the fairness of the offering to residents of the state. Again, certain offers may be exempt from these rules.

Because of the costs and difficulties involved with preparing these offering documents, virtually all film financing projects are structured to fall within one of the exemptions to the federal and state laws. Even if exempt from the documentation requirements, however, the state and federal laws continue to apply to protect the investor from fraudulent misstatements or failures to disclose material information. Since the laws cover the offers to sell as well as the sales, the filmmaker must be careful to avoid casual conversations about the availability of interests in the film. In other words, posting e-mails to newsgroups or listservs should never be part of the film financing strategy.

1. Federal Securities Laws

Although federal law covers all securities, it categorically exempts from registration a variety of transactions. First, it does not apply to nonpublic offerings.[7] Under this exception, the sale to Aunt Betty would most likely not be governed by the federal securities registration requirements if she were truly a blood relative. Were she a family friend called "aunt" out of respect, the answer under the securities laws would change. As a result, the nonpublic exception is rather narrow and difficult to rely on.

At a minimum, nonpublic transactions are conducted directly by the issuer (the company) without any finder's fees or other fees paid for identifying the investors, and without any public advertising, broadly defined. These limitations also apply to many of the other exceptions to registration under both federal and state laws.

In addition to nonpublic offerings, the federal laws generally do not govern transactions that occur completely within one state.[8] To meet this test, the business entity must be formed in the selected state, every offer and sale must occur exclusively in that same state, a significant portion of the business activity must occur in that state, and the interest must come to rest in that state. For example, if all offers to finance the film took place in California, the sales were in California to residents of California who did not move during the next nine months, the LLC or corporation was formed in California, and much of the production occurred in California, then only California law would apply regarding the sale of securities and no federal registration would be required.[9]

In addition, and perhaps most significant, the federal law exempts transactions that are limited to investors with the financial resources and personal savvy to take care of themselves. These are accredited investors, individuals with income of $200,000 annually or assets of $5,000,000 and the ability to understand the risk involved in complex business arrangements (or advisors who understand). Federal law presumes that these people are sufficiently sophisticated that they will ask the right questions and will protect themselves from poorly understood business transactions. The law also correctly assumes that only people with substantial income can afford to take the significant risk involved with these types of small offerings.

The most important of these federal exemptions is known as Rule 506. It provides a series of clear guidelines regarding the person to whom the private interests can be sold without having to register with the SEC. Rule 506 allows for an unlimited number of accredited investors and up to 35 sophisticated investors. Each of these categories is separately defined in the regulations. Broadly speaking, an individual will be treated as an accredited investor if he falls into one of three categories:

1. any director, executive officer, or general partner of the issuer of the securities being offered or sold or any director, executive officer, or general partner of a general partner of that issuer
2. any natural person whose individual net worth, or joint net worth with that person's spouse, at the time of his purchase exceeds $1,000,000
3. any natural person who had an individual income in excess of $200,000 in each of the two most recent years or joint income with that person's spouse in excess of $300,000 in each of those years and has a reasonable expectation of reaching the same income level in the current year[10]

This is not the exclusive list. Some banks, nonprofit organizations, and other entities are also accredited investors. If a person falls within this category, the federal law does not require that the information regarding the financing be in any particular form, so long as the information is fully disclosed to the investors' satisfaction.

In addition to the unlimited number of accredited investors, Rule 506 can be used to offer or sell to as many as 35 other sophisticated investors. The rule provides that "[e]ach purchaser who is not an accredited investor either alone or with his purchaser representative(s) has such knowledge and experience in financial and business matters that he is capable of evaluating the merits and risks of the prospective investment, or the issuer reasonably believes immediately prior to making any sale that such purchaser comes within this description." The purchaser representative must himself be a sophisticated investor, capable of evaluating the risks and merits of the investment. For these sophisticated investors, however, more detailed disclosure is required, making the inclusion of one or two sophisticated investors potentially more difficult than their investment is worth. Given the high-risk nature of film investment, private solicitations are better left with those in the accredited investor category, to the extent the filmmaker has that choice.

As an alternative, although generally a dangerous choice because of the lack of any limits on liability, general partnerships have one primary benefit. They generally have no securities issues because every participant is an active member of the organization, which creates an almost automatic exception to state and federal securities laws.

2. State Securities Law

The rules governing securities sales grow even more complex when dealing with state laws. For offerings not involving publicly traded companies, state law often plays the more important role in governing the nature of the transaction. Because state laws vary so greatly, there are few generally applicable rules.

The first step is to consult a qualified securities attorney in the state where the offering will take place. Generally, if the offering is nonpublic, with no advertising and no commissions or finder's fees paid, then the sale to sophisticated investors will require a minimum of mandatory documentation. Similarly, if the interests are provided to only those people having a direct working relationship with the project, there may be few mandatory requirements for documentation. As discussed below, however, the company always has the obligation to provide all the material information to the investors. Many of the states' laws simply assist the filmmaker in meeting this obligation and should serve as a guide rather than a burden.

G. Tax Issues

In any industry, one critical aspect of business planning depends on the impact of tax planning. Taxes affect both the cost of raising capital and the profits earned each year. As such, anticipating the tax effects to the film company is a necessary part of the planning process.

The goals in tax planning are to minimize the total amount of tax due and to ensure that any tax obligations that do arise can be covered with cash payments. Since every dollar saved will be able to go directly into the film, and the profits will go to the film's investors and participants, thoughtful early tax planning sets the stage for good management throughout the project.

1. Benefits for Certain Business Forms

Corporations are separate taxable entities. As a result, the profits earned by the corporation are taxed. Any dividends to the shareholders are also taxed to them. This dual taxation generally results in a higher aggregate tax. Similarly, any losses are attributed to the business rather than the shareholders. Losses to the corporation do not create any potential tax benefits to the shareholders.

In contrast, general partnerships, limited partnerships, and sole proprietorships are not taxed directly. Instead, the profits and losses are taxed directly to the owners. This reduces the tax liability when there are profits. If the income of the participants is in a lower tax bracket, then the difference is even larger. The only difficulty is that the tax liability and the payment obligations apply to the investors regardless of whether the distributions have been made by the partnership.

The LLC allows the maximum flexibility because the tax choice can be made at the beginning of its formation. By making a tax election, the LLC can be taxed as either a corporation or a partnership.[11] Similarly, a corporation can make a Subchapter S election, and also be taxed as a partnership. The Subchapter S election limits the types of stock that the corporation can issue. An S corporation can issue only a single class of stock, although voting rights can be varied. This restricts the S corporation from reducing the ability to structure unique deals in response to particular financing opportunities. Nonetheless, investors are often more familiar with S corporations than the newer LLC, and some investors are reluctant to use the LLC rather than the more familiar corporate form.

Withdrawals from both S corporations and LLCs have similar consequences. For a corporation such as an S corporation, the purchase of the stock will be a capital transaction generating a gain or loss for the shareholder with any payment that exceeds the investment resulting in a capital gain. As a consequence, the payment by the corporation is not deductible to the corporation. For partnerships and LLCs, the payment for the partner's or member's interest will not be a deductible expense either, so that the remaining partners or members will continue to have the same obligation.

C corporations serve the interests of the investors most effectively. Assuming the investment cycle will be relatively short, the value of the stock is most efficiently valued only at liquidation rather than every year. The tax losses may not be of significant value in contrast with the benefit of holding the security until it is liquidated, deferring all gains or losses until that stage. Corporations are strongly favored for technology investments that have the possibility of expanding into the public markets. While this is not a significant possibility for most film companies, the structure and familiarity may further encourage capital investment.

2. Benefits for Certain Financing

Often the film company values not only cash contributions of investors but other forms of contributions—professional services, equipment, cast participation, locations, and many other attributes of the film. This may have an unintended tax effect. When a service provider receives shares or an interest in exchange for his service, this results in taxable income to the service provider. If the service is exchanged for stock, partnership, or LLC interest, then the payment is presently taxable.[12] In contrast, the share of future profits or revenue should not be taxed until the revenue is actually earned. Given the significant risk of no actual earning, this should be taken into account in structuring the transactions.[13]

Another of the tools provided to the partnership and LLC form is the ability to allocate gain, loss, deductions, and credits in manner that maximizes their value to the participants. In many situations, the filmmaker will have significantly less ability to offset any losses against other income than some of the investors. This may be an additional benefit provided to investors that can create opportunities for financing.

3. Contribution of Property

Unlike contribution of services, contribution of equipment or property (but not rental) in exchange for partnership or stock interest does not result in any tax liability. If the filmmaker contributes camera equipment and computer equipment in exchange for its value, this results in no tax liability. The same rule applies to intellectual property such as the screenplay.

If the partner receives a distribution within two years, however, the IRS may treat the transaction as a sale to the partnership and create addi tional tax liability. This has the potential to increase the tax liability for the successful filmmaker if the transaction occurs within the two-year period.[14]

Contribution rules are particularly important to consider when planning the business structure. The exchange of a screenplay for an LLC position or stock will generally be considered a contribution in exchange for property not subject to immediate taxation, while the same interest given to the filmmaker as payment for the obligation to write the screenplay would be a payment for services and presently taxable. Both timing and characterization are very important. Before signing any agreements, the filmmaker or her attorney should consult with a qualified accountant to ensure that the tax consequences are understood fully.

Budgeting

THOUGH SOMETIMES IT is the most creative part of a film, a carefully crafted budget provides the pivotal road map for the entire film project. Whether the film is expected to cost $2,000 or $200,000,000, the film budget must present a spending plan for every dollar to be expended on the production. In addition, the budget serves as a guide that the pieces of the film are proportionate to one another. If each cast member receives tens of millions of dollars, then the film generally should not have homemade special effects.

The budget will be dictated by choices that may change dramatically depending on locations, size and prominence of cast, stunts, and the effects needed both during and after principal photography. For independent and guerrilla filmmaking, the key is to identify the cornerstone elements of the film and build the budget around those items. If a particular location must be used to tell the story, a particular cast member becomes essential to the financing, or a special effect defines the story, then that element should be identified and its costs determined. Thereafter, the remainder of the budget can be structured to keep the production in harmony with that item.

The budget process runs from inception of the project through the completion of the finished negative. Neither the prints used to show the film theatrically nor the advertising and promotional budget is included in the budget numbers used for production. For studio films, prints and advertising often equal the costs of the film production and, for an inexpensive film, may greatly exceed that cost.

A. Purpose and Usefulness of the Budget

The budgeting process has a number of important internal and external purposes. It sets the framework for all the decisions regarding the film. For example, if an independent film will be made on a minimal budget, then certain items must drop close to zero. The movie will be filmed locally or in areas that can double for other locations simply because the budget cannot accommodate travel expenses or other costs that will not ultimately appear on the screen. The science fiction genre has become so effects laden that low-budget science fiction films have nearly disappeared.

1. Direct Consequences of the Budget

First, the budget sets the tone of the picture. Broad categories of no-budget, low-budget, medium-budget, and high-budget each set in motion assumptions about the film. No-budget films, such as Kevin Smith's *Clerks*, create a certain rough ambience about them. Even modest success can often result in large percentage returns. At the other extreme, high-budget films must be blockbusters to justify the expense, resulting in ever more lavish productions and increasing expectations. Independent filmmakers often want to create the impression that their film cost more than it did to improve the advances made when sold, but understate the cost when shown to suggest that the filmmaker is more creative than was suggested. For example, it was rumored that Miramax spent close to $1 million to finish the $30,000 *Blair Witch Project*.

Second, the scope of the budget will directly affect the amount of money that needs to be raised. As discussed earlier, certain investment strategies are based on the total amount of funds sought. If a movie is financed using one of these fundraising techniques, then the filmmaker must pay close attention to the financial caps placed by the securities regulations.

Third, many of the collective bargaining agreements between the industry unions and the filmmaker base minimum payments on the size of the budget. The lower the budget, the lower the required minimums will be to use SAG actors.

2. Hollywood's Budget Magic

Driving Miss Daisy, a modestly budgeted film, worked as an award-winning off-Broadway play with a budget of thousands rather than millions of dollars. Many television shows' two-episode season openers would work just fine as feature films. Both *Star Trek* and *X-Files* have had more compelling television productions than some of their films.

The union fee structure has something to do with the budgeting sequence. Because payments are based on medium and length, the same directing or acting job must pay higher for a feature film than for television. If the minimums go up, then the other fees are ratcheted up as well. The net effect is an absurd situation whereby a $30,000 student film may get theatrical release while a $3,000,000 studio-financed project may be impossible to release theatrically rather than on television.

B. The Ultimate Use of the Budget

Despite the importance of a budget, it is a planning tool that may be changed often during the planning stages of the project. For an independent filmmaker, there may be a variety of budget scenarios based on best-case financing and worst-case financing. Certain scenes may be noted for possible revision based on the budget consequences. Like modern theatrical writing, the filmmaker writing a low-budget film must treat the financial limitations as a structural framework into which the story is crafted. If no flashback to the Eiffel Tower is possible, a close-up of a toy replica in a store window might do the trick.

Once the financing begins in earnest, however, the role of the budget changes. Ultimately, the budget plays a pivotal role in identifying the costs of every element of the project to the financial participants of the project. This includes the investors, the lenders, the completion bond company, and the unions. Once a commitment has been made, there can be few significant changes without approval. No matter how artistically compelling, a filmmaker may not unilaterally decide to film for an extra two weeks to capture the light. Nor can he drop a name star to pay for those weeks, unless he has the permission of the lender or completion bond company. Even investors might get upset by such a change, so the documents must be very explicit regarding which decisions are subject to change and which are not.

C. Anatomy of a Budget

Those fees that set the pricing tone of the project are described as "above-the-line" costs. These include leading cast members, the director, the script, and the producer's fee. In the studio world, these are often negotiated in coordination, so that star salaries are proportionate and the director has a deal somewhat similar to the other above-the-line participants.

The remaining cast, locations, sets, costumes, permits, equipment rentals, and other expenses are itemized below the line. These costs tend to vary considerably less. The cost of a location permit, for example, does not change based on the fame of the cast. The budget must also reflect the postproduction, including the editing, sound, addition of special effects, and titles.

A budget is comprised of the summary page, known as the top sheet, and a series of department-by-department itemizations for that budget. Even if a film tops $200 million, every roll of tape must be budgeted, receipted, and credited to its particular account. The numbers may get large, but the attention to detail rarely diminishes. Throughout the course of the production, the actual expenses are compared to the budget to calculate the production's accuracy in planning and to make those adjustments that are needed to keep the project on time and on budget.

D. Insurance and Completion Bond Requirements

In addition to the cost associated with the mechanical processes of filmmaking, certain expenses are part of the risk management for the production. Except for the tiniest of productions, each film company must carry a variety of insurance, including workers' compensation insurance;

cast insurance; liability insurance on the negative and videotape, sets, equipment, and property; and errors and omissions insurance to cover problems with the script such as defamation or copyright infringement. The budget should have a contingency amount, typically 10 percent of the total budget.

Finally, for many films, the project must be protected with a completion bond. The completion bond company agrees to pay those fees in excess of the 10 percent contingency. This insurance is expensive in both financial and practical terms. The completion bond company retains veto control over cast and crew and can take over the production if either the shoot begins to fall behind schedule or reshoots are necessary. The concern is focused on the budget, so an aesthetically bad but efficient production has little to worry about.

To obtain a completion bond, the production company must have full financing; complete, unambiguous ownership of the story and script rights; full insurance of the production; agreements for use of the primary locations; and a feasibility study or coverage showing that the script and budget balance. The steps necessary to obtain a completion bond make it significantly less likely that it will be needed, so for many film projects the process serves as a good exercise in planning.

E. Deferrals and Contingent Fees

Royalties, profits, and residuals come out of income, so these are not included in the budget for a typical film. For independent filmmaking, however, deferred compensation—reflecting income earned but not paid to cast, crew, or other parties—is an expense incurred as part of the negative cost of the picture. This expense should be included in the budget but separately identified. A $50,000 film may have a deferred compensation of $30,000 and cash needs of $20,000. Any contracts or other provisions reflecting return to investors would be based on the $50,000 budget amount rather than the $20,000 cash needs of the project, so the budget should make this clear. Structured in this fashion, any additional royalties paid to the deferred income participants reflect the risk of not receiving their $30,000 in earned income and are therefore much easier for the average investor to respect.

The Investors' Package

ASSUMING THAT THE filmmaker is going to finance the project independently by receiving investments from relatives and qualified individuals, the filmmaker must still determine what she must and what she should tell the potential investor. The hardest decision is how to convey the story. Few professionals, and even fewer others, can read a treatment or screenplay and capture what it will look like as a completed motion picture. The creation of a one-sheet or small poster mock-ups often elicit a greater visceral reaction than the written treatment or completed script. Regardless of how the story will be sold to the investors, there remains a great deal of information the investors should know.

A. Requirements

The key to properly structuring documentation is that all the information is true, accurate, and sufficient to give the investor a full understanding of the risks involved in the production. For the sake of both the investor and the filmmaker, the money should only come from people who can afford to make the investment or gift of the funds. The form and substance of the investment documents will depend on the legal structure selected, the amount of money sought, state laws, and the federal exemptions used to reduce or eliminate federal registration of the securities. As a result, no single document can be used for all film financing transactions.

1. LLC or Financing Agreement

For motion picture financing, the LLC serves as an excellent vehicle, because the Operating Agreement, which dictates the rights and interests of the managers of the company, can also serve as the disclosure document in many transactions. In corporations a disclosure document, known as a subscription agreement or financing agreement, must provide the same detail. Whatever the form, the heart of the process is the need to provide full disclosure of all the material facts regarding the project. This principle should guide the information—the investors are entitled to all material information.

Among the material details, the agreement must state the total amount of money to be raised and the interest each payment will receive. It must also state other interests given to the filmmaker and what payment (services, the screenplay, etc.) was given in exchange for those services. It must clearly state how these numbers can be modified by the filmmaker, if necessary.

The agreement will also provide information on the transferability of the interests, the payments to the managers (typically the filmmaker), the other income or deferred compensation paid to the managers and to other participants, and any other financial arrangements already made. If any presale arrangements have been made, any loans obtained (even credit cards), or any other material contracts signed, those should also be disclosed.

2. Private Placement Memoranda

Depending on the amount of money involved and the nature of the participants, the filmmaker may elect to use a private placement memorandum to describe the investment opportunity. These memos should be used exclusively for sophisticated or accredited investors who have the financial resources to risk a total loss of their investment in the film.

The private placement memo should include information regarding the business entity, the risks involved in the production, the film, the filmmaker, the production team, and the offering—including the financial opportunity and structure, use of the investment proceeds, the allocations and distribution of revenue, fees, and expenses. It should also provide information regarding the independent film market in general and those films that are most comparable to the filmmaker's project in particular. Finally, tax issues, termination or dissolution of the company, conflicts of interest for the filmmakers or other principals, and the effect of taking on additional financing should all be mentioned. Such a document is quite detailed and must be completed by an experienced attorney with the help of the filmmaker.

The private placement memorandum has only disclosure information; the investor receiving it has no obligation to invest. Instead, in a traditional corporate stock transaction, the actual sales document is typically a subscription agreement. The subscription agreement provides contractual language for the obligations described in the private placement memorandum similar in detail to that of the Operating Agreement. Such terms may include limitations on the transferability of the stock, identification of the obligations of the investors, the rights and returns expected, and any other contractual protections offered by the film company or waived by the investors.

Private placement memoranda and subscription agreements provide much greater detail of the business and the transaction than may be necessary for a small-film budget. Ultimately the choice will depend on the amount of disclosure necessary to explain the transaction adequately, the expectations of the investors, and the sophistication with which the investors spend their money. The key must come not from the financial return—which is extremely speculative—but from the commitment to tell the filmmaker's story or otherwise support the filmmaker in her career.

3. Other Documents

In addition to the legal structure selected, the finalized budget must be provided. For this purpose, the budget selected must accurately reflect the actual production. A statement should be included that the budget reflects the good faith plans of the filmmaker, but that it is subject to change throughout the project.

Similarly, a production schedule should be provided to give the investors an idea of the time involved in the preproduction, principal photography, and postproduction. The planned distribution strategy should also be mentioned. Again, these documents must clearly explain that they are good faith planning devices, and that the filmmaker expects them to change as circumstances dictate.

B. Optional Information

In addition to the requirements listed above, the film package can be augmented with additional information generally designed to encourage the investors. Like the earlier information, this documentation must be both accurate and helpful or it should not be included. There is no standard or set package. If a movie is to be based on a play, then reviews of the play might be helpful. If the movie will be a documentary, then newspaper stories about the topic might provide the potential investors with insight into the project. The more creatively tailored to the filmmaker's vision, the more likely the package will elicit positive responses.

1. Director and Cast Information

Investors react like any other audience. The cast information and photographs are often a movie's strongest selling point. Even if the cast is relatively unknown, strong backgrounds may instill confidence. Nonetheless, remind the cast that embellishments can be costly, and the information should not be overstated. The same holds true for the director and other key production personnel. If the person has professional expertise that enhances the film, then that information should be used as part of the package.

2. Distribution Information

Any distribution guarantees must be disclosed, particularly if they affect the possible returns the film company will see. If there are no distribution agreements in place, then the film company may be wise simply to explain that it will seek distribution of the finished film in all media. Describing the best-case scenario would be misleading, and describing the range of possibilities will ultimately prove fruitless and depressing. Assuming that the risk has already been explained elsewhere, there should not be any need to identify the particular odds of selling the film or receiving an award from a film festival.

3. Comparisons with Other Films

Like the discussion of distribution possibilities, the comparison with other films is a dangerous exercise in disclosure drafting. Offering documents that list the top five independent films and their return on investment is wholly inadequate unless the documents provide information such as the average return or the number of films that do not receive any distribution at all (a number that has probably reached into the thousands annually). Like describing a lottery jackpot without disclosing the odds of winning, comparing the current project to the most successful independent films is misleading at best. For any sophisticated investor, it demonstrates a lack of professionalism on the part of the film company.

In contrast, comparisons with other films for the purpose of communicating the story, the genre, or the visual style have far fewer drawbacks. Describing a spoof comedy as in the tradition of *Airplane* and *Scary Movie* does not suggest that it will have the same box office success, but it does convey the nature of the content well.

The filmmaker should identify the film package information based on what she would be informed by and would respect. Independent filmmaking is an incredibly high-risk financial proposition. Stress the passion and commitment rather than trying to sell the wild but quite rare successes.

C. Getting Hold of the Money

Whatever the financing structure selected, most of the money will not be used until principal photography commences. Only a modest portion of the financing should be allocated to the early preproduction stages of the transaction. As a result, most of the funds will not be needed until later in the project. This allows the film company time to continue raising funds while it is in the process of preproduction.

1. Escrow Accounts

The greatest risk for any investor is providing seed capital for a business that fails to get started. In that situation, the investor has nothing to look to for any return. Most investors, therefore, are quite unwilling to provide funds to the production company unless they know that the other money sought will also be collected and the project can at least attempt to meet the specified targets.

On the other hand, although promises are nice, nothing is as secure as cash in the bank. A subscription agreement often provides that each investor's participation is due when the minimum investment amount has been sold. When that commitment occurs, the company notifies all the investors, and they each send in their payments, which may work well in a large commercial setting. For most small ventures, however, the risk is simply too great that an investor will renege, whether for personal or for financial reasons, resulting in the filmmaker's failure to secure the minimum amount of capital.

An escrow agreement provides an excellent alternative for this problem. The escrow agreement provides that the funds raised from the investors will be deposited and held in a segregated account (or with a separate escrow company, if necessary) and that the funds can only be released for use once the contingencies are met. The most typical contingency would be that the minimum capital investment has been raised. It could also apply to casting or other key elements of the film.

The escrow need not require that every penny be raised before the funds are released. Instead, the agreement may provide that if the capital sought was $1,000,000, reflecting the amount necessary to complete the film, then the escrow funds could be released at $800,000 because that amount reflects a sufficient amount to complete principal photography. Presumably, a filmmaker should have an easier time raising editing money if a high-quality shoot has already produced sufficient footage to create a good movie. Investors may feel sufficiently comfortable to agree to escrow provisions with such a clause. Similarly, the reduction in budget may mean the elimination of certain scenes. The documents can give the filmmaker discretion to begin with a budget of a lesser amount or wait for the larger amount, so long as the investors can understand the choices involved.

2. Waivers

While some investors may require the protection of the escrow accounts, others may be more generous. The filmmaker may request those investors to waive the protections provided by the escrow accounts. Those investors who see any return on investment as secondary and the film project as the primary purpose may be willing to release their investment even prior to the funding of the entire minimum capital amount. These investors should sign a waiver of any rights for the monies to be held in escrow and explicitly grant the film company permission to use the funds for the purposes of raising capital and conducting necessary preproduction activities. The filmmaker may consider structuring the offering so such investors receive a premium for their additional risk (such as their interest being sold at a 10 percent discount from the price of the other investors).

The access to funds and the ability to gather enough capital to begin the project should be the final business issue in the making of the movie. With full disclosure, complete financing, presales and loan agreements in place, and the money released from escrow because it has been raised or waivers have been signed, the filmmaker is finally ready to add the creative process to the business process. She is one step closer to making the movie

Filming the Movie—
Preproduction and Production

Assembling the Production Team

WITH THE BUSINESS structure in place and the rights secured to the story, the next step in the filmmaking process is the lengthy but critical process of preproduction. An axiom of good filmmaking is that 90 percent of the work is good casting. This is true for the people both in front of and behind the camera.

A. Unique Opportunities as an Independent Filmmaker

The opportunity to make movies in new and different ways should be exploited whenever possible. The odds for success in Hollywood are painfully low for all participants, and perhaps especially for women. There are role models, however, in every aspect of the industry. Sherry Lansing, Dawn Steel, Lili Zanuck, and Kathleen Kennedy, among many others, exemplify quality producers.

Many other women have moved from actor or writer to producer, director, or both. Again, strong examples abound: Liv Ullman (*Faithless*, *Private Confessions*), Nora Ephron (*You've Got Mail*, *Sleepless in Seattle*),

Kimberly Peirce (*Boys Don't Cry*), and Jody Foster (*Flora Plum, Home for the Holidays*) are just a few of the many powerful women who have leveraged independent productions to redefine their career paths in a manner that can overcome the additional hurdles faced in Hollywood because of stereotypes and residual discrimination.

This is equally true with regard to race and other insidious stereotypes. Filmmakers such as Spike Lee, John Singleton, Arlando C. Smith, Robert Townsend, Mario Van Peebles, and Keenan Ivory Wayans are also independent filmmakers who have staked their claim by creating strong identities in themselves and their work.

Digital filmmaking and low-budget projects are particularly well situated for the growth and talent of individuals who are struggling against barriers to their professional development. Fortunately, in the independent filmmaking arena, filmmakers do not have the luxury of indulging in counterproductive, inappropriate racial or sex discrimination. As a result, independent films may provide the most important vehicle for professionals looking to expand their skills into new areas and for women and minority filmmakers to have the opportunity to prove themselves. Fortunately, the audience truly is colorblind and gender neutral. The audience sees only the sounds and images on the screen. The filmmaker controls those choices, but the audience will see only the result of those choices. The opportunities are real.

B. Who, What, and When to Hire

Perhaps the single greatest flaw in American filmmaking is the overwhelming number of people involved in the production process. Independent filmmakers do not have this luxury and, as a result, they can avoid some of the pitfalls of an overblown production.

The preproduction team creating the film should evolve as the project nears principal photography. Qualified individuals should be identified early and kept up-to-date on the preproduction process, but they should not begin to work on the film until their particular services become essential. This both reduces costs and streamlines the information flow of the project. Since most film shoots operate in barely contained chaos, the better the information flow, the less time is wasted on distractions or costly mistakes.

The initial team is typically made up of the producer, director, and screenwriter (though in an independent film, these may all be one person). To move forward on the project, even the solo filmmaker needs someone to work as collaborator. The process is far too lonely not to share the tensions and triumphs with someone. Filmmaking teams such as Joel and Ethan Coen and James Ivory and Ishmael Merchant have had longstanding success in part due to the healthy collaboration.

On the other hand, many of the tasks identified for preproduction can be carried out by one or two people, if they have the skills to accomplish the task (or if the filmmaker cannot afford to hire anyone else to help). For example, if the producer cannot provide the skills necessary to create the budget and estimate the coverage or costs of the production, then this becomes the first critical hire on the project. As described earlier, the accuracy and completeness of the budget is crucial to the film's operations. Similarly, since casting is often a long process, the person in charge of casting must be identified, and if it is neither the director nor the producer, then the casting director must be brought on board early in preproduction as well.

The next round of hires often involves locations for the filming. The settings are often integral to both the story being told and the costs of telling that story. A location manager and location scouts must be assigned the task of identifying the interior and exterior locations where the film may be shot, identifying the proper parties for arranging permission to shoot at those locations, and creating a feasible production schedule. On smaller films, the director typically serves as location manager, working with volunteer location scouts to help with the early legwork.

Next, the directors of the creative elements must be identified and incorporated into the process. If there is to be a director of photography separate from the director, early input into the locations, lighting, and visual style of the film becomes crucial. Similarly, if costumes, sets, props, lighting, special effects, or stunts play heavily in the film, then the person in charge of that creative area should become a central figure in the preproduction planning. For low-budget projects, however, these departments are luxuries. Actors wear street clothes, apply their own makeup, and manage their own action. There is no need to add directors and designers when the scope of the project does not call for their services.

C. Striking Deals—What Matters

In any film production, whether the budget be $2,000 or $200,000,000, there are only three significant points of negotiation—credit, compensation, and control. In the independent film world, the amount of compensation is necessarily modest. The perks that go with compensation—private trailers, limousines, staff, etc.—simply do not exist.

As a result, both credit and control become more important in the negotiation process for landing cast and crew. Fortunately, neither credit nor control has a direct effect on the cash available to complete the movie, so thoughtful choices by the filmmaker can still provide positive incentives for all the film participants.

D. Screen Credit

Providing screen credits acknowledges the primal need for personal recognition. It serves as a thank you and it permanently recognizes the work done by the person named. Screen credits also work to promote the individual or company named, conveying the status of the person to future employers and peers. As a result, it is a valuable commodity that should not be squandered.

Screen credits fall into two basic categories—those on "card" at the beginning of the film and scrolling credits at the end of the film. End credits are usually provided in a single typeface, moving relatively quickly across the screen, and, as a result, there are few serious negotiations about the end credits.

The opening credits are much more contentious. Professionals and audiences treat the first name shown as the "star" of a film—certainly the actor with the most clout regarding the production. If two names appear at once, the upper left is considered to be first position, before any names shown on the remainder of the screen. Those names that appear before the film title itself have more importance than the names that follow the title of the movie. Because these are accepted industry practices, the cast members and audience will accept these so-called rules, even if the filmmaker would like to ignore them. In addition to rules regarding placement, the size of the typeface can also suggest importance. If the cast named after the film title is in smaller type than the stars who precede it, that further separates out the remainder of the cast.

Cast members are not the only parties seeking to have their names in the opening credits. Film producers (perhaps including individual investors), writers, and the director are all typically credited. Rarely do these names go before the stars or the title, but all placement is subject to negotiation.

1. Union Requirements

Credits are one of the most important keys to continued employment in the entertainment industry. For a writer, director, or actor, the receipt of a credit helps establish a benchmark for future employment negotiations. As a result, trade unions such as SAG, the Directors Guild of America (DGA), and the Writers Guild all set policies that require their members receive minimum credit and, in the case of DGA and the Writers Guild, govern who can receive credit for the direction and writing of the film.

The union rules require that any dispute over directing or writing credits be resolved by an arbitration process run by the applicable union. The Writers Guild Screen Credit Manual reports that the Writers Guild handles over 150 credit disputes annually.[1] For Writers Guild writers, the writers must either agree unanimously as to the writing credit or submit the work to Writers Guild arbitration. The finished film and all the written submissions made by each of the authors are submitted to the arbitrator, who makes a determination regarding the contribution of each author. For most writing credits, there can be no more than two writers credited. A similar process is used for directors, but this is generally utilized much less frequently.

2. Optional Suggestions

For films that are signatories to union contracts, these rules must be followed. The good news is that the union arbitrator, rather than the filmmaker, must decide which writer or director deserves the name recognition for the work. For non-union films, the Writers Guild process can be a guide, but making highly contentious credit decisions is likely to create trouble. Unlike the Writers Guild policy, for non-union films, there is no reason not to credit everyone who legitimately worked on the film with some credit or recognition. The employment contract should, therefore, guarantee that the person's name will appear in the end credits of the film so long as that person was not in breach of the contract. The contract can also provide that the person will receive credit for the task, such as writer, if that person was the only person to provide the service, and the credit will be shared if others provided a similar service. The contract should also provide that the determination of the credits is solely at the discretion of the film company and not subject to appeal or arbitration. Taken together, this approach and these contract provisions should limit the problems over credits for most independent film companies.

3. Credits as a Marketable Commodity

Credits can be valuable to a host of other participants in the filmmaking process beside the cast and crew. Independent films often list "special thanks" to the individuals and companies that provided service, but this undervalues the assistance and softens the service provided. New York City, for example, requires that films using the valuable and free services of the New York City Film Office give the office an end credit. Being able to tell the lawyer, accountant, or restaurant that, as part of the project, they will be given credit in the film may have more than a passing value. The promise of a screen credit for "legal services provided" in addition to the promise of at least deferred compensation would likely convince many attorneys to assist independent filmmakers.

Further, the rigid, union-negotiated rules of film credits need not be followed by independent filmmakers. Treat the Hollywood norms as guides, but do not be bound by them. If the movie was inspired by a person who did not otherwise participate in the film's production, feel free to give the "inspired by" credit. If the film is based on a stage play, then prominent screen credit may be the way to induce the playwright to risk allowing an independent production company to have the film rights. The key is to recognize the high value and low cost that credits provide for the filmmaker. This is one of the few advantages non-union movies have over union productions, and the filmmaker should take advantage of it.

E. Compensation Packages—Making the Deals

Many independent films are created as professional stepping-stones, providing concrete evidence of one's professional skills, and creating the first paid work experience. As a result, even modest payments become very important for many of the participants. Nonetheless, as mentioned earlier, truly modest payment raises employment law concerns because of minimum wage laws and other employment obligations.

For most participants in the independent film, however, these legal concerns take second place to the psychological and professional importance of working rather than volunteering on the film project. This need should be respected.

1. Salaries and Per Diems

The basic payment system for most films is a flat fee. The cast members and crew members involved in the entire production are guaranteed a certain amount of money for the work. Payments of the fee are typically apportioned based on the planned number of weeks for the production. Except for those production members actively involved in preproduction, payments do not begin until principal photography. Some small payment can be made during the rehearsal period, if it is extensive.

These norms for payments track the traditional structure for most film-making, which assumes little rehearsal and tightly scheduled shoots. For independent filmmakers, these customs need not be followed. To the extent they are varied, the payment systems should also be varied. For example, if the filmmaker adopts a theater model for preproduction, then extensive rehearsals of the entire script may be done over a period of four to six weeks. The filming can then take place over a period of a few days rather than weeks. This model works best in a film that uses few sets and camera setups. A handheld camera walking with the cast through the sets as the scenes unfold needs to be well choreographed, but once staged, the natural flow of the action seems organic to the film. For such a shoot, the rehearsals become integral to the production process, while the length of the principal photography is substantially reduced. The timing of payments must be varied to reflect these choices.

In addition to salaries, the cast members and crew members may be paid per diems. These are modest payments based on the number of days worked. With the possible exception of the above-the-line participants,[2] the per diems are the same amount for everyone on the film. For non-union productions, per diems are not required, but they often supplement craft services (food service on the set) or assist with significant travel to the shooting location. The amount is intended to cover food, gas, and lodging (if the shoot is away from the production center). Even if the entire salary is deferred, payments of per diems often help ensure that the cast and crew can afford the gas to get to the set.

2. Deferrals

One very effective way of extending the amount of money raised to make the film is to defer expenses. Theoretically, if all the costs were deferred, then the film could be produced for no money, and all budget expenses would be paid from the film's future revenues. While this is not typically possible for all expenses, participants in the film project are often willing to defer all or part of their salaries. The true deferral simply puts the payments off until the film begins to receive revenues. Since the salaries are budgeted costs, they must be paid before any capital is returned to the investors or profits are paid to any parties.

A common source of confusion is the order of deferral payments. If the film is sold for an amount greater than the total deferred expenses outstanding, then everything is paid simultaneously. If, however, money trickles in, then it is important that the priority of payments be clearly spelled out in the employment contracts or in other agreements incorporated into the employment agreements by reference.

First, each class of deferments should be treated "pro rata," or in proportion. This means that all salary deferrals for all participants are pooled together. If the film company receives $5,000 to be applied to the salaries, then the $5,000 would be distributed to all the participants on a dollar-for-dollar basis. If the total pool was $50,000 in deferrals, then each participant would receive a payment of 10 percent of the amount deferred. The filmmaker could choose to pay the deferrals on the basis of the number of participants rather than the amount owed, but this would mean that some participants were paid in full before others. Either approach works so long as the system used is applied consistently and agreed upon in advance.

Second, any other classes of payments should also be spelled out. For example, it may be that all expenses, including equipment leases, credit card expenditures, invoices, etc., must be paid in full before any of the deferrals are paid. If this includes ongoing expenses such as office rent, then that must also be specified. Theoretically, all costs other than the deferrals should have been covered by the capital investment, but in the frequent situation where there are budget overruns or not enough capital, then the agreement should state whether the credit cards are paid before or after the deferrals. In addition, the producer's fee may be treated as a separate payment, to be made either before or after the other deferrals, depending on the needs of the producer.

Finally, the filmmaker may be receiving payment for many different aspects of the project. To the extent he is wearing different hats (director, actor, screenwriter, editor, producer, etc.), the tasks that entitle the filmmaker to additional compensation should also be clearly identified in advance. The filmmaker may provide that his producer's fee is deferred until after all the other deferrals are paid in full, but he will still be entitled to his deferred fee as a cast member and as the screenwriter. To avoid bad feelings and legal problems, such a structure must be quite explicit in the budget and contracts. As long as the system selected is clear, fewer problems will arise later.

3. Profit Participation

The other source of payment to the film participants flows from profit participation in the film. Studio films are notorious for definitions of profit participation 20 or more pages in length that make it almost unheard of for even the greatest blockbuster to actually turn a profit. For independent films, however, the successful project will return a profit that is not hidden in the studio overhead or other charges to the film.

Profit must still be defined. It comes after the expenses are paid in full, the entire investment is returned to the investors (often at 110 to 125 percent of the amount invested), and a reserve fund is made for ongoing operations of the film company. The remainder of income should be profit. Except as provided in the profit participation agreements, all profits belong to the film company and those, in turn, belong to the shareholders or members of the company. As a result, profit participation arrangements must be carefully specified in the offering documents for the film company.

Filmmakers may find it helpful to create a profit participation pool of some percentage of the profits, anywhere from 10 to 25 percent. In this way, the investors can be told that 10 percent of all profits are apportioned among the members of the cast and crew. That number will not change even though the exact participation within the pool may continue to fluctuate as participation points are allocated for cast and crew during negotiations. The filmmaker then designates that the pool has a certain number of points, say 100 or 1,000. These points are then incorporated into the employment agreement. The points not allocated can be returned to the investors, retained by the filmmaker, or paid pro rata to the pool. Any of the options work, as long as the choice is made in writing as part of the initial employment contracts.

Although even more contingent than deferred salaries, profit participation may be the most valuable aspect of the compensation package. For those rare blockbuster films, the profit participation points can be exceptional income. The contract, therefore, should also be very clear about when they are earned—upon successful completion of the employment task rather than upon signing the employment contract. If an actor leaves the film because a paying job is suddenly available, that actor should not remain a profit participant. Instead, if the director can negotiate to shoot sufficient coverage to work around the actor in exchange for keeping some of the deferrals and profit participation, the contract provides the filmmaker with negotiating leverage.

4. The Unions

Each union requires that a guaranteed minimum amount be paid as compensation, representing salaries and per diems. This allows union members to negotiate larger amounts and profit or revenue participation above those minimums. The unions will not allow deferred compensation.

Despite the basic rigidity of the union costs, there is some flexibility. SAG, for example, has low-budget contracts that significantly reduce the minimum salary requirements for low-budget films and allow actors to work without compensation on bona fide student projects.[3] There are a number of different low-budget agreements that vary primarily by the size of the budget, but also by the limitations imposed on distribution. As a result, some of these contracts may be more restrictive than the film-maker wishes to use.

One technique that avoids this problem is to pay the union members their full wages, including all pension and health costs. The participants, in turn, agree to invest their entire net salary in the film. Such an arrangement must be established early in the negotiations, and the union participants should receive both generous profit participation in their compensation package and the same return as other cash investors. Given that many actors working on low-budget films are more concerned with remaining eligible for health benefits, financial concessions that protect those minimums are treated favorably. By reinvesting the actors' net income, all union financial obligations are met, the cast members do not risk jeopardizing their union status by working on a non-union shoot, the professional quality of the production is generally improved, and the resources needed to make the film are not substantially reduced. Finally, as members of the production company, the participants should be sufficiently involved in the production to avoid most problems with the sale of securities to them.

F. Control During Production

The third primary negotiation point for most major hiring decisions concerns the allocation of control over the film project, and how the balance of control may change throughout the production process. Perhaps one of the most famous of film legends is that Sylvester Stallone received one or more offers to produce *Rocky* that he turned down because those offers did not include a guarantee that he would play the title role. His perseverance reflects his understanding that the role was far more important to his career than the credit and money he would undoubtedly have earned for the screenplay.

For the filmmaker, control should be the primary concern. In decisions involving the business structure, the hiring of the management team, financing, and distribution, the filmmaker should be sure to insist on control to the greatest extent possible. Unless the money or other rewards become so rich that the filmmaker is prepared to take them and run, control over the film should be the touchstone for all decisions.

If the filmmaker assumes ultimate control, then the other participants in the filmmaking process necessarily will not have control. Nonetheless, the other professionals have many of the same concerns that the filmmaker does, and as a result, reasonable authority and responsibility must be delegated by the filmmaker to these professionals as well. Further, to be successful, the filmmaker must assemble a competent, professional team. Professionalism includes respect for others and requires the filmmaker trust the assembled professionals to make competent decisions.

1. Artistic Control

The filmmaker must establish the mood and tone of the film. As he shares this vision with others—the cinematographer, the location manager, the designers of sets, costumes, props, lighting, sound, and music—the director should allow those individuals to suggest ways of achieving his goals. Even the writing must be shaped carefully to fit within the tone and mood to be achieved. Casting choices are based on the decisions that shape or reshape the script, and will inform every choice in direction and editing.

If the filmmaker is not the director, then the collaboration must be even more closely structured. Directors are often hired to fulfill the vision of the producer or story writer, but this relationship can easily turn into conflict if the two visionaries do not see the same goals. Schedules for collaboration must be agreed upon in advance. If the director does not wish the intrusion of the filmmaker, then the filmmaker should choose to select another director early in the project before such a choice dramatically affects the budget or morale of the film.

Artistic control should not be left to unspoken assumptions. In the larger-budget union films, rules of control have evolved over decades into complex collective bargaining agreements that balance the interests of the writers, directors, crafts, and talent against the interests of the producer and financial backers. These models may not be relevant for independent films and are particularly unrepresentative when the filmmaker plays more than one of these parts.

The film company should instead adopt explicit job descriptions for the key participants, clearly explaining to whom each employee reports. The contracts should specify that the employment is "at will." Although the compensation is most likely based on a fixed amount, the contract should provide that if the employee is terminated prior to completion of the project, then only the portion of the fixed amount that has accrued to the date of termination is paid. This is true for both paid salary and deferred salary. The filmmaker should also choose whether or not the portion of any revenue or profit participation accrues as well.

The structure selected should also be followed. The director should work closely with the cast and the directors or designers. The directors and designers, in turn, should be responsible for and have full authority over the workers within their areas. For example, if the job descriptions place the job of costumers as being supervised by the costume designer, then the director should work directly with the designer rather than giving any of the costumers inconsistent orders. In this manner, the information flow is maximized, confusion is minimized, and the designers are given the courtesy and professional respect they deserve, while the director retains ultimate control and the ability to terminate, if necessary.

2. Management Control

Like artistic control, management control requires a strong command system. In a very short period of time, a company that did not previously exist will suddenly employ dozens (or hundreds) while spending thousands or even millions of dollars in a brief period of time, only to once again collapse down to a few people with little or no activity. The most popular person in the company becomes the person with the checkbook. The most important person becomes the comptroller.

The professional titles should be matched to business duties, since legal obligations attend to titles such as president of the corporation or managing member of the LLC. These obligations should be vested in the filmmaker as the person who has the authority to carry them out on the project rather than using them as "credits" to be bargained with. To clarify the ultimate management and control of the production, the filmmaker should hold a key management position in addition to his artistic title, putting all other employees within his professional jurisdiction.

The producer has the business responsibility for managing the organization. If the filmmaker is the director of the film, and holds the position of president of the film company, then the producer may be a corporate vice president. In an LLC, the Operating Agreement must also be explicit that the filmmaker has primary authority, with the producer having that authority delegated by the filmmaker.

As a practical matter, however, the director will have his hands full making the movie. The producer must manage the business decisions. This may include coordinating with the line producer, location manager, and others to be sure that schedules continue to function; every expenditure is within the budget as well as authorized for current payment; and all laws, regulations, and agreements are signed and followed.

Occasionally, decisions will meld the art of commerce and filmmaking involving both artistic sensibilities and the business management decisions of the film project. Weather can wreak havoc on film schedules, and decisions to postpone, relocate, or eliminate scenes are necessarily a compromise between the business and artistic interests. Most decisions, however, tend to be either artistic choices (e.g., the color of a set) or management ones (e.g., the budget to build a set). The producer and director must each know when they must consult the other. They should also meet regularly to keep each other apprised of the ongoing progress. Separately, each then manages the people and decisions for which he or she is responsible. In this way, the structure encourages the most efficient and least contentious planning process possible. This is not to suggest there will not be problems, merely that the problems will not be caused by simple confusion and misunderstanding.

3. Resources to Outsource

Some of the more important but mundane tasks of the film can be readily outsourced for arguably less money and certainly greater efficiency. The management of the film company remains responsible for these outside vendors, but their services make the process more professional and better structured.

The most important area to outsource is the payroll function. As mentioned earlier, payroll has a host of legal obligations regarding taxes, insurance, withholding, and reporting requirements. All of these obligations can be transferred to a payroll house rather than being handled them internally. There are many firms that handle basic payroll, including a number that specialize in the motion picture or entertainment industry.[4] The services should be able to accommodate any union obligations the film company has undertaken, and some will be able to continue to provide residual payments that will come due as income flows from nontheatrical media.

Either as part of the bundled payroll service or separately, the employment taxes should be outsourced as well. This increases the chance that proper tax filings will be made not only in the first year of the film production but in years to come when fewer people remain professionally associated with the project.

Similarly, services provided by lawyers and accountants are typically outsourced as well. To the extent that any management function can be provided by a professional who has experience in the motion picture industry and can provide the service for a price comparable to that of the film company's internal personnel, the filmmaker should consider outsourcing the task. If the failure to perform the task will result in legal liability or risk injury, then the choice to outsource becomes the better course of action.

G. Insurance

In addition to the completion bond, there are a number of other types of insurance that should be considered by every film company. Ultimately, the amount of insurance depends not only on the budget but on the level of protection the participants in the film deserve.[5]

1. Workers' Compensation

Required in many states, workers' compensation insurance provides automatic medical insurance for work-related injuries. Where required by law, this coverage is not optional and must be included in the production budget. Even if voluntary, participation in a state workers' compensation system provides an essential protection for the cast and crew at a cost much lower than most private insurance systems.

2. Property Damage Liability Insurance and Auto Insurance

For any production shooting on location, property damage liability insurance must be available to protect the film company and the locations on which the company operates. For each location, the property owner will be added to the policy as additional insured. Some municipalities will also require this protection. Similarly, comprehensive general liability and auto liability insurance for production vehicles used during the filming both on and off camera remain a necessary part of doing business.

3. Equipment Insurance

The rental value of film and lighting equipment represents only a tiny portion of the total value of the equipment. As a result, the rental fees may directly include equipment insurance fees. If not, the equipment owner will invariably require insurance to protect these assets. Given the number of things that can go wrong, this is certainly valuable coverage for most productions. As digital equipment drops to consumer prices, however, the particular nature of the equipment used will dictate whether or not this insurance is necessary.

4. Errors and Omission Insurance

Errors and omission insurance protects the distributor (and potentially the exhibitors) from liability based on the content of the film. The insurance company defends lawsuits and indemnifies or pays for the cost of any losses that arise from defamation, invasion of privacy, or copyright liability as well as other lawsuits based on titles, piracy, plagiarism, or theft of ideas. Particularly given the more controversial nature of independent films, the purchase of errors and omission insurance is critical. Often, this purchase may be left to the distributor or at least until the time of distribution. The danger with deferring the purchase is that script changes necessary for the purchase of the insurance may cause minor inconveniences during the shoot but will be extremely costly and difficult after the cast has dispersed and the sets are no longer available.

5. Other Coverage

In addition to the first four categories of insurance listed, there are a number of other policies that may be necessary depending on the shoot and the budget. These include specific insurance policies for aircraft, watercraft, animals, and flights. These additional protections may be useful—and occasionally even required—but only in select situations. The elements of the production may also be insured, including the props, sets and wardrobe (as one policy), the cast, the film negative, and other media. Finally, insurance may even be available against the weather. Given the size of the investment, the filmmaker can select what degree of risk he feels appropriate for the production. Given the other risks involved in an independent film production, however, these insurance policies are not particularly popular with independent filmmakers.

8

The Key Members of the Independent Film Company

ALTHOUGH MANY OF the roles that must be filled have already been discussed in the context of financing and planning the production, brief job descriptions may be helpful to understand the broader role each of these participants plays in the filmmaking process. The variety of jobs does not necessarily mean the same variety of personnel. A truly guerrilla documentary can be created by a single person. Nonetheless, that filmmaker still serves in each production job, alternating as her own producer, director, writer, and editor. The cast, sets, costumes, and other elements are taken as they are found, but decisions regarding their inclusion are continuously being made by the director. As a result, the filmmaker has many of these tasks imposed on her as well.

A. The Producer

1. Job of the Producer

The producer provides the key leadership, management, and supervision for the entire film project. This includes the "creative, financial, technological and administrative [process] throughout all phases from inception to completion, including coordination, supervision and control of all other talents and crafts, subject to the provisions of their collective bargaining agreements and personal service contracts."[1] Like the CEO or president of a corporation, the producer is responsible for all final executive decisions and personally participates in many of the choices made in every aspect of the project.

A good producer must have a solid grasp of the financial, artistic, and technical aspects of filmmaking. Often the task requires that the producer bring strong-willed professionals together to make hard decisions that balance the financial resources against the filmmaker's vision and the technical limitations of the project. Experience, problem-solving skills, and strong management techniques are the cornerstones of being a good producer.

Executive producers are generally involved in the project only indirectly, serving to help raise funds, or coordinating multiple films at the conceptual level. Few independent films have executive producers except as a way of securing additional capital by providing the credit for inactive but essential financial participants.

Associate producer is another title that is often liberally distributed to production participants who undertake many of the producer's duties in coordination with the producer or by the person's own initiative. Although this credit is sometimes used in bargaining, independent filmmakers may wish to grant associate producer status to the individual who stands out throughout the production process as the unsung hero, who went well beyond the job description or pay to ensure that the project was completed.

2. If the Producer Is Not the Filmmaker

The Producers Guild of America distinguishes between entrepreneurial producers and employee producers. In the independent filmmaking context, the entrepreneurial producer is the filmmaker—the person who initiates the project on her own initiative. An employee producer is a person hired by the financier of the project to manage the film's production.

If the filmmaker is not the entrepreneurial producer, then the filmmaker must take pains to ensure that the employee producer is under the direction and employ of the filmmaker rather than the distributor or other financier of the project. As between the director and producer, the producer's control of the budget gives him primary authority over the film. A filmmaker can retain control of her film only to the extent that the producer answers to the filmmaker and no one else.

This is not to suggest that the filmmaker should not employ a producer or use someone who has the experience, problem-solving skills, and management strength that the filmmaker (and most artists) may lack. To the contrary, an independent professional will add perspective to the project, allowing the filmmaker the ability to make prudent, responsible choices. Even if the producer can be overruled, the advice and alternative viewpoints are invaluable to healthy production choices.

3. How to Select

Unlike some other independent film roles, the producer is only valuable if successful. On-the-job training can occur, but the experienced producer adds an incalculable value to the production company. If there is no one willing to work within the production budget, it is better to spend whatever money is available (whether in salary, deferrals, or revenue participation) on an experienced consultant who can provide some regular guidance throughout the film project.

If there is no experienced producer, the job falls to the filmmaker, so the filmmaker should be reluctant to hire a producer unless that person is truly qualified. There is nothing inappropriate in the filmmaker retaining the credit as sole producer, or coproducer if that is the reality of the production, so long as the sole producer credit has not been granted as part of anyone else's employment agreement.

In choosing to hire a producer, the filmmaker should do more than review the person's prior credits. Producers can range in participation dramatically, so have extensive conversations with the producer's former directors and others. These conversations should help the filmmaker better evaluate whether the producer is qualified, and whether the style and approach to filmmaking is compatible with the filmmaker's goals and expectations. More than anyone else, the compatibility between producer and director is critical for the filmmaker. It may also help to meet with the prospective producer on a few occasions, discussing the project and soliciting advice. A prospective producer should be willing to invest a little time up front as a way of doing his own due diligence on the film.

(Remember, the producer has to decide whether this is a film and film-maker with whom he wishes to be associated as well.) This rehearsal period for the producer and filmmaker provides a good opportunity to test the strengths and styles of the two individuals, so that each can assess whether the combination will be successful or not. The most successful of producer/director relationships can last decades, growing the careers of both participants.

4. Deals for the Producer

The entrepreneur producer is invariably among the most highly compensated participants in the film project. Often the producer's salary is relatively modest, but the producer will seek a significant percentage of the revenues. In terms of financial rewards, a filmmaker who can serve as her own producer should expect to see a much larger return than one who works with an experienced producer.

Producers are engaged to be in the project for the long haul. They should agree to be available for all of the preproduction, principal photography, postproduction, and, as reasonably necessary, all the marketing and distribution issues thereafter, including the supervision of the foreign language versions, dubbed editions, special edits, and other longer-term projects.

A producer may be interested in long-term relations as well, including a right of first refusal on the director's next project, or at least on any sequel or prequel undertaken during the three years following the initial theatrical release of the film. The compensation package may even extend to a small portion of any sequel and prequel rights or right exploited in other media, such as television or live theater.

B. The Writer

1. Job of the Writer

The motion picture writer may be the loneliest person in Hollywood. The job may include the development of the story, the treatment, or the shooting script. Each of these tasks, however, is done in relative isolation. To protect the writer from loss of credit and status, the Writers Guild insists that the writer's credit be highly restricted and noncollaborative. While this does not stop collaboration from occurring, it illustrates the noncollaborative nature of the writer's role in the process. The job for the writer will depend significantly on the relationship of the story to the screenplay.

a. Spec Script

When a screenwriter creates a script on speculation (i.e., "spec script"), the writer has created a finished draft of the complete screenplay that she can offer for production to producers, directors, and companies, ready to go. A spec script may be based on a story idea original to the writer or based on an existing story in the public domain. Occasionally, the spec writer will actually purchase the literary rights to the source work herself. Given the low chances the project will be produced, however, the costs associated with purchasing the underlying literary rights make this approach infrequent and rarely successful.

Many independent projects use another form of spec script. In this case, the filmmaker approaches a writer and offers her the opportunity to write the script for the project. Any payments for the script are dependent on whether the filmmaker likes the submission. This form of spec script writing is prohibited for members of the Writers Guild, since the screenwriter assumes all the risk of the script not being accepted, and the finished script cannot be used by the writer with a different producer, since it is based on the story provided (hopefully, in writing) by the filmmaker.

b. Original Screenplay

The majority of film projects stem from the hiring of a screenwriter to write an original screenplay based on an idea of the filmmaker's. The screenwriter is then hired as an employee by the production company to complete the screenplay. In this process the writer usually submits a first draft, meets with the producer or producer and director to review their thoughts and ideas on the script, and, based on their notes and the meeting, revises the script into a final draft. There may be multiple interim versions until the screenwriter considers the work the final draft, although multiple submissions are not contemplated under the Writers Guild minimum structure. In this scenario, the production company is the copyright holder of the script, and the writer is paid for the submission whether or not the film is eventually shot and distributed.

c. Nonoriginal Screenplay

A nonoriginal screenplay differs from an original screenplay because the story idea or source material already exists. If the film will be based on an existing stage play, then much of the story and dramatic structure will already be in place. Even some of the dialogue may reappear. The film may be significantly different, or it may change only the physical attributes of the project, opening the scenes up from the confinement of the stage. In order to engage in the script development process, the production company must own the rights to the source material or at least have nonexclusive permission to use the material. The production company may have purchased the film rights from the playwright or novelist, or be using true-life stories compiled from newspaper accounts. In either case, the screenwriter bases her work on the materials and rights acquired by the production company.

d. Rewrites and Polishes

The writing process seems never to end. Final scripts are often revised on a daily basis for a variety of reasons. Casting choices and locations each dictate certain changes to the script to better integrate the people and places used over those merely described. The thoughts of the cast members often reshape their characters to enrich the characters within the setting of the story. Humor described in print sometimes fails to translate to the screen.[2] Changes in participants among the producers, directors, designers, and cast change the expectations. Finally, some people always tinker, not knowing when to leave well enough alone.

The difference between a rewrite and a polish is that a rewrite may be a substantial reworking of another person's final script while a polish should be focused on details, particular lines of dialogue, or punching up the script with some added humor. Both are provided by additional screenwriters who revise the final draft of the script. The process can continue indefinitely. Invariably, directors and filmmakers also serve in this capacity, at least to some extent. For union productions, advance notice and other guidelines exist to protect union writers from losing screen credit to this tinkering, but true collaboration or rewriting by the filmmaker can meet union muster, if done properly.

2. Protecting the Filmmaker as Story Writer

Often, the filmmaker will write the initial treatment for the project well before engaging a screenwriter. The filmmaker must be cautious, however, to protect herself from losing any advantage in the creation of the work. Stories abound about similar projects racing through production to be first to market. This can happen because public domain literature[3] has become popular on stage and in print, because historical stories gain modern relevance, or just by random chance.

If a filmmaker were to meet with a writer and suggest a story for the writer to create as a spec script, there is no legal limitation on the writer regarding the script eventually created. Instead, the filmmaker must take concrete steps to protect herself in that situation. First, the more concrete the story provided by the filmmaker, the more likely the story will be entitled to copyright protection. Copyright law does not extend to ideas, merely their expression. The law will treat a detailed plot or treatment as protected expression rather than the mere story or idea. Copyright will protect the filmmaker to the extent that the treatment is written down in a tangible form. The oral pitch will not be entitled to copyright protection, but the written treatment will. The filmmaker may wish to register the treatment with the Writers Guild (described below) because it provides evidence of the creation of the treatment. Writers Guild registration does not provide any additional legal protection.

Second, the filmmaker may wish to require that the writer (as well as producers and others) sign a nondisclosure agreement. The nondisclosure agreement merely provides that the information disclosed will not be used except for the disclosing party's benefit, unless the information becomes generally available to the public without the fault of the recipient of the disclosure. These are not common in Hollywood, but they have become ubiquitous in the software and other intellectual property industries. If the agreement used is narrowly focused on the film information and allows the writer to avoid the contract's limitations, and if the information is made available from sources other than the film company, then the use of a nondisclosure agreement may be appropriate. Realistically, few producers, distributors, or financiers will be willing to sign a nondisclosure, but the spec writer should be willing. For the writer, it provides protection of the idea behind the film rather than the copyright protection that extends only to the expression.

3. How to Select

The selection process for the writer or writers depends on where in the production cycle the film presently stands. Despite the position of the Writers Guild, many writers are willing to write scripts on spec, even for a production company that owns the underlying story idea and rights. The best way to know whether to buy a script is to read it. In addition, this risk is not significantly different from the risk taken by the filmmaker who will sell the finished film through a film festival, but only if the audience receives the film warmly. On the other hand, this same offer should not be made to more than one writer at a time. To do so shows a lack of respect, if not bad faith, on the part of the filmmaker. The writers should not be bidding or competing against each other.

The primary alternative to using spec scripts requires that the filmmaker rely on previous screenplays and credits received by the screenwriter. When applicable, the filmmaker should compare the writer's script to the finished film to better gauge the work actually contributed by that screenwriter. Given the constant rewriting process, knowing a screenwriter from her filmed work may not show the true picture. Many new writers, however, are not likely to have produced many films with credits. By reviewing their own spec scripts, the filmmaker can assess their writing styles and techniques.

A reasonable alternative that up-and-coming writers may appreciate would be to require sample pages, rather than the full screenplay. In this way, the writer can submit some portion of the film drafted on the basis of the filmmaker's materials and directions, but not be forced into the labor-intensive process of creating an entire screenplay. In this way, the filmmaker can assess the timeliness of delivery, the style of writing, the ability of the writer to listen to suggestions, and the artistic sense of the writer for the filmmaker's material. Otherwise brilliant writers may fail on any given project if they do not have the right eye for the imagery sought, ear for the dialogue, or taste for the story.

4. The Role of the Union

The Writers Guild represents professional screenwriters. A film company may become a signatory to the WGA Theatrical and Television Basic Agreement (commonly called the Writers Guild Minimum Basic Agreement, or

WGA-MBA) simply by contacting the Writers Guild. If the writer is a Writers Guild member, then union rules prohibit the writer from working with a non-union company. Whether the individual writer chooses to follow this rule, however, is the choice of the writer rather than of the production company. The only danger in working with a union writer on a non-union production is that she could change her mind and refuse to deliver a script without the film company signing the WGA-MBA.

The WGA-MBA provides for two different minimum rates. Low-budget films, those budgeted below $5,000,000, require a minimum that is roughly half the fees for a high-budget film costing $5,000,000 or more. In 2001, the Writers Guild minimum for purchase of a screenplay was $35,079 for a low-budget film. If the writer was employed to provide a treatment as well as the screenplay, that amount increased to $52,210.

The WGA-MBA amounts are often useful for negotiations even when the writer is not a member. In determining the appropriate deferred compensation, the WGA-MBA minimum amounts provide an excellent guide. In addition, depending on the size of the budget, it may be appropriate to provide some percentage above minimum when all or most of the writer's fees are deferred. In this way, the writer may earn 150 percent of minimum in the event the film fully covers its deferred costs.

5. Deals for the Writer

The WGA-MGA provides an excellent structure for negotiations whether or not the writer is actually a member of the union. Compensation is linked to the type of writing requested, with a greater amount of money for writing both the treatment and the screenplay than for writing the screenplay alone. Similarly, writing an original screenplay is worth more than writing a screenplay based on literary rights owned by the production company.

The payment should be based on delivery of both a first draft and a final draft. The number of iterations between should be specified in the contract, such as a first draft, intermediary draft, and final draft. If the production has cash available, then the writer should be paid a portion of the total amount due at the delivery of each installment. Conversely, a schedule should be used that has incentives for early delivery, and should include the right of the production company to reduce payments for late delivery or to terminate the agreement.

Even if the majority of the salary will be deferred, the screenwriter should receive some cash payment at each delivery point. Unless all salaries are deferred, the screenwriter should not be singled out for complete deferment. Similarly, under the WGA-MBA the screenwriter's minimums are automatically increased if the production budget exceeds the low-budget minimum. Tying the deferred salary to the production budget (with both a floor and ceiling) allows the screenwriter to benefit proportionately from any significant increase in the project's scale. Though highly imprecise, providing the screenwriter(s) a minimum of 1 percent of the film's total production budget may reasonably approximate the negotiated fees for films in the low-budget and blockbuster range alike.

Perhaps the most important aspect of the remaining contract provisions involves identifying the screenwriter in the event there is a controversy over the writer or writers on the project. The WGA-MBA includes mandatory arbitration provisions. Even without a union writer, the filmmaker should retain the right to award credit based on the contribution provided; limit the number of parties entitled to screen credit (perhaps subject to the producer's discretion); and incorporate an arbitration clause, so that the determination can be made without resorting to a court proceeding in the event of dispute. Additional interests, such as profit or revenue participation, should be available only for the credited screenwriters. The total participation may be divided among the credited writers (and earned by a single writer if that writer receives sole writing credit).

In addition to salary, the WGA-MBA provides that the screenwriter should have some access to the shooting set. This should be done as a professional courtesy and can be included in the contract for those writers receiving writing credit. Similarly, the writers receiving writing credit should be afforded the opportunity to screen the movie at a time when any feedback may still be valuable to the editor and the filmmakers. The writers should also be included in the promotion of the film, included in all written materials, and potentially included at junkets and film festivals as well.

Despite some competition between writers and directors over the paternity of a project, the writer remains a highly dedicated part of the creative team who will often provide a great deal of additional, uncompensated assistance to help get the project completed and distributed. Industry custom provides a great deal of helpful guidance, but participants and resources should not be lightly dismissed simply because of those customs.

C. The Director

1. Job of the Director

According to the Directors Guild of America (DGA), the director "contributes to all creative elements relating to the making of a motion picture and participates in integrating them into a dramatic and aesthetic whole."[4] This somewhat vague description captures the essence of the director's role. The director (typically the filmmaker but not always, as described above,) supervises all the creative elements of the project, imprinting her vision of the story, sound, design, and essence of the film into the project. Technically, the director need only be responsible for the actions of the cast and the camera; in reality, the director remains integral to the entire production.

Unlike the screenwriter, the use of multiple directors occurs rarely and results in significant confusion when it becomes necessary. The director is usually attached to the project early and thereafter participates in all the other employment arrangements for the production. The director should know about, or help decide, virtually all issues involved with the production, including the casting, employment of other creative personnel, and creative decisions involving script, locations, set design, scheduling, and postproduction editing. The producer generally has authority over the director, but throughout most of the preproduction and principal photography, the director has the practical control over much of the project. In the typical case, the director begins his involvement about the same time as the script is being created.

If the director joins the production after a final script has been delivered, there is a strong chance that additional writing will be requested by the director. The director will work with the producer and location manager on locations, revising the budget to accommodate the choices made. The director should also participate closely in the casting decisions. During the principal photography, the director coordinates the creative elements of the film, directing the action and filming each day and typically reviewing videotape or rushes of the previous shooting each night.

When the filming is completed, the director will assemble his cut of the film. At a minimum, the director should be given the opportunity to create an initial cut of the film. The producer or filmmaker should provide comments to the director, who may wish to act on those comments to revise the edit of the finished film, or else the director will have completed his work, leaving final tweaking (or more significant editing if the parties do not agree on the film) after the director has completed his work. The director will also participate in the promotion of the film in all venues.

2. How to Select

If the filmmaker is not the director, then the selection of the director becomes a critical step in the production process. The wrong choice can cripple or kill the project. Because of the practical difficulty in terminating a director, the filmmaker must work closely with the prospective director to determine whether the visions of filmmaker and director are mutually compatible.

The first step is to review the previous projects helmed by the potential director. Thorough due diligence is a must. The filmmaker should speak directly with the producers on those projects, along with cast members, production crew, and others. There is no meaningful process that can serve as a tryout for the project. Filming is dependent on too many choices; the early work may not be indicative of the final project. The filmmaker should pay particular attention to the comments of former cast members who have worked with the director. The cast may be in the best position to gauge the effectiveness of the director on a project, and if a former cast member is reluctant to work with the director again, or has significant doubts, the filmmaker should be very active in determining whether problems may come to this project as well.

3. The Role of the Union

The DGA represents directors, assistant directors, and unit production managers in film, radio, and television. The role of the DGA has traditionally been to provide representation on issues of credit, control, and finances since its inception in 1939. Because the motion picture has evolved into a director's medium more than the medium of any other artist, the union focuses primarily on its relationship with the studios. Within the independent filmmaking arena, the filmmakers are typically the directors, so the union provides little relevance. Nonetheless, the DGA Minimum Basic Agreement provides for compensation minimums, mandatory credit, and rules on the relationship between the director and the production company. These serve as useful guidelines even in the non-union context of low-budget filmmaking, and are mandatory for any union production.

The DGA does offer a "side letter" that serves as a rider to the DGA-MBA, providing reduced director minimums. The side letter is not a standard agreement so much as a term sheet that can be used by the union and the producer to negotiate a mutually agreeable package. The DGA states that it is willing to "defer or waive other initial compensation (e.g., Vacation and Holiday Pay, Overtime, and Completion of Assignment Pay) until the project reaches a negotiated 'break even' point."[5] As the DGA explains, it "utilizes a pattern agreement as a basis for negotiations, [but] producers are encouraged to meet with a representative of the Guild to discuss any issues that are of concern to the Company or to the individual production." Despite the somewhat vague terms of the side letter, the DGA reports that more than 70 productions have taken advantage of the reduced costs for experienced union directorial talent. Most important, the side letter allows a member filmmaker to stay in compliance with her union obligations while developing her own independent film.

4. Deals for the Director

Whether or not the production is governed by the DGA-MBA, the agreement provides useful guidance on the proper relationship between the director and filmmaker. To the extent the filmmaker is not the director, certain protections may be modified; however, most of the director's creative rights are essential to a quality production and should be honored for the sake of the project rather than because of the collective bargaining agreement.

Before the employment begins, the filmmaker should go over certain items identified in the DGA-MBA with the prospective director. Unless the director comes into the project knowing these items, the relationship may get off to a rocky start. The DGA-MBA requires disclosure of the following:

1. budget for the film or at least its top sheet
2. proposed shooting schedule
3. names of artistic and creative personnel already employed
4. all existing film contemplated to be used
5. any rights of script approval or cast approval contractually reserved to any person other than the filmmaker and producer
6. story and scripts presently available
7. any other artistic and creative commitments

These disclosure items really detail the significant issues that the director and the filmmaker must agree upon when structuring the film project. The scheduling, budget, and creative decisions will dictate as much about the film as any choices made during the filming process. A director who does not participate in those decisions is at a severe disadvantage, one which he may be unable to overcome.

In addition to the common understanding, the director also has concerns regarding issues of compensation, credit, and control. The director's compensation package will most likely include some combination of salary (paid and deferred) and either profit participation or revenue participation. Unlike producers, directors only occasionally participate in revenues rather than profits. To the extent that the filmmaker is attempting to lure a well-respected professional director to work on a low-budget independent film, the filmmaker can offer revenue participation in exchange for substantially lower budgets and resources than the same director has traditionally been given. In contrast, the opportunity to direct a feature film is a highly prized opportunity that relatively inexperienced directors will jump at for very modest compensation.

Director's credit has not historically proven controversial. The DGA-MBA requires that the initial director receive credit if he has completed 90 percent of the film. If more than one director is used, a choice can be made to award both credit. The general assumption is that the second director is the person with the greater influence on the final look of the film and invariably has the better relationship with the production company. The contract should, therefore, provide that the director will be guaranteed director credit only if he has completed 90 percent of the principal photography. Otherwise the filmmaker should retain discretion on how to award the film credit. In this way, a subsequent director who shoots as little as 25 percent of the footage may still dramatically reshape the project and therefore be awarded either sole or shared direction credit.

Unlike director's credit, "a film by" credit has proven to be highly controversial. This credit, which is not specified under any union agreement, has increasingly been granted to the director. In the independent filmmaking world, this should be the credit of the filmmaker, if anyone. The slowly developing trend is to provide this credit only to directors who are also credited on the script. Given the procedural hurdles of a director receiving script credit, however, it may also be appropriate in those situations where the director is a substantial noncredited writer on the project.

The most contentious relationships involving directors' contracts stem from issues of control. The producer controls the budget, but the director is responsible for the need for all expenditures (though not necessarily able to authorize those expenditures). The same relationship applies to hiring, selecting locations, and many of the production decisions. As a general matter, the contract may simply provide for consultation by the director with the producer on these issues, but that contract will be highly unsatisfactory if relied upon. The DGA-MBA takes the opposite approach, identifying which support staff can be selected by the producer (such as the unit production manager) or by the director (the first assistant director). Essentially, every issue that is subject to prior disclosure is under the final control of the producer, but the producer must provide the director opportunity for meaningful consultation on those issues. Perhaps more significant than the right to consult on significant changes is the opportunity to know of these changes prior to scheduled filming. For example, significant changes to stunt work require advance notice to the director, who may object to the change if there are legitimate reasons for the objections.

Finally, under the DGA-MBA, the director must have some assurance regarding his participation in the postproduction process, even after his director's cut has been delivered. Assuming the director does not have "final cut" authority over the film, he must still be allowed to participate in the postproduction process. Since the final look of the film becomes so essential to a director's future, anything less than reasonable consultation seems highly inappropriate. Unless the director has been terminated for cause or has become an obstruction to the editing process, he should be included throughout the process, at least as an advisor to the filmmaker or producer.

D. The Production Team

1. Jobs of the Unit Production Manager and First Assistant Director

The team of unit production manager and first assistant director fill out the senior management of the film production. These positions implement the decisions and directions that the producer and director make, respectively. The UPM provides the logistical detail of the production, working through the details of the budget, production logistics, scheduling, finance, travel, and myriad additional detailed logistical issues that affect the film. The UPM will negotiate many of the agreements for the production and arrange (and rearrange) the production schedule.

The first assistant director runs the set, ensuring that each day's schedule is ready for the director, that the call times for shooting, costuming, and makeup are coordinated so that each cast member can be costumed and ready in time for the scheduled appearance. The first AD works with the cast and serves as an intermediary between cast and crew whenever necessary.

Any significant changes made by the UPM must be filtered through the first AD so that the production can continue to operate smoothly. Like the relationship between producer and director, the relationship between UPM and first AD must be one of respect and constant communication. Respect between producer and director will set the tone for the rest of the production. That is equally true between the UPM and first AD.

Although the tasks are interrelated, they are not interchangeable. The first AD must monitor and participate in the ongoing production and coordination throughout each day of the shoot. The UPM, in contrast, will often be working on what comes next, adjusting production schedules to account for weather or other uncontrollable variables, revising the budgets as expenses come due, and preparing for the design and logistics issues that are on the horizon throughout the production. Even in the smallest of films, both of these roles must be filled continuously. For an independent film looking to reduce the number of participants, the film-maker is more likely to collapse the producer and UPM successfully than to collapse the UPM and first AD into a single job description. Similarly, independent directors often have to manage their own sets, so the direc-tor may face the burden caused by losing an assistant director, but that would not place the director into the producer's role.

2. How to Select

The primary criterion producers consider to choose the UPM and direc-tors consider to choose the first AD is comfort. More than any other posi-tion, these two roles are extensions of the needs of their supervisors. Trust, confidence, and rapport are essential for the producer with his UPM and the director with his first AD. As a result, wide latitude should be given to individual preference in this selection process.

If someone is to be hired who has not worked with either the director or producer before, then the key is to look for a track record involving organization, efficiency, initiative, attention to detail, and experience on film sets. These two roles serve as the engine on the project, propelling the cast and crew late at night, early in the morning, and into long week-ends when everyone would rather be doing less. They are also the face of the production, because the producer and director do not spend as much time among the rank-and-file production personnel as do the UPM and first AD. As such, the tact, respect, and professionalism utilized (or for-gotten) reflect directly on the production company, director, and producer. The employer should be concerned about these attributes as well.

Often, production assistants move up through the ranks to become sec-ond ADs and eventually first ADs. Others may follow a similar track to UPM. In this way, even a low-budget project may be able to identify some-one with strong potential and a reasonable amount of experience.

3. Deals Structures

Both the first assistant director and unit production manager are covered by the DGA. For a union shoot, the DGA-MBA provides the minimum compensation and credit obligations. As with the directors, the side letter agreement may be used to reduce the costs to employ union talent in these roles. The side letter may also allow for limited non-union personnel in these areas, particularly if an experienced director or producer can use the opportunity for training and promotion of someone who has worked on prior union productions.

E. Cast

1. The Actor

The actors portray the characters in the film. More formally, acting may be defined as "the performing art in which movement, gesture, and intonation are used to realize a fictional character for the stage, for motion pictures, or for television."[6] The task is as simple as that, and perhaps remains the most difficult process in the creative arts. Film roles are portrayed by experienced professionals with years of training to capture their emotion on film. Other roles are portrayed by untrained individuals who simply appear on screen in the manner sought by the director of the film. Casting choices are often the most fundamental to the entire project.

For independent films, the filmmaker may be a cast member rather than one of the other participants in the film. When the actor has some degree of fame, this may be the opportunity to both star in the film and direct the project, as Ed Harris did so successfully with *Pollack*. For less well-known actors, the choice may be to produce an opportunity to star in a role that no other producer would offer. Particularly for minorities and women, independent films offer the ability to create opportunities rather than to wait for Hollywood to offer them. Many independent films may be fueled, at least in part, by the desire of actors to play these hard-to-find parts.

a. Casting Directors

In productions with more than the most modest of budgets, casting directors provide the producer and director with information and suggestions on the cast members to be sought, based on breakdowns of the script and suggestions made by the producer, director, and casting director. An experienced casting director has access to talent agents representing union talent, a database and personal knowledge of the cast members' experience, and some insight into cast members' income histories and box office appeal. By utilizing historical information about the cast members' prior film contracts, the casting director can help negotiate reasonable salaries for the cast and avoid unnecessary delays as unrealistic choices.

For many independent films, the producer and UPM must fill the role of casting directors, soliciting the talent agents of potential cast members. To the extent that the producer and director have personal working relationships with any of the preferred cast members, these relationships may serve better than any formal process to interest the actors in the project.

b. Breakdown Services

Casting directors rely heavily on breakdowns of the script to create a brief synopsis of each character in the film. Breakdown Services, Ltd., has been the leading company providing this service, free to casting directors and producers, for over 30 years. Breakdown Services' staff writers read and analyze approximately 30 scripts daily.[7] Talent agents download the casting information directly from the Breakdown Services Web site. Using the breakdowns, talent agents may submit cast members or contact the casting director or producer with possible talent for the production. Given the growth of the Internet, Breakdown Services also allows the actors to see the breakdowns directly in some situations, with the producer's approval. In addition to Breakdown Services, Ltd., new Internet-based companies are now beginning to provide similar services.[8] The growth of the Internet and rapid changes in Internet business may lead to significant changes in how casting information is distributed over the next decade, as well as shift the participants in the industry.

The breakdown service provides an efficient method of providing detailed cast information to the talent community at little cost or trouble to the producer. The true work comes next, sorting through the potentially thousands of submissions to narrow the field and begin the process of auditioning.

2. Talent Agents and Managers

For union projects, the primary official contact flows from the casting director or producer and the agents for the talent. Talent agencies will receive the breakdowns of the script and, at the same time, the casting director will be contacting the agents for the star talent that the filmmaker has in mind for the key roles. Occasionally, the agent will be interested in the project. More often, filmmakers identify stars that are not within budget for the independent film, not available for the production schedule, or simply not interested in working on an independent film. With tremendous perseverance, however, the filmmaker will begin to generate interest by actors whom the filmmaker might wish to cast.

The talent agent's obligation is to maximize her client's income and professional opportunities. Occasionally, a talent agent will see a script that she believes will transport her client's career. More often, however, the talent correctly sees the opportunity to participate in an independent film as the loss of the opportunity to work on a higher-paying, higher-profile project. (This coincides with the agent's own income, typically 10 percent of the client's revenue.) As a result, talent agents may often be a hurdle rather than an aid to independent film production.

A talent agent will typically suggest a number of other, less-established clients who may be appropriate for the roles identified in the breakdown sheets. Among these less-known performers may be some stellar talent. One of the true successes of the independent film process flows from the opportunities given to undiscovered talent both behind and in front of the camera.

To attract strong, well-recognized talent, however, the filmmaker should use whatever resources she has to contact potential cast members through informal means. This is where personal and professional relationships make the largest difference. On a low-budget project, a single known star may guarantee at least a video distribution agreement. Such a "bankable" star will encourage financing, improve press coverage, and lend credibility to the project. Once an actor becomes interested in the project, the negotiations will still be conducted by the talent agent. It is important, therefore, that the filmmaker work to keep the talent agent somewhat positive toward the project, so that she does not convince the actor not to pursue the role.

Some talent also have personal managers. For non-union talent, a personal manager may be the only professional willing to assist the person. Managers should not negotiate contracts or help to procure employment. Independent filmmakers should use these managers as a sword rather than a shield. To the extent that an independent film role opens an actor to a broader range of roles or might serve to reinvigorate an overly narrow career, the manager may see long-term value in such a relationship. Managers, therefore, are a useful avenue for the filmmaker to pursue talent. In contrast, managers should not be pursuing job opportunities; that is the exclusive obligation of talent agents. Filmmakers should be leery of any manager acting as an agent. Such a manager may be trying to act as an agent without complying with union rules or financial limitations imposed by agreement on registered agents. This practice is inappropriate, and may also lead to complications if any dispute arises involving the agreements. As a result, the filmmaker should always work through the actor's agent unless he or she is unrepresented.

3. Advertisements

In addition to the formal processes using casting directors and breakdown services, a myriad of online databases have developed that allow actors to submit their pictures and resumes for review. Unless the film requires someone of truly unique talent (such as a 4' 9" soprano or a sword-swallowing juggler), these databases may be of limited value. On the other hand, some of these databases allow the filmmaker to post casting requirements or breakdowns directly. For non-union shoots, this may greatly expand the range of possible talent available.

One of the premier traditional print resources now boasts newspapers and Internet resources. Backstage[9] and Backstage West (which acquired its Los Angeles competition, Drama-Logue) publish short cast descriptions for both union and non-union productions. These listings are free and widely read. For many independent projects, most of the cast members come either from personal relationships or these advertisements.

4. Auditions and Casting

For motion pictures, casting can take one of three general formats. For well-known performers, no true audition is required. Instead, a meeting or interview will be held between the actor and director to discuss the part and give both parties a chance to get acquainted. While there will be some discussion of the character and the vision of the director, the actor will not be expected to perform the part. This meeting may include some readings from the script, but these are not necessarily required.

A more formal audition may also be held. In this setting, the director, casting director, and perhaps the producer or UPM will observe as an individual actor presents a scene from the production, often together with another actor who has already been cast. If, for example, the film is to star a particular lead actor, that actor may be willing to work with the director to allow the director to see her with a few different actors in the role of the male lead. In this way, the director can better judge the chemistry between the leads.

At the other extreme is the cattle call. This invariably humiliating experience allows the producers and director to observe potentially hundreds of unknown actors reading for roles in the production. Actors with any modicum of success will not participate in these, but for unknown actors, cattle calls represent an opportunity (admittedly much like a lottery ticket) to land a smaller part on a production. Casting directors who submit breakdowns through Breakdown Services may not then use cattle calls to review the talent submitted. The cattle call should really be used as an alternative to requesting that actors submit resumes directly. Also, since the process is painful for both the actors and the producers watching the process, cattle calls should not be used unless the production seriously plans to cast from the process. As a backup plan, it is far too time-consuming and disrespectful of the actors. Where it will result in actual casting, however, many, many actors are willing to endure the process.

5. Screen Actors Guild

Film actors and extras are represented by the Screen Actors Guild (SAG), which provides for minimum salaries, pension, and health care benefits for its actors. SAG also governs work conditions on productions. The minimum salary for actors depends on the production budget, the amount of time the performer will be in principal photography, and the agreement signed with the union.

Regardless of whether a union contract is signed, the independent filmmaker should abide by the SAG work condition requirements designed to provide a safe working environment. Almost every major film accident occurred because the work schedules were violated or safety rules ignored. Most independent films do not have the resources to survive even a modest accident, and no film is worth risking the lives of cast or crew.

SAG provides a range of contracts ranging from major studio production contracts to contracts designed for student films shot for academic credit. Because of the number of types of contracts and the constant fluctuation of these agreements, the filmmaker should contact the closest SAG office early in the preproduction process to determine whether a union agreement can be arranged. The obvious benefit of shooting under a SAG agreement is the ability to cast professional actors. If even one of the preferred cast members is a member of SAG, then the production must enter into a SAG agreement.

Perhaps the biggest drawback to a SAG production occurs if the film is to be made outside of a traditional SAG market. SAG operates approximately two dozen regional offices, each having a carefully mapped geographic zone. Shooting outside those zones can increase the costs under the SAG agreement considerably, so locations may be selected with this in mind. Alternatively, if a particular location is central to the film, then it may affect the filmmaker's decision to use union talent.

6. Extras

SAG now provides for union representation of extras, having merged the former Screen Extras Guild into the SAG union. The union agreement requires that a specified number of union extras be hired before non-union extras be allowed to be employed. The particular number depends on both the contract under which the production is authorized and the location of the shoot. For contracts involving low-budget projects, this requirement may be minimal and may be waived in some situations. Again, this is an area that the filmmaker must discuss with union representatives early in the production process.

7. Contract Issues

In addition to the primary issues of compensation and credit, cast members are generally concerned about their obligations to the production—mostly regarding the production schedule. The filmmaker will generally be required to accommodate the schedules of the key cast members, particularly if they are working below their normal salary to participate in the film. In addition to the dates of principal photography, the contract must provide that the actors will be available for any necessary reshooting and for postproduction looping or dubbing. The contract will typically call for a minimum number of days of looping that are included in the contract and a pay scale for additional days needed.

The talent agreements should also include contractual obligations to promote the film. For stars working below their normal salary, a contractual commitment to promote the film may be difficult to negotiate, but it should be part of the package for other cast members. Even a small amount of promotion may be critical to the success of the film, so the filmmaker should work to encourage participation, contractually or not.

If there is a possibility of generating additional revenue through children's products, soundtrack albums, or other merchandise, then the contract should specify that the film company has the right to use the names, likenesses, and publicity rights of the actors on these products. The provision should limit the use of each actor's publicity rights to products directly associated with the film, and should include a royalty payment to the actor. The royalty will typically be based on a percentage of the income paid to the film company for that item or items. The filmmaker should avoid agreeing to pay a percentage amount unless the percentage is based on the filmmaker's income. If the filmmaker were to offer a percentage of retail sales, for example, the filmmaker might well owe more than she earns, and she could have no method for auditing the obligation.

Equipment and Locations

THE LEGAL AND business choices in this chapter should be secondary to the aesthetic production goals of the filmmaker. The digital revolution has dramatically affected the choices of equipment available, and the business practices are slowly adapting to that change. The ability to digitally alter the location during or after the shoot creates an entirely new set palette from which to paint the images. Each choice affects every other choice.

A. Types of Equipment and Contracts

1. Cameras and Lights

The production company will rent a package of camera equipment and lighting equipment, plus stands, electrical generators, and other related equipment for the film production. Perhaps the hardest choice to make at present is the medium on which the "film" will be shot. For the first time in a century, the independent filmmaker has a choice of formats, including the 35mm print, 16mm film stock—the traditional staple of the independent filmmaker—and a number of competing digital media. The choice of medium will be based on cost and ease of use as well as the overall look being sought.

The medium chosen will dictate a number of other choices. Because 35mm film requires significantly more lighting power than any other format, lighting equipment must be selected to complement the shooting format. The size and weight of the camera will require that most moving shots use dollies or similar equipment. Steadicam equipment, which allows a 35mm camera to be operated in a "hand-held" fluid fashion, can be rented, but this choice also requires that the camera operator be experienced wearing and operating this large piece of equipment.

Eventually, digital equipment will render the 16mm format obsolete. Whether that era has already arrived remains unclear. Sophisticated digital equipment is readily available in some cities but remains hard to rent in other areas. The quality of 35mm prints created from moderately priced digital equipment has not yet gained widespread acceptance. Still, the ease of shooting, the low-light range of digital equipment, and instant recording ability all make digital a strong contender for independent filmmaking.

Rental prices will vary significantly from company to company and region to region. Be sure to shop around. In some areas, it may be cheaper to travel considerably to rent the equipment than to pay local prices. The contract should always be between the production company and the equipment supplier. The filmmaker should try to avoid being personally liable for rental fees or for any damage to the equipment. Often the rental fee will include insurance. If the production company carries adequate insurance, it may offer to include the rental company as an additional insured on its policy rather than paying again for the equipment insurance. Flexibility on this point will vary from company to company. Be sure to include insurance and other costs in the comparison of contracts. Finally, weekly rates may vary significantly from the base rate of equipment. Some companies apply a weekly rental fee equivalent to three or four days of rental. Careful planning is necessary, however, because most contracts do not allow for extensions to convert a daily rental into a weekly rental. It may be cost-effective to rent for a week rather than renting for two days if the production schedule proves to be overly ambitious.

2. Weapons

Filmmakers often wish to use real weapons in the creation of certain scenes. While this is commonly done, independent films that intend to use fewer personnel and guerrilla filming should be ready to comply with detailed, time-consuming regulations and supervision. A handgun or rifle remains a weapon subject to licensing and permitting requirements even if it is not operable on the set. If it has been permanently disabled—the interior components rendered unworkable—then it may not be subject to licensing requirements, but even that will vary from jurisdiction to jurisdiction. While it's a good idea for safety purposes, temporarily disabling the weapon will not change most licensing requirements.

In most jurisdictions, even if no film permit is required for the production because it is filming exclusively on private property, the production company must still have a film permit if a weapon will be used. In one instance, a shot was fired as part of a lawful, independent shoot on a private farm. The police were called to the scene of the shooting, and the production was shut down with substantial fines levied for the false alarm generated by the production. Had the production obtained a permit, the police would have had a record of the planned shooting on the set, and the production could have continued.

The Massachusetts Film Office provides a representative example of problems that may arise for companies planning to use weapons.

> Massachusetts has one of the toughest gun laws in the country. Property masters or armorers who are nonresidents and wish to possess firearms in the Commonwealth while filming, must obtain a temporary license from the Massachusetts Firearms Records Bureau. A non-resident gun permit is valid for one year at the cost of $10.00.
>
> The permitting procedure requires the applicant to submit a copy of a current license to carry firearms issued by the applicant's home state. If no such license is required in the home state, documentation attesting to the applicant's good character including a criminal-free record must be secured from the Town Chief of Police and State Bureau of Criminal Records. . . . Allow seven to eight weeks for the entire permitting process. . . .
>
> Once a weapon is in Massachusetts, it may only be transported in a locked box by a licensed person. If the weapon is aboard a safe within the prop truck, the driver of that truck must be licensed. Transportation captains in Massachusetts routinely assign licensed drivers to drive a prop truck when weapons are involved. Actors do not need to obtain a license to handle prop weapons on the set if a duly licensed person is also on the set to immediately supervise

weapon use. Strict attention must be paid to supervision. Please be advised that a firearm that is temporarily inoperable is considered a weapon in Massachusetts and must be treated as such.[1]

3. Stunts and Special Effects

Stunts and special effects both involve specialized activities with significant degrees of risk. Stunts typically include fight scenes, falls, or other highly choreographed movement. Special effects typically involve pyrotechnics—explosives or fireworks—which require state licenses and local permits, even on private property. Both should be conducted using experienced professionals, no matter what the production budget.

For pyrotechnics, a license is required in most jurisdictions. Attempts to create homemade effects can result in serious injury. Unlicensed attempts may void the production's insurance coverage and will certainly make the participants in any accidents personally liable for the losses. If injury or expenses related to an unlicensed accident disrupt the production budget, the personal liability of the filmmaker might conceivably extend to the investors, because the filmmaker's personal negligence personally cost the production its opportunity to be completed. Needless to say, unlicensed pyrotechnics should be avoided.

Even relatively simple stunts should be done only under the careful supervision of a stunt coordinator. Of course, the line between action and a stunt is not always clear. Common sense should serve as a guide. If the action, done improperly, could result in one of the actors being seriously hurt, then it should be treated as a stunt and conducted only after it has been well rehearsed and all risks minimized.

4. "Renting a Crew Member"

Just as stunt coordinators and special effects experts are employed for specific tasks, technical experts such as the gaffer (electrical experts) or key grip (movement of lighting and camera) are specialized professionals. Particularly for small, digital productions, using handheld cameras and limited professional lighting may substantially reduce these tasks. For non-union productions, professional trade union positions may be unnecessary. In certain situations, however, experts may be required. Rather than hiring the person for the entire project, it may be possible to enter into a special arrangement that covers only the particular scenes needed. This is not necessarily compliant, however, with the union obligations of the gaffer or key grip. Asking a professional union member to work on a non-union project is risking that the person could be forced to leave the set if requested by a union representative, or may simply change his mind. This risk can be minimized if the person is hired for a short duration to assist with particular segments of the film.

Alternatively, the producer may determine that the project is complicated enough to require a union crew. The International Alliance of Theatrical Stage Employees (IATSE, or IA) provides locals for all below-the-line production personnel. Generally speaking, IATSE does not cater to independent films and provides few accommodations for these productions.

Other professionals, notably the director of photography and the sound mixer, are often package rentals along with their own equipment. In this way, the production may rent equipment and have the operator supplied. Producers should be sure, however, that the production requires the professional services in addition to the equipment. The producer will have far less control over these packages than she would if she were hiring the equipment from a rental house and employing the professional separately. On occasion, this can limit the producer's discretion over the quality of either equipment or personnel. The producer must carefully scrutinize the references of anyone offering a package. Nonetheless, experienced sound mixers and directors of photography provide welcome efficiency and cost-effectiveness for the independent filmmaker.

B. Selecting Locations

The location should be treated as one of the characters in the script. In a visual medium, location choices convey much of the story. Independent filmmakers often choose to blur the locations selected, but this denies the filmmaker one of his chief assets. Instead, effective use of the film permitting process and solid legwork will allow the filmmaker tremendous flexibility in the locations represented in the picture.

1. Use of the Soundstage

The Hollywood of the 1930s built tremendous soundstages where controlled environments could be used to create any set imaginable. The obvious benefit is control. These enclosed spaces provide for excellent sound and allow the production company to reproduce exactly the environment envisioned by the filmmaker. In addition, small portions of rooms or spaces can be constructed, allowing the camera to move into spaces that a 35mm camera could never enter in the real world.

The film industry has witnessed another transformation as the soundstage of the 1930s has been augmented by non-Hollywood locations such as the Long Beach geodesic dome (former home to Howard Hughes's *Spruce Goose*) and other major facilities. These environments have been converted into soundstages in which other "locations" can be built. This trend blurs the distinction between soundstage and location shooting. These spaces are not owned by the studios and exist outside of Hollywood. They are typically rented on a long-term basis so that multiple sets can be constructed in the space. Soundstages also provide certain efficiencies because all the production facilities center on a single location. Hollywood soundstages may be too expensive for all but the largest of independent films.

The independent filmmaker, however, may use the soundstage effectively by using larger spaces as one-stop locations for multiple sets. Using shuttered warehouses, school buildings during summer break, or other available spaces, the filmmaker may enter into a single lease that provides him with a range of environments that can be adapted to various scenes needed throughout the film. Legally, the issues are the same as any location shoot (discussed below).

2. On-Location Shooting

The modern trend for filmmaking—both independent and studio pictures—has been to move out of the studio and onto natural locations. This trend includes a certain amount of set decoration that occurs on location. If a filmmaker selects a neighborhood because of its period houses, then modern attributes must be hidden or removed. A 1950s film cannot retain visual credibility if the featured exterior has a satellite antenna.

Location shooting agreements enable the production company to use the property for purposes of filming, to portray it in the film, and to alter its name or image in any manner. The film company will generally pay for the right to use the property. Any alterations to the property should be specified very carefully in the agreement. Usually, the film company will agree to restore the property to its original condition. When appropriate, however, the film company can agree to make modifications to the property that the owner is permitted to keep, such as repairs to the exterior, repainting, etc. Whether in the contract or not, the filmmaker should identify the property owner and the tenant (if different) and name each of those parties as an additional insured to the film company insurance.

The filmmaker should also be prepared to discuss details about the shoot. The property usage agreement may need to specify the use of electricity, telephone, water, or other utility services, provide for late-night usage that could entail asking the residents of a residential property to stay at a hotel, and detail the parking requirements. In Los Angeles, property owners are very sophisticated about the use of properties, while in other parts of the country, even the smallest of feature films is a rarity. Filmmakers should also be prepared to work with commercial property owners regarding business loss during the period of production. If a filmmaker proposes to shut down a retail business during filming, the business owner will want to be compensated for the lost revenue. Even if the film's eventual release will result in improved traffic to the store, most shop owners will insist on current payments.[2]

Although a property owner has very limited rights to stop the use of a property photograph, the same location agreement should also provide for the right to make pictures and films of the property. Additionally, a paragraph acting as a general release of all claims against the film company for use of the photographs (such as defamation, rights of privacy or publicity) should be included as well—just in case.

Famous buildings require slightly different agreements. Although the owner of a building may have no right to the copyright in a publicly visible building, it may have trademark rights if the building serves the corporation in that capacity. In addition, the building may have ornamentation—sculpture or murals—that are protected by copyright. In such cases, express permission from the copyright and trademark holder are highly recommended. The First Amendment may serve as a valid defense to any claims for a documentary filmmaker, but for a feature film, there is ample opportunity to secure the rights to film. Finally, it should be noted that the copyright and trademark rights holder in this situation might not be the tenant of the building who has the exclusive right to grant access. Instead, the building owner (usually through the property management company) and perhaps the original artist must be contacted to gain full permission for the filming.

3. Permits and Requirements

In New York, California, and other major metropolitan locations throughout the United States, a filmmaker must obtain a film permit in order to conduct any commercial filming. This often does not apply to news filming and may be inapplicable either under the terms of the film ordinance or the First Amendment for documentary filmmakers. As a general rule, film permitting requirements are designed to protect the community from the disruptions caused by large productions, and a small digital camera is an advantage as it will generally go unnoticed on the city street.

Whether a film permit is necessary from a practical standpoint, the permit process in most major areas has become increasingly simple, and the filmmaker may find that the local film commission provides significant assistance to the making of a film. Most film offices have libraries of available locations for shooting. They also have experience in various locations throughout the area, and they can work with the filmmaker to minimize the disruption that may be caused to areas in which the filming takes place.

General requirements for acquiring a film permit are few. The nature of the production must be specified, with particular attention to the number of trucks and parking requirements. Any weapons or pyrotechnics must be detailed, and their use processed through the fire marshal or other specified authority. Finally, there will be a minimum insurance requirement. If the filming will take place on city, county, or state property, then the film office will also require that fees be paid for the use of the property, usage restrictions are met, and the jurisdiction is named as an additional insured on the film company insurance.

As cities and states have begun to recognize the tremendous economic value filmmaking offers to local communities, most film offices have streamlined the permitting process and provide very pro-filming resources that are fully available to the independent filmmaker. Film offices— particularly that of the Mayor's Office of New York, the California Film Commission, and the L.A. Film Office (the Entertainment Industry Development Corporation, or EIDC)—all provide tremendous resources for independent filmmakers. Other cities and states, attempting to compete with L.A. and New York, have also grown in scope and resources. Independent filmmakers should take advantage of these resources to the greatest extent possible to improve the quality of the production and reduce costs.

Shooting the Film

A WELL-ORGANIZED production should anticipate most legal and business issues before arriving on location. To accomplish this, the filmmaker must use good planning and professional organization. Typically, this job falls to the location manager working in conjunction with the unit production manager (UPM), or the producer.

A. Scheduling

Filmmakers schedule the film around those resources that cannot be controlled. This means that the luxury of filming the script in chronological order is a rare occurrence. Among the uncontrolled resources that must be managed are the schedules of the stars, particular locations, weather, and budget. First, stars often have only limited dates available to shoot— particularly limited dates for the low-paying independent filmmaker. These dates will set the start dates and end dates of the shooting schedule. Second, if certain locations may only be available during a particular week, then other choices must be made to accommodate that week. Third, weather is an uncontrollable variable. Indoor shooting days should be left until the end of the production so that, if inclement weather hits, those indoor days can be moved up. This way, the production will not be shut down waiting for the weather to change. Fourth, budget constraints must be considered. There is no reason to pay people who are not working, so, typically, the larger production days are grouped first, and people are slowly let go as the shooting schedule calls for fewer and fewer people.

Because weather constantly changes, as does availability of cast and crew members, even the most rigidly fixed schedule is likely to be changed throughout the production schedule. Proposed changes must be evaluated against the other constraints of locations, cast, and budget. The UPM must be sure that everyone involved in the production is kept constantly aware of the changing schedule. Contracts for locations and equipment should specify target dates but allow the filmmaker to adjust those dates as required by the production.

B. Preparing Locations

Location filming adds realism to movies and expands the range of tools available to set designers even when the designer modifies the location to represent other spaces (such as using futuristic architecture to represent science fiction settings). Well in advance of the day of filming, the location manager must provide the property owner with a contract that specifies exactly what changes are to be made to the location and how those are to be made. Typically, all modifications to the property will be temporary, so the contract should provide for a schedule that includes preparation time, a period of filming, and a period for striking the set and returning the location to its original condition.

1. Working the Neighborhood

If the changes are significant or will affect neighbors, then the location manager should contact those neighbors as well to let them know what is happening and, to the extent possible, enlist their support. This is particularly true if the production will shut down traffic to streets, even for short periods of time. Even a modestly sized independent film company can be quite an intrusion into a neighborhood. Trucks carrying lighting, electrical generators, film equipment, sets, and costumes, and the cars of cast and crew add up to a logistical invasion larger than most construction projects. Even a guerrilla filmmaker working with a single handheld camera will need neighborhood support.

To avoid or minimize disruptions, the filmmaker must communicate closely with those affected by the filming. At least two weeks prior to the scheduled shoot, the location manager should contact the owners of all the properties that may be affected by the shoot. The location manager should inform the property owners or occupants of the date of the proposed shooting; the nature of the filming, that it is an independent feature (and include some promotional information regarding the film, if it will be helpful); the nature of the shooting (exteriors, interiors, moving vehicles, etc.); the scheduled starting time and approximate end time of the filming; and the needs of the company. If sound matters, then she should request that no lawnmowers be used. If a historical period is being re-created, then modern cars may need to be removed.

Be sure to give the name, telephone number, and e-mail address for the film company's contact person—and respond immediately to any request. A follow-up should be made the day before the shoot. For most properties, the participants typically will be quite helpful.

Business owners will be concerned about interference with their customer traffic. Filmmakers must be prepared to avoid disruption or to work with affected store owners. In some cases, this may include negotiating with a local chamber of commerce on behalf of a large number of retailers. Here, timing becomes critical—interrupting business is much more expensive in December than in January.

2. Closing Streets

Given the start-and-stop nature of filming, the filmmaker should consider using intermittent traffic stops. Rather than closing the street, production could stop traffic only while the cameras are running. For many films, intermittent traffic stops are all that will be necessary to capture the necessary shots.

If a street must be closed for any significant period of time, the film company must work closely with all the regular users of that street. To close a street, a local film permit is absolutely required, unless the jurisdiction does not issue such permits. The permit is typically conditioned on the film company providing alternative parking, patrolling the intersections (or hiring off-duty law enforcement personnel to control traffic), and gaining the permission of the affected residents or businesses. To get such permission, payment is sometimes necessary, but tactful requests, permission to observe the filming, or an offer to provide pastries or cold drinks often suffices.

C. Daily Requirements

Unlike military invasions, even the largest films interact with the local community when on location. Independent filmmakers should utilize their environment even more heavily. By working with local vendors, the film company may reduce its expenses and improve its relationships— particularly important if the location selected will be used for any extended period. The local Home Depot often benefits tremendously from location shooting. Film companies can also arrange to provide prepaid coupons to local restaurants in lieu of craft service, if it can be arranged in a cost-efficient manner.

1. Set Preparation—Utilities Basics

All but the smallest sets require significant electricity, water and sewage capability, and the ability to control sound. Unfortunately, these needs are not necessarily compatible. Each of these choices must be planned in advance with careful attention to local regulations.

Electrical power may be obtained through portable generators or temporary power drops attached to utility poles (provided by the local electrical utility), or by tapping into the existing electrical service of the location. The choice of electrical source will depend on the size of the production, the resources available, and the duration of the shoot. A small guerrilla filmmaker should be able to plug lights directly into the location if an agreement has been made in advance. A large production will need to bring its own generators unless it plans to use the location for a significant length of time. In that case, arranging a power drop with the local utility will become cost-effective. A second advantage of using a temporary power drop is the avoidance of the noise and fuel consumption of portable generators.

If portable generators are selected, the location must be carefully mapped to park the generators sufficiently far from the shooting so that the noise of the generators does not interfere with the production sound. Large power lines will snake from the generators to the lights and production equipment. The scale of this equipment increases the complexity of location shooting considerably, adding to the size of the crew and the scope of each location used.

Water and sewage are also important parts of any location filming. Water availability varies dramatically from area to area. In urban areas, water hook-ups are often provided from the location because the cost to the landowner is not significant. Where well water is used (and in areas facing drought conditions), access to water may be costly and difficult. If the location will not provide water, then the local utility must be contacted to use a hose to a fire hydrant, if available, or to provide other suggestions for temporary connections.

The same approach applies to toilets and sewage. The scale of the production will dictate the size of the facility necessary. If the location has facilities, arrange to use them. If that cannot be done, or if the size of the production makes that impractical, then the company will need to rent a "honey wagon"—a trailer with dressing room and bathroom facilities built inside. Most honey wagons will need water and sewage hookups, although storage tanks may also be available. In addition, portable toilets that do not use local water may also be rented if no other alternative is available. These choices are all more expensive and cumbersome than making arrangements with the location, so the contract with the location should be negotiated with these needs and expenses in mind.

2. Parking

Often overlooked, crew parking is a significant logistical component of location shooting in some areas. In a small production, this can include extended parking for 10 to 20 vehicles. In a larger production, the necessary campsite area should include enough space for individual cars; cast trailers—mobile homes starting at 35 feet in length; a honey wagon ranging from 35 to 65 feet in length; a 35-foot trailer for wardrobe, makeup, and the grip truck; and a much larger truck for lighting and electrical production equipment. Add the portable generators and the parking area can grow to the size of a small college. Locations that can provide support for these needs must be selected. If necessary, the automobile parking can be moved to a remote location and the production can use a van or car as a shuttle between the parking and the rest of the camp.

D. Staying in Control

To keep the location operating smoothly, the location manager must work closely with the unit production manager (UPM) and first assistant director to ensure that the location is used as efficiently, productively, and legally as possible. Efficient use comes from coordinating the shooting schedule and the activities of the cast and crew on the set. Productive use comes from maximizing the amount of usable film shot—by creating multiple scenes at each location so some areas can be prepped while others are being used for filming. Legal use includes compliance with the location permit and its restrictions as well as compliance with any location agreements.

1. Logistical Planning

Coordination is the key to controlling the logistics on the set. When dealing with rental of equipment for the film location, scheduling and availability of equipment is critical. In areas familiar with the motion picture industry, equipment rental companies have a great deal of expertise. In other areas, however, local vendors may not be familiar with the production company's needs. The UPM must be sure to negotiate with these companies and put the dates and times for each piece of equipment into the contract. The location owner must be fully apprised of the equipment coming so that there are no surprises the morning of the shoot when the trailers and equipment roll up.

To be cost-effective, timing each piece of equipment is also critical. It may be more cost-effective to rent a location for an extra day, allowing a smaller design team more time to prepare the set. This means that the set designers and crew may have a different start date than the grips and electrical. The honey wagon may not appear on location until the third day. By scaling the activities, costs can be controlled, but the UPM must truly understand the activities occurring on the set at any given moment in time. Scheduling should take place on an hour-by-hour basis rather than day-by-day.

2. People Planning

Hour-by-hour scheduling is essential for effective management of locations. Idle cast and crew reduce efficiency, while a missing cast member can bring the entire production to a halt. Since the UPM manages the crew and the first AD manages the cast, the two must carefully coordinate call times and the day's schedule to be sure that the right people are always available and planning to work on the same scenes.

Independent productions are generally less structured than larger-budget studio films, and crew members may be willing to pitch in to help with needs outside of their primary responsibility. By having the ability to work on both today's and tomorrow's shooting schedule, crew members can be kept involved more effectively than in traditional shoots.

3. Budgeting and Cost Control

The original budget for the film should be treated as a historical document, retained in its original form as a tool for comparison. That budget will begin to deviate from the actual expenditures before the filming even begins. As a result, it will need to be updated constantly to reflect the actual expenditures and to project the expenditures necessary to complete the film. For example, if the screenplay costs included an additional, unbudgeted polish, the money for it must come out of some other area or the total cost of the film increased. Most independent films cannot afford to increase the budget, so something else must go. If the choice is to eliminate a location and its associated costs, the set budget must reflect this change, or the elimination of the location will merely allow the set designer to spend more on other locations. Both the budget and the schedule must reflect every change. Interim budgets should be kept on file.

The need to account for actual expenses becomes most pronounced during location shooting. In the heat of the afternoon, crew members are often sent out to buy necessary but forgotten items. These last-minute expenses can add up. For a small independent film, such expenses can overwhelm the budget. Receipts should be turned in within minutes of the expenditure and must be turned in by the end of each day. Even on the largest studio shoots, every dollar spent must be accounted for with a receipt. Every receipt must reflect a particular budget item. If someone is sent to Target, Wal-Mart, or Home Depot to pick up some necessary items, the register receipts should be separated by budget. Gaffer's tape should be on one receipt and wood screws should be on a second, so the accounting properly reflects which departments are charged with the expenses.

Just like the daily rushes, the filmmaker must look at the expenditures daily to ensure that the production remains on time and on budget. If either the schedule or the budget starts to go awry, the filmmaker should make adjustments. The earlier adjustments are made, the smaller they generally need to be. Careful management can keep problems to a minimum.

E. When Things Go Wrong

Even if the filmmaker makes the best possible choices and works as carefully as possible, the complexity of a motion picture almost guarantees that things will go wrong. Locations that have been contractually secured suddenly become unavailable, cast members get sick, sets that look ideal in model form do not allow the action to take place properly, the weather will not cooperate—the list of possible problems is endless.

Some solutions should be prepared in advance by the filmmaker. The filmmaker can anticipate some problems by identifying simple scenes that can be shot in readily accessible locations to cover previously scheduled days. The budget should include a contingency line—typically 10 percent of the budget—not to be used unless a true emergency develops. Backup locations should be identified for all the major locations selected, so that there is someplace to go when things go wrong.

Other problems are less susceptible to advance planning. If a key cast member becomes unavailable, a double can be used and the dialogue later dubbed in, but this has limited effectiveness. Often, it is better to adjust the script than to try to hide the missing cast member.

The most important aspect of crisis management is quick communication throughout the production. The filmmaker and key personnel must agree upon a strategy to solve the problem as quickly as is reasonable. All of those key personnel must understand the final decision made. Each must communicate the changes to the cast, crew, and vendors affected by the change. Today, e-mail and Web pages can be used to give everyone a place to look for the latest information, call sheets, and changes. If a Web page is used, it must be kept up-to-date. Confirming telephone calls should be made to the cast and crew so that no members of the production are left unaware.

If the communication works effectively, even significant changes can be made with a minimum of intrusion. Things will go wrong. The good producer and filmmaker thrive on these moments of change to energize the creative spark of the production. If the business and legal considerations needs are met, then the creativity can be unleashed most effectively.

Selling the Movie—
Postproduction, Distribution,
and Marketing

Music and Sound

For most modern films, music has become an integral element of the storytelling process. Music can be used to accentuate the action. Evoking the emotional response sought by the filmmaker, it can come from natural sources, such as a car radio shown onscreen, or it can be created directly by the characters in the film. Each of these different types of music not only plays a different role in the story but also has a different legal relationship with the filmmaker. Music performed by the characters in the film is labeled foreground music. In contrast, both the original musical score composed for the film and any recorded songs played in the film are considered background music. Because the rights for licensing music for film, television, and video games have become the most intricate licensing of any copyrighted works in the law, each type of music must be treated separately.

A. Introduction to Motion Picture Music Licensing

The filmmaker wishing to use a recording of a popular song must enter the byzantine world of music licensing. Since *American Graffiti*, the modern film musical has been reinvented as a greatest hits collection of popular or cutting-edge genre music. The filmmaker of these movies also takes on the role of record album producer, collecting the right mix of sounds and artists—collected from a variety of songwriters, singers, music publishers, and record labels. Each has an interest in the copyright used in the film and each must be represented in the licensing process.

1. Two Different Copyright Holders

The recording of a popular song is protected by two separate copyrights. First, the composition (the lyrics and the written music) are protected by a copyright held by the composers. The composers may be represented by a songwriting team, such as Lennon and McCartney, a team of the composer and lyricist, such as Rodgers and Hammerstein, or a single person. Regardless of the number of composers, they jointly hold a single copyright.

Second, the sound recording of the song is protected through a copyright held by the producer of the song or the record company that manufactured and distributed the song. The performers on the recording are not protected by copyright, but look to employment contracts with the record company for participation in the song's revenue.

In this way, Motown Records owns the recording of "Trouble Man," a song copyrighted by singer and composer Marvin Gaye. If the filmmaker wishes to use the song, then the composers (or the publisher to which the composers have assigned their rights) must license the song. If the filmmaker wishes to play the Motown version of the song, then both the representatives of Marvin Gaye as composer and Motown as owner of the sound recording will need to grant permission to use the work. In addition, because of a long, strained history, there are a variety of different rights that must be identified and licensed separately. Failure to include any of these discrete rights in the contract can create substantial problems when distributing the film or they can result in the entire film being unmarketable in some or all markets.

2. Types of Rights Necessary

Every film distributor today intends for each film to be shown theatrically and on premium cable, broadcast television, cable television, non-network broadcast television, and home recording machines (VHS tape, laser disks,

DVDs, etc.). These markets are to be exploited worldwide. In addition, the Internet is quickly evolving into another film distribution media, both for downloads and for streaming performances. To exploit these markets, the distributor must acquire a number of different legal interests. Most distributors expect that the acquisition of these rights has been arranged or accomplished by the filmmaker.

a. Public Performance

The public performance right in music protects the copyright holder from any public performance of a copyrighted work without authorization. The performance of the song in the movie theater and on television both constitute public performance rights that the filmmaker must acquire before the movie can be played in the theater or broadcast on television. Historically, this right was reserved only for the composers in the song, not the record company in the sound recording. Recently, however, sound recordings were granted a limited public performance right for digital sound recordings. This new right may extend to some digital films as well.

b. Reproduction

The right of reproduction protects both the composers and the recording companies from unauthorized creation of copies of a sound recording in any medium. Most consumers view this as the rule about taping radio broadcasts or ripping CDs, but in a commercial context, this applies to making prints of a film embodying songs and sound recordings and, more important, creating copies in all the VHS tapes and DVDs.

If the filmmaker contemplates a soundtrack album, then the reproduction right must extend to use in this format as well.

c. Synchronization

In addition to the statute-based rights of public performance and reproduction, copyright recognizes a distinct right to associate a song with a particular audiovisual image. Whether used for films, television, or commercials, the right to synchronize the pictures with the sound is a distinct legal right that must be separately protected. Although the law allows some sound recordings to be made using a statutory or compulsory license,[1] these provisions apply only to nondramatic works and cannot be used for copies made as part of an audiovisual work such as a film soundtrack.

B. The Music License

The industry tradition has been to create a series of contracts for each of the types of rights, rights holders, and media.[2] This can result in an absurd number of separate contracts and confusion regarding the use of the music over the life of the film. Every Hollywood studio has a large team of lawyers and paralegals who focus exclusively on the music licensing issues for their productions.

1. Music Clearance Services

The independent filmmaker must find a way to accomplish this same task so that the filmmaker holds the rights necessary to distribute the film. If the music sought is held by the larger record companies and publishing houses, then the most efficient approach may be to work with a music clearance service. In some cases the company may be the licensing agent for the film. For example, the Harry Fox Agency, a division of National Music Publishers' Association, Inc., is the source of both the composers and the record companies. Filmmakers may find that, despite the size of the Harry Fox library, the types of works available (in both genre and fame) do not suit the filmmaker's goals.

Similarly, for more generic music, a music production library will provide a helpful source of music in a wide array of styles, instruments, and arrangements. These production libraries own both the composition and sound recording copyrights, so they provide one-stop shopping for the musical needs of the production.

Another type of bureau provides a clearinghouse service. These companies do not own any rights in music themselves, but they serve to locate the rights requested, help establish the pricing, and ensure that the appropriate rights are identified. Some of these companies are listed in Appendix E.

In addition, independent filmmakers may wish to take advantage of the Music Report. The Music Report is actually an arm of Breakdown Services, Ltd., and provides a breakdown of the musical needs for the film, just as Breakdown Services does with the script for casting. The Music Report distributes the list of the screenplay's song needs to subscribing music publishing houses and record companies, who will then submit songs to the film company for consideration. While there will be times when the filmmaker cannot substitute anything else for a particular song, there are many other instances where a song must merely connote an idea, genre, or age. Less well known but more cost-effective choices may be as compelling as the obvious first choices identified in the screenplay. Since this service is free to the filmmaker, it provides an excellent opportunity that should not be overlooked.

2. Essential Terms

The essential terms of the music license are suggested below. For some of these choices, the costs may be prohibitive and the filmmaker must choose to do without the desired song or risk buying something less than all the rights that may possibly be used.

a. Term

The rights should last in perpetuity. Although some contracts provide for five-year terms, this means that future sales of rights can be frustrated by the inability to acquire (or even identify) the rights. At a minimum, the renewal provisions should guarantee the fee and the right to exercise the right. Nonetheless, too much can go wrong, and a new owner of the music rights (such as a company that purchases the music library in a bankruptcy sale) could demand exorbitant fees for the new grant of rights. Of course, if the movie is never released or has only a short run, then the cost savings of the shorter term will be worthwhile. Since this is generally not the bet being made by independent filmmakers, a short music license term is probably the wrong place to save unless the savings is truly dramatic.

b. Territory

The territory should be worldwide. In fact, some contracts now specify "the universe" rather than the world. Given the growth of the International Space Station and the length of copyright, which could well extend over a century, the universe may be the more appropriate territory. There is no reason to license anything less than worldwide, because even short delays involving licensing the soundtrack at the time of foreign distribution may frustrate the distribution agreements.

c. Media Covered by License

The standard contracts will typically require a list of media. Given the rapid change of technology and the guarantee that the growth of technology is highly unpredictable, the media should be "all media now known or hereafter developed." This should also avoid future conflicts over various forms of Internet distribution and whatever will come after.

Older contracts may list theatrical exhibition, television (be sure to include free and pay or further identify the various tiers of broadcast, satellite, and cable television), foreign distribution, and specialty markets (16mm prints, airplane cuts), but will often omit some of the home distribution technologies that include videotape, laser disk, DVD, etc. The list of media for both the public performance category and the home use category are evolving and both should be defined broadly.

d. Public Performance Rights

Most music license agreements are drafted very narrowly. As a result, traditional contracts recognized that the public performance rights were only necessary in those media that were distributed to the public. The license of a song in a film covered the theatrical exhibition and broadcast rights. Home presentation of a VHS tape does not require any public performance right, so many contracts do not give any public performance rights for VHS tapes or similar products. Nonetheless, videos are often shown in schools, community centers, and other smaller public venues. Without the public performance rights in VHS tapes, DVDs, etc., the filmmaker cannot authorize any such performances. For some independent films, the guerrilla marketing planned could be frustrated by the failure to secure public performance rights across all media.

In addition, the need for public performance rights in digital works is relatively new and virtually untested under the law. If the Internet or other interactive digital technologies grow in bandwidth and sophistication, the digital performance interests in sound recordings may become a significant right. All filmmakers, but particularly those digital filmmakers hoping to exploit the Internet for some portion of the film's distribution, must purchase the limited public performance rights from the record company.

e. Reproduction or Mechanical Rights

The right to reproduce a song is often limited to the home media market (VHS tapes, DVDs, laser disks, etc.). Nonetheless, each print of the film also includes a mechanical reproduction of the sound recording and the composers' song, so the license to reproduce the song (known as the mechanical license) should also include all media. The mechanical license applies to both the composer and the record company if the record company's original recording is to be used.

f. Synchronization Rights

The right to use the song in conjunction with the visual image is an aspect of the public performance right. As such, this provision is essential in the composers' agreement but, because of the new digital performing rights, it is advisable in the license from the record company as well.

g. Scope of Usage

The contracts will narrowly limit the way in which a song may be used. First, the song may not be altered (although it typically can be used in part rather than in its entirety). This means that the lyrics cannot be changed. If a song is to be featured in the foreground because it will be sung by a character as a parody or otherwise changed for dramatic effect, then this particular usage must be separately negotiated—and such permission will not be granted lightly. The filmmaker's rights will be nonexclusive, allowing the copyright holders to license the song to other films as well.

Second, the song can only be used in conjunction with the entire film. Permission to use a song in the film's commercials or trailers must also be negotiated separately. The use of the song as part of a music video based on the film must also be separately negotiated.

Third, the filmmaker must provide credits for the composers, publisher, performing artists, and record company from which the rights were licensed. These credits generally appear in the end credits.

h. Fees

The range of fees can vary greatly, depending on the popularity of the song, whether the music is used in the foreground or background, whether the music is featured in the story, the budget of the film, and other songs being licensed. Typically, the U.S. theatrical and television broadcast rights are contracted on a flat fee basis. Outside the United States, theatrical performances are covered by licenses provided by performing rights societies. The mechanical rights are increasingly based on a royalty fee tied to the number of units manufactured or sold. To get a general idea of the range of licensing fees and structures, the filmmaker or his attorney may wish to consult with *Kohn on Music Licensing* by Al and Bob Kohn, which provides a list of licensing ranges for the various types of licenses needed.

3. Alternatives to the Music License

The independent filmmaker will often choose to avoid licensing songs. The costs and administration simply outweigh the benefits to the story and film. Such a choice will not prevent the use of music; it will only change its source. As an alternative to licensing popular song recordings, independent filmmakers may exploit songs no longer protected by copyright because the work is in the public domain. They may also create original songs for the movie, or purchase the copyright to the music. In these cases, unless the sound recording is also in the public domain, filmmakers commonly choose to record the music specifically for the motion picture. Regardless of the source of the song, original recordings greatly reduce the scope of rights to be licensed.

C. Work for Hire: Composers and the Film Score

The original film score is the background music written specifically for the motion picture. Composers such as Elmer Bernstein, John Williams, and Danny Elfman have created intricate orchestral works for film that rival the great opera scores and symphonies of past centuries. Generally, after a series of meetings between the filmmaker and the composer regarding the goals for the music overall and for each scene, the filmmaker provides the composer with a rough cut of the edited film. The composer creates the score, which is then modified and refined until the musical beats within each measure align perfectly with each frame of the picture. Arrangements are made—either for a live orchestra or for an electronically re-created performance—and the music is recorded as the finished cut of the film is played. Like foley artists, the musicians carefully play to match the images and timing on the screen, accompanying the film as an orchestra would accompany a ballet or opera.

The musical track is recorded separately so that it may be incorporated into the final prints of the film. For foreign distribution, the sound and dialogue tracks are delivered separately so that the original dialogue can be replaced with a dubbed soundtrack.

1. Work-for-Hire Productions

For the filmmaker, the legal relationship with the original composition is a work made for hire or a complete assignment of copyright. Under copyright law, certain types of works can be created that vest the copyright in the employer rather than the employee. The first of these two situations occurs when an employee creates a work in the regular scope of his employment. So, for example, if the film company were to employ the composer for a reasonable length of time for the purpose of writing compositions for the motion picture or pictures created by the film company, then the film company, rather than the composer, may be considered the copyright holder of the composition. Courts look at the nature of the employment relationship with heavy emphasis on tax status, withholdings and insurance, the ability to control the work, the actual control of the work, and the ability to add additional projects without additional pay. It would not be good planning to rely exclusively on the employment relationship. At a minimum, the employee should have an employment agreement that carefully specifies that the compositions are created on behalf of the employer and are intended to be treated as work for hire.

The second category of work for hire provides greater certainty. For nine categories of work, an employer can specially commission works. Among the nine categories are motion pictures and audiovisual works. This is very important because most musical commissions are outside the scope of this category. The filmmaker can specially commission the work as a work for hire. The agreement must be in writing and signed by both parties. The agreement should be signed before the work is begun, but certainly the earlier the better.

2. Assignments of Copyright

If the film receives worldwide success, the work-for-hire provisions may create additional difficulties. Some countries do not recognize the work-for-hire concept, rendering any such understanding unenforceable. To protect against this problem, the employment agreement or agreement for the special commission should also include a paragraph stating that any rights not granted as a work for hire are irrevocably assigned by the composer to the filmmaker in perpetuity. This means the composer cannot reclaim the rights, and the grant will last forever. (A reversionary right in U.S. copyright law makes this contractual promise limited to approximately half the life of the copyright. This is why the use of the work for hire is more useful in the United States, while the assignment is more effective abroad.)

The composer may insist on a third alternative—licensing the score for the motion picture but retaining all other rights. In this situation, the rights of the score's composer would be the same as those of the composers for any single featured in the film.

D. Performers

In the United States the singers and musicians performing on a song have no interest in the copyright. As a result, no particular contract language is necessary to protect the filmmaker's copyright in the work. Despite this, however, a performer may protect himself from the unauthorized use of his performance. As a result, the film company should be sure that every singer and musician has signed a contract that specifically authorizes the film company to record the performance and assigns any copyright interest in the film company.

As an added precaution, the language should also include a work-for-hire statement in the form suggested for the composer of the film. The assignment language may help avoid problems involving the interpretation of the contract in foreign jurisdictions, and the work for hire may anticipate any additional changes to copyright as it continually increases the range of possible copyright holders.

Postproduction

WITH A TREMENDOUS amount of coordination, communication, concerted effort—not to mention a little bit of luck—the filming has completed. Realistically, some of the postproduction work often begins even as the principal photography continues. As the filming takes shape, the director will identify particular shots to begin assembling a very preliminary cut.

A. Editing

Editing is an artistic process. The proliferation of "director's cut" editions illustrates that there are many correct choices that can be made within the editing process. It also shows that the directors often continue to think about the choices they had to make on their films. Nonetheless, the process of editing allows the director to find the horse hidden in the marble, cutting out all the footage that does not help tell the story.

1. Timing the Editing Process

The purpose of the preliminary assembly merely lets the filmmaker know when the minimum coverage has been shot. Particularly for tightly budgeted independent films, compiling a preliminary edit of the film will allow the filmmaker the opportunity to determine when she has enough film to tell the story. Many compelling scenes never make the final cut of a film. Independent filmmakers simply do not have the luxury to waste time and money on anything that will not ultimately appear onscreen. If the script has a scene that is interesting but not essential, film it later in the production schedule. That will allow the filmmaker to drop the scene if time and funds require hard choices.

Once principal photography ends, the real postproduction period begins. Following the wrap of principal photography, the director should take a short break to regain some perspective on the footage and regain some physical strength from the rigor of the shoot. The director must look at the footage as a fresh observer rather than responding to the conditions of the filming. The director should begin to work with the film editor (if there is a separate editor working on the project) as soon as the director can treat the film with renewed enthusiasm and new objectivity.

2. The Director's Role

If the filmmaker is not the director, then the role of the director must be carefully determined when the director is hired. Directors Guild of America (DGA) union rules obligate the producer to allow the director to deliver a cut of the film. Even if the production is not governed by the requirement, it serves as a good minimum standard. The director should have the best ideas about the film that's been shot and story being told. As such, he should provide the primary structure to the final film. If the producer and filmmaker do not like what they receive, then they are free to change it.

3. The Editor's Role

The role of the professional editor will vary dramatically, depending on the budget of the film project. In larger productions involving IATSE (International Alliance of Theatrical Stage Employees) union crews, the editor (or editors) must also be a member of the union. At the other extreme, many independent films are edited by the filmmaker on an AVID, Final Cut Pro, or Adobe Premiere software. When an editor is used, the director and editor will typically work closely throughout the filming so that the director can identify the scenes he prefers from the dailies and explain the nature of the shots. As this process continues, the editor can work to compile the film as the director focuses on the principal photography, allowing the first cut to be completed within days following completion of principal photography.

4. Rough Cuts

Once the director and editor have viewed the first cut, the real work of sculpting the film begins. Scenes are deleted, reordered, and tightened. The running time starts dropping dramatically. Ultimately, the final rough cut must be made to meet all contractual requirements. The length of the film must meet any contractual obligations, and the content must be trimmed to anticipate any contractual obligations to achieve MPAA ratings ("R" or "PG-13").

The editing process should also anticipate the need for multiple versions of the film. Additional shots should be identified for the broadcast television version of "R" movies, airplane edits, and foreign jurisdictions (where censorship rules may vary considerably). Identifying the coverage shots as part of the editing process may save significant time and effort—if not sanity—when the distributor calls.

Whether to open the editing process to others remains a highly individual choice. Producers will wish to see the film early in the process, but an uncompleted film may be more dangerous than the screenplay. Relatively few observers have the experience to watch a film without the score and sound effects and needing minor adjustments. Also, the editing process has been further complicated by the evolution of digital editing technology. The traditional scratched work print creates a particular image that is quite distinct from that of a final film. A digital file will look perfect—even if the edit is unfinished. As a result, digital viewing may be even more misleading than the scratched print once relied upon.

5. Final Cuts

At some point, however, the director must determine that the film is "finished." At this point the director delivers the film to the producer and together they review the film. Ideally, the producer adores what has been done and accepts the film without comment—but ideals are rarely achieved. Instead, the producer will give notes and comments to the director, who should then be given the opportunity to respond to the suggestions with another cut.

Who determines when the edit is complete will depend on the director's contract. Given the risks involved in independent production, the filmmaker should concede the contractual right to final cut only as a last resort. If the filmmaker is anyone other than the director, however, then the filmmaker should be equally insistent that she will control the final film edit. Even if the director controls final cut, various distributors in foreign markets and some media (such as broadcast television) still insist on the power to alter a film to fit the needs of the marketplace.

B. Sound

The music, dialogue, and sound effects combine to create a powerful element to any film. By operating at the level of the audience consciousness, music can dramatically alter the emotional impact of a scene. Music can swell to give gravity to a simple visual image or turn a tense moment into a lighthearted sequence. Sound effects can emphasize action, turn small visual effects into overwhelming events, or even add characters off scene. The offscreen cry of a baby changes every moment—whether a romantic tryst or an attempted car-jacking. Dialogue should remain natural and balanced throughout—the bare minimum for a competent production.

1. Separate but Equal Soundtracks

Each of the three separate sound sources—music, dialogue, and effect—must be kept separate to allow the sound editor to control the project. Occasionally, individual segments of dialogue must be changed—either for effect or to meet censorship obligations. In other situations, the entire dialogue track must be replaced for Spanish, French, or other distribution. Choices of music may need to be changed for either artistic or legal reasons. As a result, most distributors will insist on receiving the three separate tracks for dialogue, music, and effects. If available, each of the three tracks should be recorded in stereo or some proprietary enhanced stereo system such as Dolby.

Although it may be somewhat counterintuitive, part of the sound editor's job is to separate out some of the recorded sound into the separate tracks. Dialogue is typically further separated into separate tracks by character.

2. Source Music

Given the need for separate soundtracks, music recorded live as part of the filming can create difficulties for later mixing of the film. The legal licensing does not change whether the music is recorded in a studio or live on the set. One benefit to recording music on location is the match of the sound with the location's background environment. For very low-budget productions, recording source music may make sense because the filmmaker takes what she finds, but for most productions, studio recording may be preferable.

To synchronize the performance of the musicians on the film, a playback recording will be used. A previously recorded studio session will be mixed and played on the set. The performers will play along to that track so that they can match the physical movements to the earlier recording. The playback recording is replaced with the studio recording in the final mix.

3. Score

The score cannot be finalized until the cut is locked—edits should be made so that the timing can be exact. The traditional process included matching the score to a print of the film (often a black and white copy of the edit print). Today, given new film editing and music technology, the composer can time the score directly to the digital file playing on the computer.

Low-budget filmmakers should consider hiring composers who can not only write the music but also arrange and play the music on digital equipment. There may be as many untried film composers finishing music school as directors finishing film school. The musical triple threat— composer/arranger/performer—can significantly enhance the overall production for far less than any other solution.

4. Cue Sheets

If a more traditional approach is used, the composer must provide different musical notations to create the score. First, the composer will develop musical timing sheets that provide descriptions of the scenes and the associated music associated with each beat. More important, the composer will refine this into musical cue sheets, which track each musical moment.

The cue sheets include the cues for the score, effects, and dialogue. Each cue is tied directly to the edited film by footage or frame number. The musical cue sheets are part of the written sound description and will be required by most distributors. The cue sheets are critical for foreign distributors to be able to dub the dialogue without disrupting the remainder of the film.

5. Sound Effects and Foley

The original recording may include many of the sounds necessary to make the film sound realistic—or stylistic—as required by the filmmaker. Nonetheless, a good many of these sounds need to be enhanced by the effects editor. The choices for sounds dramatically shape the impression of each scene, and the sound effects can significantly shape the sounds and the overall film.

Foley is a particular type of sound effect created by working in a soundproof stage. The foley artist works with a variety of props and floor surfaces to create the sounds to match the action on the screen. He acts out the sound effects, synchronizing the sounds live to the film.

6. Dubbing

Often, filming conditions simply do not provide for good sound recording. An actor dangling from a building buffeted by wind may be difficult to mike. Even without stunts, the same problem occurs when car traffic obscures the audio. In such situations, the sound editor will use ADR (automatic dialogue recording) to re-record the missing dialogue. In other situations, the dialogue may need to be altered because of mistakes or other necessary changes.

If significant use of ADR or looping is planned, the production schedule should be organized to ensure that the cast members are available for the duty. Matching dialogue is difficult enough without losing the cast to other projects and delaying the sound editing. For smaller films, scheduling may make ADR a difficult choice. To the extent possible, good location sound should be used over reliance on ADR.

7. Background Sound

Spending a small amount of additional production time to make sure the sound is recorded effectively during the filming can save the filmmaker substantial money. Looping dialogue over the edited film adds substantial cost, can create scheduling conflicts, and slows postproduction. Equally important, the sound editor needs to record ambient sound for every set. The background sounds of a silent set create the base line for later dialogue editing and whatever looping is required. The investment in this minute of audio production can save significant money in the long run and should never be missed.

C. Testing the Picture

Film directors often feel that audience testing exemplifies the worst excess of corporate Hollywood, allowing a kid with a response card veto power over the director's vision and integrity. While the feeling overstates the importance of particular response cards, test audiences play a highly controversial role in the development of films.

An audience test involves taking a nearly completed film to an audience demographically selected for the target age and sex. (Studios also select geographically, which applies both to regions and, unfortunately, to race or ethnicity.) This cross section of the target audience views the film and comments on what they have seen on small response cards. The audience is also carefully watched to gauge its reaction.

If the audience is representative and the questions on the cards appropriate, the filmmaker can learn a great deal about whether the choices made have the desired effect on the audience. If the audience is not representative or the questions were asked incorrectly, the test audience can lead to a wild round of counterproductive edits and reshoots. Unfortunately, there is no way to know whether the audience is right or wrong.

The greatest problem directors face with test audiences is that the producer controls the process and the outcome. Directors often invite preview audiences—friends, colleagues, and others—to watch the early edits of the film and provide comments. This previewing is not significantly different than the test audiences. What differs is the director's ability to accept or reject the criticism. Since the primary benefit of working independently is the control it provides the filmmaker, the filmmaker should control this process as well. That does not necessarily mean rejecting the test audiences, if offered by the distributor, so much as controlling what the producer or distributor can do with the information.

D. Control of the Final Picture

When the director has finished the film and made those adjustments suggested by the producer, he delivers his final version of the film. At this point, the producer has the ability to make additional changes to the film without the permission of the director.

In rare situations, the director negotiates for "final cut." Final cut affords the director the power to control the theatrical version of the film. This is the ultimate power in the production hierarchy and is granted only rarely to the most powerful of directors.

The filmmaker may retain final cut for her independent film in a number of situations. If the filmmaker is the director and has financed the film without entering into a negative pick-up or distribution agreement, then the filmmaker retains the power by default. The filmmaker should not grant such control to the producer unless the producer demands it as a condition of financing the film. Even then, the demand may make the cost of the financing too great.

If the filmmaker is the producer, then she should retain control over the hired director. The filmmaker may agree to consult with the director in this situation, but final control should be retained. The final editing of the film should be consultative, if possible, so that all of the participants in the process walk away satisfied with the outcome. This becomes critical when it is time to market and promote the film. Nonetheless, the contracts must be explicit regarding who retains the ultimate control of the film. Only one person can have the final cut. Absent any contract language to the contrary, that is the producer of the film, the CEO of the production company that owns the copyright in the final motion picture. If any variations are required, they must be spelled out very carefully in the employment contracts.

Even control of final cut will not end all editing of the film. Censorship needs will differ in various media and markets. Certain words cannot be spoken or images shown on broadcast television or in many countries. The distributors will demand control over the editing to make the film salable in those markets.

E. The Ratings System

One of the typical delivery requirements is a rating from the Motion Picture Association of America (MPAA). The rating is a voluntary designation provided by the MPAA that suggests audience guidelines. The rating system has tremendous influence on the marketing and sale of films in the United States, however, because of how ratings are put to use. Stung by public pressure, exhibitors will generally not allow minors under 17 years old to attend movies rated R or NC-17.

Many newspapers and television outlets will not accept advertising for NC-17 or X-rated films.[1] The MPAA ratings are trademarked and highly controlled. No filmmaker can designate her film as having achieved a particular rating without the certification of the MPAA.

To obtain a rating, the filmmaker applies to the Classification and Rating Administration of the MPAA and pays a relatively modest fee. If the rating is higher than that sought, the rating can be appealed. Appeals are difficult to achieve, however, requiring a two-thirds vote of the Appeals Board to overturn the initial rating. More frequently, small changes to the language or length of scenes are made that will satisfy the ratings board and allow a lower rating to be applied.

Independent filmmakers should be able to require the domestic distributor to shoulder the cost and administration of the ratings process. There is no value to rating a film until it is ready for commercial promotion, so any expenditure before this is premature. By the time a rating is necessary, the distributor is better equipped to initiate the process.

F. Delivery Elements

1. The Negative

Independent filmmakers face a difficult choice when selecting a medium because certain distributors will insist on a full panoply of traditional delivery requirements. The most critical delivery item is the original negative of the cut, finished film and the accompanying optical soundtrack. In addition, distributors typically request an internegative—another copy of the negative used to strike prints and protect the original negative. Some distribution agreements will also call for an interpositive—a print of the film used to make the internegative.

For a digitally created film, these elements are unnecessary and would create an unwanted expense at distribution. The digital image (or 16mm image) must be transferred to a 35mm print, but this is done using the cut finished film, not all the stock shot. Filmmakers should be sure not to agree to deliver elements that they do not need to create or have the money to make. If the film is stored electronically, then the internegative is an unnecessary step. The original negative should be used for the striking of prints and, if it becomes torn, another negative created from the electronic file. Since the number of prints needed for an independent film is often very small, the additional expenses are unnecessary.

2. Sound and Music

The delivery of sound is a critical component of the final delivery requirements. As described above, the filmmaker must work carefully to separate the sound into its three separate tracks. The typical distributor will require a magnetic track on 35mm separated for dialogue, music, and

effects. An additional request may be for a stereo or Dolby version, resulting in a six-track mix of the tracks.

In addition to the recorded sound, the written materials necessary to
create the movie must be delivered. The written material includes copies
of the music cue sheets with the necessary timing, the title of each composition, and copyright clearance information such as copyright owner
and publisher. Some distributors may also require the actual music license.

3. Titles and Credits

Just as the distributor demands various formats of the titles, it will also
typically require that the titles be made available both in the final film and
as a separate negative and interpositive. Of course, the filmmaker's list of
contractual credits must also be complete and supplied to the distributor.

4. Other Media Formats

Some distributors require videotape versions of the film on one-inch
videotape that can be used as the videotape master. While this should be
the distributor's obligation, the filmmaker will want to control the transfer to the smaller 1.33:1 television ratio. The filmmaker may actually create cover shots so that certain scenes are composed separately for the
wide-screen 1.85:1 aspect ratio.

If the filmmaker has shot additional coverage scenes for the video format, then the distributor will request access to the additional material for
its own editing. Similarly, the distributor will want coverage shots such
as cut-outs, trims, and second takes if it has any right to edit the final film
for distribution in foreign markets, television, or other arenas where different content or language issues may arise. In this case, the distributor
will also require the accompanying sound effects, dialogue, and music that
applies to that material.

5. Lab Access Letters

Many of the production elements are stored in a film laboratory rather
than with the filmmaker. This facilitates production and distribution. The
labs act as an escrow agent, holding the negatives and other elements of

the film, so that the distributor or distributors can gain access without gaining ownership. To grant the distributor access to the lab, the filmmaker signs a simple letter that grants the distributor permission to access the lab's stored materials. The letter grants the lab permission to produce whatever versions of the material are necessary for the distributor, and requires that nothing will be removed from the lab without both the filmmaker and the distributor being notified. In this way, neither can disrupt the business of the other.

6. Promotional Material

The independent filmmaker typically has the poorest ability to help with the promotional requirements asked by distributors. Although most distributors will cut their own trailers, they will expect that the filmmaker has cleared the music for such a use. They will also seek a variety of photographs of the cast and the shoot to be used in the production. Typical requests include 25 to 100 color slides of the film and as many in black and white; contact sheets and negatives of additional photographs of the production; color and black and white negatives and prints of the cast and key production employees; and press books or press kits, if any exist. Often none of this material has been created. The filmmaker should remember to shoot a few rolls of film so that some marketing materials are available, but she must also remember to be clear with potential distributors so no demands can be made after the contract is signed.

More important than production photographs, the filmmaker may be requested to provide the artwork and materials for the one-sheet poster of the film. While the distributor may wish to control all the marketing, the filmmaker should try to meet this demand as a way to control the style and tone of the promotional materials. On the crass assumption that people are generally lazy, the filmmaker may be able to control substantially more of the marketing campaign if she voluntarily creates the initial materials as part of the distribution package.

7. Documentation

The required range of documentation will vary considerably from distributor to distributor. The filmmaker should be prepared to provide a certificate of copyright and a statement certifying that the distributor has exclusive rights in the territories granted under the agreement. The transfer of exclusive rights to the territories should be filed with the Copyright Office, and copies made available to the distributor upon request.

Some distributors will require a written synopsis of the film, and most will require a copy of the final screenplay and shooting script. In addition, distributors may ask for certification that the film has received a particular rating from the MPAA. For independent films, the distributor should handle this obligation.

Depending on the scope of the distribution agreement, the distributor may require Errors and Omission Insurance to be obtained by the filmmaker, and may require that all the contracts, chain of title, license agreements, and other documentation relating to the filmmaker's valid ownership of the film and its constituent elements be provided. The documentation requirements will vary greatly by distributor and should be treated as subject to negotiation.

G. Storage and Delivery

The designated film lab should serve as the repository for the original negative of the film, the final soundtracks, cut-outs, and the alternate scenes and other footage that could conceivably be used to continue distributing the film. Everything else will reside with the film company—or more likely in the garage of the filmmaker.

If the film is shot on 35mm, then hundreds of hours of undeveloped film stock may be stored. Similar hours of images will be stored on removable hard disks or other digital storage media. Material that may be necessary for distribution in additional markets or territories should be included in the lab storage, while the remainder can be kept at home.

The lab access letter serves as the primary vehicle for delivery. Rather than providing physical copies of most materials, the filmmaker can provide access to the bulk of the material required by distributors. By limiting the ability of the distributor (and the filmmaker) to remove the film without notice or permission, the lab help protects against any unscrupulousness of either party.

The filmmaker must assume that the distributor could go bankrupt or fail to make payments at any point. Although this most likely will not happen, the mere possibility that the original negative could be handed to the distributor and lost or destroyed invokes a filmmaker's nightmare that no amount of money could rectify. The filmmaker must be careful to give only copies of documents and film elements. If the distributor breaches its contract, the filmmaker must be in a position to grant the rights in the film to a new party. If the first distributor has physical custody of the film, the filmmaker is at its mercy.

Finally, the production budget should include the cost of a long-term lease of a storage facility for the documents, film, and other materials. Film must also be treated with particular attention to temperature and humidity, so the types of storage must be carefully selected. Ironically, the good news is that most independent films will succeed or fail rapidly after their release, and the extra storage can be either justified or eliminated shortly after the film comes out.

Theatrical Distribution

THIS CHAPTER ON theatrical distribution and those on marketing and ancillary markets apply only to those filmmakers who did not enter into a negative pick-up or other arrangement that sold the entire marketing of the film to the film's financier. Once the filmmaker has sold the marketing and distribution rights, the filmmaker's role, except his capacity to participate in the marketing events for the film, is usually finished. In the current film economy, however, most filmmakers are left to scratch up sufficient funds to create the film, then use the finished print to sell the distribution rights.

A. How to Entice and Select a Distributor

The goal of the filmmaker is to create the best possible market opportunities for the distributor. This requires that the filmmaker take certain strategic steps. While none of them is mandatory, they each help increase the odds at least slightly that the film will be sold to an enthusiastic distributor.

1. Show Only Final Product

The filmmaker should show only the completed film unless there is no feasible alternative. The ability to watch a film with the sound incomplete, the color not balanced, or cuts missing, like the skill of reading screenplays or watching dailies, is one few people actually have. Worse, distributors will not recognize that they do not have the ability. Many of the subtle techniques operate below the audience's consciousness. If the technique were noticeable, it would detract from the film. The better the final film, therefore, the less effective the unfinished preview.

If the filmmaker cannot afford to finish the film, he would be better advised to create an extended trailer of the film, along with a one-sheet poster and production stills. The distributor needs a good trailer and promotional material to sell the film; the quality of the film itself is secondary. For the filmmaker faced with the hardest decisions regarding the last few dollars in the production budget, the trailer and promotional materials should be the priority unless the film can be completely finished—not just rough cut.

2. Sell the Biggest Market First

Distribution costs for a studio film often exceed the total costs of independent films. Each 35mm print of the film may cost $3,000 to $5,000, so a wide distribution of 2,000 screens can run as much as $1 million in print costs alone. Print advertising costs often run between $20 million and $50 million, depending on the size of the release and the intensity of the campaign.

Although independent films are rarely treated to this level of marketing, the filmmaker should not ignore the scale of the market costs. A print advertising campaign may not result in theatrical ticket sales, but the same film that bombs at the box office may soar to the top of the video sales or rental charts with almost no additional marketing. A distributor who controls both theatrical and video distribution should be much more willing to invest in promotion than a distributor that owns either. The combined budget of the two markets will invariably be less than what a single distributor would spend on the two markets.

The filmmaker should incorporate this marketing reality into his sales strategy. Early in the selling cycle, the filmmaker should insist that the

U.S. market be sold only to distributors who can exploit all or most of the domestic markets. Only if the filmmaker can close on complete domestic deals should he start to market the film to distributors who specialize in smaller media.

3. Know the Film

Perhaps the hardest job of the filmmaker is to realistically assess the value of the film. The filmmaker knows intimately what the film cost to make but has little idea how many people would be willing to pay full price to see it at the movie theater. If the filmmaker wants to have realistic conversations with the film distributors, he must develop some perspective on the film. This cuts both ways. Early in the sales process, the filmmaker may believe that his work should win all the Oscars. After a few months of distributor rejections, the filmmaker may think that the film should be allowed on public access television, even at 2:00 A.M.

Realism helps build credibility with the distributor, assists in properly positioning the film within the distributor's catalog of films, and creates a realistic basis for the contract negotiations. Without these attributes, even the most marketable film may go unseen.

Knowing the film is most critical when the filmmaker has choices regarding the distributor. If the filmmaker receives multiple distribution offers, knowing the film will enable him to match the film to the strengths and successes of the distributor.

4. Enter Film Festivals Selectively

The independent film marketplace is something of a community. For filmmakers consistently creating independent work, the premiere film festivals are the professional equivalent of the Academy Awards—an opportunity to move among peers as leaders in the industry. New filmmakers can learn a great deal about the realities of the industry.

Film festivals serve as an efficient way to get the filmmaker's film in front of a paying audience and potential distributors. Most films are made to be viewed in social settings. Comedies are always funnier to a viewer laughing along with a live audience. Film festivals provide a powerful marketing opportunity and a far superior way to display the film to a distributor than with a videotape in an office.

The filmmaker must still be careful. Not all festivals are alike. Local festivals may create opportunities for press coverage, and travel fees are eliminated in the filmmaker's home town. In every other situation, the filmmaker should show some selectivity. The more prestigious North American festivals include the New York Film Festival, the Toronto International Film Festival, the Montreal World Film Festival, the Telluride Film Festival, and the Sundance Film Festival.[1] These are highly competitive, but the exposure should help improve the chances of distribution for most films. That is not to suggest that getting into one of these festivals will guarantee a distribution deal. The New York Film Festival shows approximately 50 films annually, the Sundance Film Festival screens approximately 100. Only a small percentage of the films shown at even these festivals go on to theatrical distribution.

Even if the festival situation seems hopeless, there is a silver lining. The filmmaker should aim to do more than simply tell the film's story. Film festivals put the filmmaker in a room with thousands of other filmmakers, producers, distributors, and others with the same passion and profession. Even if the film does not end up in theatrical release, it may impress producers looking for talent on other projects or actors willing to take a risk on new material. The opportunities are real.

While some festivals are stellar events, others are of less value. The filmmaker must be selective or the submission fees and time commitments may undermine any value of the festivals. Adam Langer's *Film Festival Guide* identifies 500 festivals. The filmmaker should undertake to know what films have previously come out of each festival, whether a festival serves as a true marketplace for distribution deals, and in what regard a festival is held by the independent film community.

5. Go Where the Buyers Are—Attend Film Markets

In addition to the competitive film festivals, many films debut at film markets such as the American Film Market, held every February in Santa Monica, or the Cannes Film Market, held in conjunction with the Cannes Film Festival. These are predominantly transaction markets, with international sales agents attending screenings to purchase content. These markets are likely to be more financially rewarding than the more generally visible film festivals.

Typically film markets are huge, week-long affairs with thousands of participants. While there may be some panels, mixers, and other secondary activity, the primary goal is to put film content in front of sales agents and distributors. Filmmakers may try to be strategic about participation in film markets as part of an overall distribution strategy. The filmmaker may reduce the film's marketing guarantee requirement if he sells his film at a film market prior to a significant festival award. In contrast, the distributor may anticipate better response from competitions than what actually occurs, so that the guarantee advanced would be higher. Ultimately, such timing is dictated by luck and serendipity.

B. Knowing the Distributors

The filmmaker should know who the significant distributors are to quickly assess the credibility of the distributor's interest and enthusiasm.

1. Majors

The seven major motion picture producers are each major motion picture distributors as well. The vast majority of films produced in the United States are released domestically by these. They are vertically integrated telecommunication giants, which own production, distribution, and even the manufacturing facilities for videotapes and DVDs.

The seven companies are Warner Bros. (AOL Time Warner); Universal Studios (Vivendi International); Sony Pictures Entertainment (formerly Columbia Pictures); Paramount Pictures (Viacom); Twentieth Century Fox (News Corp.); Metro-Goldwyn-Mayer (MGM/UA); and Walt Disney Co. (Disney, Inc.). Although the corporate ownership has varied considerably over the past century, the roster of film studios has not varied significantly since the early days of the MPAA.

2. The Mini-Majors

In a category of its own is Dreamworks SKG, the modern answer to Mary Pickford's United Artists. Formed by Steven Spielberg, Jeffrey

Katzenberg, and David Geffen in 1994, Dreamworks has challenged the majors in feature films, animated films, music, and television production. It is also rapidly developing its own distribution channels.

All of the seven majors except MGM also own smaller film production companies. (MGM no longer has the presence of the other companies but, as the successor of both MGM and United Artists, retains great historical importance.) Although each company is operated in its own unique, idiosyncratic fashion, the smaller, wholly owned companies often make their own purchasing decisions.

Miramax has grown into the preeminent home of sophisticated independent films, despite its ownership by Disney. New Line and Fine Line are AOL Time Warner companies, as is Castle Rock. Fox and Sony each have "classics" companies that are more closely integrated with the studios.

3. Leading Independent Producer/Distributors

In addition to the companies owned or associated with the majors, a few independent producers have become havens for independent films. These include Artisan Entertainment, Lions Gate Entertainment, and a host of increasingly smaller companies that have less theatrical impact.

Also important in the mix are the television powerhouse companies of Showtime and HBO. These two companies purchase a tremendous amount of content for premium television distribution, including a significant amount of independent fare. Jerry Offsay, president of Showtime Production, has carved a unique niche for his television network by selecting highly regarded independent films that are sometimes considered too controversial to sell elsewhere. Showtime and HBO do not compete for theatrical distribution, so a filmmaker can leverage a sale with either of them into validation of the marketability of the film with distributors that otherwise might not have been interested.

4. Everyone Else

There are hundreds of independent film distributors working in the United States. Few of the remaining distributors have significant impact on the theatrical market. While most independent filmmakers do not have the opportunity to distribute their films theatrically, the possibility should not be conceded without a fight. If no experienced theatrical distributor offers a contract, the filmmaker should begin to work with the remaining distributors on how best to maximize the impact of the film.

C. The Distribution Deal

Every distribution agreement, large or small, covers the same fundamental issues. The distributor must promote the film in various media, collect payments, and share those payments with the film company. In addition to the filmmaker's delivery obligations, discussed earlier as part of the postproduction planning, additional concerns should be addressed.

1. Media and Territory

The territory of the film includes both the media and the geographic area in which the work can be shown. Unless the agreement provides for worldwide distribution in all media, this provision must very clearly spell out what countries and what media markets are covered by the agreement so that additional contracts can be negotiated to build up the worldwide distribution of the movie. For example, the provision for domestic television should include pay-per-view, pay cable, network, syndication, free cable, satellite, and any and all forms of television transmission now or hereafter existing. The section should specifically include or exclude home video. It should also specifically include or exclude interactive services such as the Internet or consumer devices such as home computers rather than television.

2. Term

The term of the distribution agreement will vary depending on the range of markets covered by the agreement. If the agreement is limited to domestic theatrical distribution, then there should not be significant activity more than one year after distribution begins. Recognizing that the distributor may need some flexibility regarding the start of the campaign, the term in such a situation should be limited to from two to five years.

Further, the filmmaker may wish to insist that the distribution rights terminate if the film has not been distributed in any of the listed markets within 18 months of delivery of the finished film to the distributor. This short drop-dead provision may be somewhat difficult to negotiate, but it provides significant protection for the filmmaker properly concerned about his film being left in the back of the distributor's catalog.

3. Advances and Payments

With significant debts generated throughout film production, the filmmaker may be most concerned about the payments to be made by the distributor. These payments serve as advances against the future income generated by the film. Advances act as a minimum payment, because the filmmaker will be entitled to keep the entire amount, without regard to the total income generated by the distribution. As income flows from the various markets, the distributor will withhold any additional payment to the filmmaker until the filmmaker has earned an amount equal to the advance.

After recouping the filmmaker's advance, the distributor will be paid a percentage of the revenue generated by the film. Payment to the distributor will be determined from the total gross income generated. The distributor will keep 20 to 30 percent of the theatrical and video income, increasing to 40 to 50 percent of the other markets. After the distributor deducts this fee, it deducts its expenses for the marketing and promotion of the film, often including its costs in attending national marketing conventions and other general overhead costs. The remainder of the net proceeds is then paid to the filmmaker.

Because of distributors' ability to manipulate reporting of gross income and expenses, the filmmaker should focus primarily on the advance. Industry practices reduce the net proceeds paid to the filmmaker to a relatively small portion of income generated.

4. Distributor's Guarantees of Promotional Expenses

Almost as important as the advance is the distributor's guarantee regarding the size of the marketing campaign. Even though costs of the marketing campaign ultimately come from the filmmaker's portion of the revenue, the larger the campaign, the more likely the film will be viewed. Without the guarantee, the distributor will have no particular incentive to get behind this picture and push for its distribution. The filmmaker can always ask the distributor to change the campaign if he feels the payments are no longer needed, but invariably the filmmaker will want a larger campaign than the distributor is willing to provide. Without a contractual obligation from the beginning, the filmmaker is at the mercy of the distributor.

5. Audits

Given the importance of the advance, payments of guarantees, and accounting of the promotional fees, the filmmaker must be able to monitor or audit the books of the distributor. More specifically, the filmmaker must have the right to have the books made available to his own accountant. Often a distributor will seek to limit access or limit the amount of time the filmmaker has to conduct an audit or bring action on one, but the filmmaker should resist losing this legal protection.

6. Foreign Sublicensing

Often a distributor will sublicense some markets or territories to other companies because it does not have the facility to fully exploit those markets. This sublicensing arrangement can be as efficient as any attempts of the filmmaker to track down those markets and cover them with different distributors. Often, however, the sublicensee is actually a company owned by the distributor itself—meaning that the distributor is making the profit as the sublicensee and charging a premium for its licensing fee. Unless the total fees are capped, an unscrupulous distributor can earn twice the revenue by sublicensing to its own subsidiary. Filmmakers should be careful to cap the sublicensing fees to limit additional revenue when the distributor owns the sublicensee.

D. Rights to Withhold from the Distributor

The distribution agreement should also be quite explicit regarding limitations on the distributor. No rights should be granted unless the distributor can exploit those rights and the filmmaker can be assured that he will see a return on the payments. In addition, there are certain legal controls that distributors often request, but these requests should be carefully limited or refused.

1. Copyright and Ownership

The distributor may need the right to edit the film for certain markets, particularly foreign markets. Nonetheless, the distribution agreement should not be an assignment of copyright and should not grant the distributor the right to remake the film or create new projects out of the story or related rights. The editing rights must be limited to those changes required by local censorship laws or changes for accommodating foreign languages. These accommodations may also include translating the title in either a literary or a conceptual fashion. Except for these specific changes, the distributor should have no power to modify the film. This limitation may not apply if the film project is purchased outright by a major studio's distribution arm, but, for all other purchasers, the copyright and ownership in the story should be retained by the filmmaker.

2. Marketing Materials

It may be the distributor rather than the filmmaker who creates the marketing campaign that defines the film in the public's mind. Particularly in a situation where multiple distributors will distribute the film in various markets and media, each distributor must agree that the filmmaker will own any marketing materials. This way, marketing materials can be used from the theatrical distributor to promote the video sales of the film, even if these are licensed to different distributors. It is also helpful if the distribution agreements expire and later interest in the film requires the filmmaker to promote the picture again. In addition to legal ownership, the contract should provide that at the end of the contract term any remaining materials be given to the filmmaker or destroyed, at the filmmaker's discretion.

3. Foreign Royalty Revenues

In addition to the legal rights afforded to U.S. copyright holders, many countries throughout the world provide additional legal protections in the form of royalties. These royalties are paid to authors and producers for the use of films in ways that may not be easily negotiated, or because the use is mandatory in that country. For example, if a film is broadcast on terrestrial television—over the airwaves—then the cable operators of many countries are allowed simultaneously to carry that broadcast on local cable systems in exchange for paying into a national fund. The owner of the film is then eligible for a portion of those funds.

Each country has a slightly different set of revenue sources, including cable retransmissions royalties (described above), surcharges on blank videotape, rental royalties, educational royalties, theatrical box office levies, public performance royalties for video, and many others. Typically, the money is collected by a national rights society similar to ASCAP and divided among the registered content owners. This means the filmmaker must register with dozens of collection societies in hundreds of counties.

Fortunately, the American Film Market Association (AFMA) provides a collection service that acts as both registration agent and collection agent for these funds. Registration is far simpler when handled by the AFMA, and filmmakers are much more likely to receive royalties through the collective powers and efforts of AFMA than through a distributor or sales agent in a particular country.

Distribution Strategy

MARKETING OF THE final motion picture is every bit as important as the film's content in creating an audience for the picture. Marketing is not a science. Spending $50 million and opening in 2,000 theaters will certainly generate millions of dollars in revenue, but it often generates far less than the print and marketing fees—let alone the film's production costs. In addition, few independent films have the marketing budgets to simply open wide and hard. Instead, the filmmaker must work with the distributor to control the marketing campaign to build audience interest in the movie.

A. Staging the Domestic Theatrical Distribution

Distributing the film requires tremendous coordination and a good deal of cooperation on the part of the exhibitors. Exhibitors are entitled to bid on each film separately, may choose not to show a particular film, and are typically rewarded with greater revenue for films that have longer stays in theaters. They also buy films for each screen (or at least each theater complex) rather than for the chain as a whole. These rules have developed over the years to protect independent theaters and small chains from the larger chain competitors.

1. National Release

Studios generally release their films nationally, meaning in each major market in North America (including both the United States and Canada) on the same date. This allows them to maximize the impact of paid advertising and drown out negative reviews with a well-financed campaign. Increasingly, the dates of international campaigns are being moved closer to the opening dates of U.S. release to reduce the window of opportunity for video piracy. Although the exhibitors negotiate individually, large national releases tend to announce the dates of campaigns, which forces exhibitors to participate or be left behind. A small theater chain wishing to be part of the release of *Titanic II* must be willing to stop showing whatever film it otherwise would play on that date to make room for the blockbuster release. National release dates of major pictures must be carefully considered lest the independent film be forced out of theaters to make room.

2. Markets Sold in the Presale Agreement

Depending on the financing techniques employed, some distribution choices may already be settled. For example, if the presale agreements call for exhibition in certain territories at specified times, these will dictate all other agreements. Presale agreements may allow some flexibility regarding the scheduling of actual release dates. For a small film, release in overseas territories should not have a material impact on its domestic release, and good reviews can be exploited as part of the domestic marketing effort. Outside the United States, dates for theatrical distribution generally have little impact on the overall marketing campaign. There is no need to hold up the distribution in India while awaiting Europe, or to let Japan have the film before Korea. Audiences do not travel to see the films abroad, the problems of piracy are not diminished, and distributors are generally not sufficiently sophisticated to create any meaningful strategy with international release dates.

If a portion of the presale agreement comes from videotape or DVD distribution, the filmmaker should be able to delay the release in that media for a specified period of up to one year so that she can take every opportunity to release the film theatrically first.

3. Platform Release

The best-known strategy for distributing an independent film is known as a platform release. The film is opened in one selected city (often New York, Chicago, or Los Angeles), selected for the size of the market, influence of the critics, and opportunity for word of mouth to spread to other areas. Assuming positive reviews and good word of mouth, audiences for that film should grow, and the per-screen revenue for that film may well equal or exceed that of the top blockbusters playing at the same time. Exhibitors are far more interested in the per-screen revenue than the national grosses because per-screen revenue translates into ticket sales and concession traffic.

After two to four weeks, press and audience reaction will generate interest sufficient to move to additional markets. If the campaign is highly successful, additional prints will be ordered and new theaters will be added to the original showings. Typically, however, the prints are shipped to the new markets, keeping the total print cost down. In this way, a movie may play 5 to 10 major markets on 1 to 3 prints.

If the film is doing well in 10 markets, then the distributor may choose to expand still further, adding an additional 10 markets, and so on, until national distribution has been accomplished. More likely, the efficiency stops well before the first 100 markets have been hit, but the film will still have had a very successful theatrical run and will be positioned well for videotape sales built on theatrical word of mouth.

The platform release allows exhibitors to gain confidence in the film, and the flexibility to add it to their schedule when the blockbusters begin to fizzle. As a result, the timing and geography of the platform release becomes highly dynamic, reacting to openings throughout the country.

4. Four Walling

A filmmaker without any other options may still buy the opportunity to have her film shown in a commercial theater. In a four-wall arrangement, the distributor or filmmaker rents the theater, rather than licensing the picture to the theater. Typically, only a filmmaker who could not otherwise attract a distributor would do this. The filmmaker pays a rental fee for the theater for a specified time period and receives all ticket sale income; the concession income may be either kept by the theater or apportioned.

Four walling may seem like an act of vanity, but it can be much more than that. Sometimes the limited run will be enough to get the local critic to see the film and elicit a positive review. It may result in generating some interest among potential distributors.

Four walling may even be profitable, particularly if the film is uniquely attractive to a specific local homogeneous audience. For example, four walling may do very well when a film is promoted exclusively within a concentrated religious community, the local gay and lesbian community, or a college campus. Other exhibitors will not be able to promote within those communities nearly as effectively as the filmmaker who has created a work geared to that particular audience.

B. Staging the Remaining Markets

The traditional cycle of film distribution starts with domestic theatrical distribution; approximately six months later the film is released on videotape, DVD or laser disk, and pay-per-view; then six months following that it is released on premiere cable such as HBO or Showtime. After that, the largest films get network broadcast premieres, then cable. This cycle releases the film in the most expensive markets first. Since theater tickets are the most expensive option for the audience, common wisdom is that once a film has been made available on HBO the chance for a theatrical market is over. While the logic may be generally sound, for independent films, there are opportunities to schedule against the model.

1. Premiere Cable as Catalyst

Short distribution windows can create a momentum of their own. Disney regularly cycles its classic animated films in and out of television and stores, so that every showing is a new premiere. (Because these films are directed at younger viewers, a large part of the audience changes every five years and the youngest viewers have never before been exposed to the work.) Similarly, a short "premiere" on HBO or Showtime creates tremendous exposure, but that exposure may not destroy the film's marketability in smaller art house theaters around the country, if the television window has closed.

Less than half the potential audience will be exposed to the film if it premieres on a single premium channel. Therefore, there may be a significant number of viewers willing to pay theater prices to see the film, and that audience will be exposed to considerably more marketing as a result of the film's short television appearance than otherwise. Of course, such a distribution scheme requires the consent of the television network and the exhibitors, but for the right movie, it creates a viable alternative.

The other unfortunate consequence is that the film loses its eligibility for Academy Award consideration. To be eligible for the Oscars, the film must play for one week in theatrical exhibition before being distributed in any other medium.

2. PBS

Like the premiere cable networks, Public Broadcasting System stations show movies unedited and uninterrupted. The word *system* in the name, however, is something of a misnomer, because each station purchases its contents individually. This creates two separate PBS markets for the filmmaker. The filmmaker may be able to sell her film—particularly if it's a documentary—to the production companies that are purchased by the PBS stations, such as NOVA, National Geographic, Great Performances, etc. The filmmaker's work may sometimes be appropriate as content packaged for such a series. The filmmaker may also license the work to any particular PBS station for broadcast. This creates more than 100 possible sales, and the PBS station can work like the premium cable stations to promote the film and expose it to a potential theatrical audience.

3. 16mm Formats

Although niche markets are shrinking, they remain unique opportunities to show independent films. The 16mm format is used primarily for colleges and schools. These smaller projectors show films in classrooms, organization-sponsored events, and school-hosted screenings. Films are typically licensed through specialty distributors who control the public performance rights of the films exclusively in this format. For the appropriate content, this market may create a great deal of interest and could lead to a cult following.

4. The Internet

One of the great hopes for digital filmmaking was that the Internet would subsume many other entertainment media. A single device, always connected to the Internet, and a ubiquitous connection through the home's internal network would replace or supplement every stereo, game system, television, computer, and many other devices. Unfortunately, the market for high-speed Internet connections has stagnated, home networks have been largely ignored, and the only pervasive entertainment uses of the system are instant messaging, computer games, and burning music CDs to be listened to away from the computer.

Against this backdrop, the dream of the Internet as a haven for independent filmmakers seems highly overrated. Certain sites such as Ifilm. com, Atomfilms.com, and alwaysifilm.com continue to show filmmakers' movies but have yet to mature as a method of generating income for filmmakers.

For those attempting to find a larger audience, the Internet can provide a form of viral marketing. Once the film is posted to a Web site (or available on a peer-to-peer network), the filmmaker can send e-mails with download information and information about the film to interested discussion boards and chat rooms. The e-mails can be made topical and informative so as not to become unwanted spam. Judiciously done, these e-mails and postings may generate significant interest in the movie. The filmmaker may be able to leverage significant hits into interest in more traditional media. Some sites may contribute some modest payment or royalty for viewership, but most simply provide the privilege of free access for the film rather than financial compensation for use of the filmmaker's work.

For short and very short projects, the Internet provides a marketplace where one did not exist before—and the opportunity to receive feedback from the public about one's work—and can be a valuable tool, even if not yet a bona fide distribution channel.

C. Direct to Video

Unfortunately, most independent films do not receive theatrical exhibition. Instead, they skip this step in the cycle and move directly into videotape and DVD distribution. Given this reality, makers of very low-budget films should consider avoiding the costs associated with producing a film of sufficient image quality that it could be shown theatrically. A direct-to-video project can be made for a few thousand dollars, even while following most of the legal guidelines identified throughout this book, and can sometimes be highly profitable.

Most videotapes and DVDs are sold to rental outlets such as Blockbuster or Wherehouse, where consumers spend $2 to $4 for the right to use the film for a few days. The rental outlet purchases the tapes outright from the distributor and does not pay a royalty based on the number of units sold. In addition, some films are sold through traditional retail and discount outlets directly to the public. National discounters such as Target, Wal-Mart, K-Mart, Costco, and Sam's Club lead direct sales. Children's titles and holiday films do particularly well because they are well priced gifts and are often purchased on impulse. Blockbusters also have success in this category.

Independent films may fit well within this marketing strategy if the content compares to the other types of films sold successfully. An independent filmmaker's retelling of *Pinocchio* may or may not garner a theatrical distributor but will likely generate some interest by retailers.

For most independent filmmakers, success should be measured as it is for fighter pilots. A successful landing or feature is any project you can walk away from. If videotape sales allow the filmmaker to recoup all costs while showing the story to the audience, the filmmaker has outperformed most in the field.

D. Controlling a Distributor's Campaign

The filmmaker may have no voice in the distributor's movie campaign unless the distribution agreement provides contractual rights to the filmmaker. Even if the filmmaker initially supplied the one-sheet, the production stills, and the other tools of the marketing campaign, the distributor may still have absolute control.

To achieve control over the campaign, the filmmaker should insist that a few key protections be included in the distribution agreement—at least for the film's initial market (whether that be theatrical, video, or something else). A minimum should be set for the amount of money the distributor must spend on printed materials and advertising for exclusively promoting the film. The obligation must be exclusive or the distributor can simply spend a great deal of money to promote its catalog of films, which includes the filmmaker's project but does not highlight it. The more detailed the type of spending, the stronger the filmmaker's control will be.

Ideally, the filmmaker should also insist on approval rights for all the marketing materials. Although this is seldom granted, the filmmaker should be guaranteed the right to consult on all such materials. While consultation serves only as a good-faith obligation, the distributor that forgets the name of the filmmaker the day after the contract is signed can then be controlled—the filmmaker can terminate the contract and start over with another distributor.

The distributor and filmmaker should also have some written plan for the distribution of the film that both are comfortable with prior to entering the distribution agreement. Although it would be unreasonable to make such a plan part of the contract, it should serve as the basis for planning and discussion. The marketing plan must be highly opportunistic and therefore quite flexible, but the fundamentals should be explicit.

E. The Credit Obligations in Marketing

Negotiations with the film's stars and key personnel may also give rise to contractual obligations regarding the film's marketing efforts. At a minimum, both the filmmaker and any distributors must respect the obligations regarding credit size and placement granted to particular cast and crew members. Additionally, some cast members may have negotiated for picture placement in the marketing campaign. In that case, the filmmaker and distributor must use the photograph of the particular cast member in the posters and marketing material.

If other cast members negotiated "favored nations" provisions regarding such contractual rights, then they also are entitled to the photo placement. These contracts can severely limit the flexibility of marketing ideas. If the distributor creates a great campaign that would violate the contractual rights of an actor, then the filmmaker must seek that actor's permission to waive the contractual obligation and use the campaign.

The original contracts for the cast and crew members should have included a provision granting the filmmaker the right to use the person's publicity rights, including name, likeness, voice, and signature as part of the marketing and packaging of the film. If that was not provided in writing, then the permission should be obtained in writing prior to using any person in the marketing of the film.

F. Marketing Campaign Independence

Distributors generally work by playing the odds. A distributor will "buy" a number of movies and then support only the movie that is easiest to sell. If one of those movies is bought without any payment of an advance or contractual obligation to spend money, then that film may sit in the distributor's catalog without any marketing effort. If that film begins to gather interest, however, then the distributor will start to actively promote it.

Therefore, the filmmaker must make every effort to promote the film herself. This may duplicate a small distributor's job, but realistically it will help the filmmaker's film to stand out from the rest of the distributor's catalog. A side benefit is that promotion often promotes the filmmaker as much as the particular story, an angle that is far more valuable to the filmmaker than to the distributor.

1. Critics and Festivals

Perhaps the easiest step in the campaign comes from garnering positive reviews for the film. The filmmaker simply needs to put the film on exhibition where critics will see it and those critics will write strong, laudatory articles about the film. The good news is that some people like brussels sprouts. No matter how quirky or idiosyncratic the film, there will be some critic out there who will rave about it. So long as the film is not a technical disaster, someone will be willing to write positive things about the content.

The hardest thing about working as a filmmaker is that the corollary is also true. No matter how brilliant the film, some critics will find the story repugnant and many will find it old hat. Criticism goes with the territory.

To manage the criticism, the filmmaker should be a bit selective. The less famous film festivals will often generate a good deal of regional press hoping to boost the films on exhibit. These festivals may be useless for attracting a distributor, but quite valuable in attracting a few solid reviews.

If the film is to be shown in a one-paper town, the paper's critic must be invited to the opening. Often critics' reputations for the types of movies they like and dislike are well known. Do not avoid a local critic by snubbing him. He is still likely to show up—just with a chip on his shoulder. If the local critic has written that he despises gladiator movies, do not premiere the newest gladiator epic there. Unless the opening is national, open in that town after some positive press has been generated elsewhere.

2. Hometown Press

When a local resident makes good, that makes local news. Often these are very kind stories, designed to make everyone feel good about their neighbors. Do not ignore the opportunity. Every bandwagon has to start somewhere, and the lightest piece of hometown fluff will still serve to pad the publicity package. If the article compliments the film, then so much the better.

3. Specialty Markets

Independent films fill an essential role in telling stories that speak to small communities rather than the mainstream. Although Spike Lee's *Do the Right Thing* and Steven Spielberg's *Schindler's List* were nationally recognized films, most such projects fizzle at the box office and as a result do not receive studio financing. Still, independent filmmakers create these movies as powerful testaments to our heritage and culture. Having made such a film, the filmmaker should turn to these communities for its first audience.

This strategy involves both the institutional community and the general community. First, within each self-identified community are organizations that serve as the focus of that community's public outreach. Enthusiastic support from the leadership of these organizations may open doors to mainstream distribution and will certainly enhance media attention. These organizations are typically part of national and international coalitions of similar organizations that share common interests. Letters of introduction from local leadership may expand the potential to reach national boards.

Second, these community organizations may be able to deliver interested audiences for the filmmaker. Particularly for a film in a small platform release or being four walled, a strong, positive endorsement by the local community newsletter or paper will do far more to sell tickets than any paid ad. The filmmaker may even consider encouraging the community group to four wall the film directly. Let the local church underwrite the costs of the evening and keep the proceeds as a fundraiser. The filmmaker will have made a modest profit and generated substantial word of mouth regarding the film.

4. Distribute Advance Copies

Nothing tells the story better than the story itself. No one sells the film better than those who believe in it. The filmmaker can combine these two truisms into a powerful marketing tool. Every member of the cast and crew has acquaintances who will be interested in seeing the project. Some of them may be helpful in finding a distributor or receiving a positive review. While most independent filmmakers offer a copy of the final film on videotape to each member of the cast and crew, most forget that the combined contacts of cast and crew may create a powerful base of people willing to screen the film. Add the investors to this group and the list begins to have some potential as a marketing tool.

Rather than distributing videotapes without introduction, the contact person from the cast and crew should draft a letter that explains why the person is receiving the film and from whom the mailing was initiated. Follow-up information should also be included so that interested recipients can get additional information. At worst, this technique serves as a nice community-building tool within the production company. At best, it may open doors the filmmaker never knew existed.

Additional Revenues

FOR FILMS THAT have been successfully distributed, additional revenue opportunities may be available. Not every film generates additional income, only those films that have been successful are able to generate any interest. For all additional revenue sources, the filmmaker must be sure to have secured the legal rights to the film's marketing materials for such use. This means signing contracts with the creators of those materials for the film in every media as well as for all products related to the film. If the distributor of the film created the marketing materials, then the distribution agreement should include a license to use those materials in distribution markets not controlled by that distributor as well as in all potential product markets.

A. Soundtrack Albums and Music Publishing

The most common additional revenue source comes from sales of soundtrack albums. If the movie uses a significant amount of music, particularly popular songs, then the collection of music as performed in the film may be quite marketable.

A soundtrack album consists of four elements. First the film's marketing materials—title and artwork—must be used or the crossover audience awareness value will be destroyed. These materials often include the names and pictures of the cast members, so the publicity rights from the cast are necessary. Second, the songs selected for the movie are selected again for the album.

Third, the versions of the songs used—the performances—are the same as the performances used in the film. This may include publicity rights from the cast members, but more likely includes the mechanical reproduction rights from the record company that owns the copyright in the recordings and the music publisher or composer who owns the copyright in the songs. The permission of the song's copyright holder need not be obtained, because the filmmaker can license the songs through the copyright office by paying a statutory license fee.

Fourth, the soundtrack album may include original music composed exclusively for the film. This copyright may be owned by the film company or may have been retained by the composer, in which case a mechanical license must be obtained to record the score and produce the albums.

Gaining permission to license a soundtrack album is much simpler when done at the time the music is originally selected for the film. All the same parties must give permission to use the music in the movie, so there is little additional obligation to license the soundtrack album as well. To avoid increasing the cost of the film, these licenses should be based on a royalty paid for the number of soundtrack albums sold. By doing this, the filmmaker avoids any costs until there is revenue.

B. Novelizations

While many films derive from novels or short stories, the story as retold in the film often makes for good reading. As a result, films are increasingly the source for new novels. Assuming the film company properly purchased all the elements of the story, no additional contracts are necessary to create the novel of the film. Many screenwriters view the novelization as an opportunity to maintain control of the story and may seek the right to be the writer of the novel, if they so choose. (This is referred to as a right of first refusal; the filmmaker is obligated to ask the screenwriter before asking anyone else.)

One compromise on the awarding of the right of first refusal to the screenwriter is to condition the grant of this contractual right on the screenwriter receiving sole screen credit, pursuant to the film's credit dispute policy. In this way, the screenwriter who truly wrote and controlled the story will receive that same opportunity with the novel, while those screenwriters who may have participated in some portion of the story can be politely told no. Of course, the filmmaker can offer the opportunity to write the novel to one of the screenwriters who received shared credit, but there would no longer be a contractual obligation to do so.

The novelization rights will be sold to a publishing house. The publisher will typically distribute the novel only in a paperback or trade paperback version. If the film is an original story, and a particularly compelling literary one, the filmmaker may seek to use the novel to promote a theatrical distribution deal.

C. Merchandising and Licensing

Perhaps the biggest windfall for motion pictures today is the merchandise tie-in. The *Star Wars* saga (perhaps the largest-budget independent film ever created) has created an empire of toys, games, dolls, and paraphernalia that now spans three decades. Like the creation of the soundtrack album, the key to merchandizing is control of the necessary elements. First, the filmmaker must control the marketing rights to the title, artwork, and photographs used to promote the movie. Second, the filmmaker or the product manufacturer must license the publicity rights of the actors.

An action figure cannot be created using the likeness of an actor without that actor's express permission. While these publicity rights are typically assigned to the film company for the ability to make and market the film, that contract would not cover the dolls or games. These items must be separately licensed, and the actors will generally receive a small royalty or profit participation from these agreements.

D. Story Rights

Finally, the filmmaker may sell the story itself. It is no longer uncommon for Hollywood to remake movies that are still available on videotape and played often on television. *Planet of the Apes* illustrates the ability to remake a film that continued to be popular with its original cast production. Filmmakers are often haunted by the difficult choices imposed by very low-budget filmmaking and may wish to revisit the material later in their careers.

Story rights may include simple remakes or expand the original story through sequels, prequels, and spin-offs. Sequels are not limited to action stories like *Star Wars* or characters like James Bond. Children's characters naturally lend themselves to multiple adventures. Character-driven stories such as *Terms of Endearment*, *The Godfather*, and *Chinatown* opened the door for continuing sagas.

The ability to exploit the story rights in new projects brings the legal analysis full cycle to the beginning of the book. The ability to create these works will depend on what rights were initially purchased, which entities own the rights, and how the financing was structured. The filmmaker should make those choices with an eye toward the film being produced and the future stories yet to be told. By controlling these rights, the filmmaker can increase his chances that he will continue participating in the lives of the characters he created and nourished throughout the filmmaking process.

Format for the Feature Screenplay

FOR THE NONWRITER, a brief guide to the screenplay format may be useful. The American motion picture screenplay format differs from its British counterpart as well as the television equivalent in small but important ways. Although the rules are quite specific, they are also quite easy to follow.

1. Scene Header

Each scene begins with a line in all capital letters, aligned on the left, with three components. First, the header indicates interior or exterior written as "INT." or "EXT." Second, the location of the scene is presented. The name of each scene should be sufficiently clear and consistent so that all designers know where and in which room the action takes place. Finally, after two dashes, the time element of the scene is given. This may be as simple as "MORNING," "NOON," "DUSK," or "NIGHT" or, if it is necessary for the script, the time can include actual time indicators such as "6:25 A.M." The scene header looks like this:

INT. TONY'S BEDROOM—NIGHT

The scene header is also where information such as the camera's point of view (P.O.V.) or camera angle would be written. P.O.V. and other similar information should be used sparingly, if at all, in a screenplay prior to the adaptation into a shooting script.

2. Scene Description and Action

The paragraph must describe the action and location of the scene. Film is a visual medium, so the descriptions are often more important than the dialogue; however, they are only a guide for the production designer and art director. The writer must find a balance between description and brevity while keeping in mind that the length of the paragraph will indicate the length of the shot.

A new scene should be used whenever the action moves to a new location or requires a change in camera setup. The paragraph should be justified on the left. Each character's name should be capitalized the first time it appears in a scene. Important sound information should also be capitalized, such as "GUNSHOTS ring out."

Here's a typical example:

> TONY stands in front of his dresser. He begins to get dressed, pausing to clasp the chain around his neck. Carefully, he dons his plain white shirt, then ties the black obi to hold it in place. SHANE walks into the room, knocking as he enters.

3. Dialogue

The name of the character speaking should be in all capital letters, centered. Immediately below the name are the "stage directions." Stage directions are also centered and put in parentheses. Stage directions should be used only when the action and the dialogue do not suggest the emotion or intent of the text. Besides, almost no actor has ever admitted to following the stage directions.

The actual dialogue is written in paragraphs with extra narrow margins of approximately $2\frac{1}{2}$ inches from the right or left. If the same character continues to speak after another block of scene description, the word continued "(cont.)" should accompany the character's name with the next block of dialogue. Here is another scene from the film script:

INT. TONY'S KARATE SCHOOL—LATE MORNING

TONY stands inside a large karate studio. From the top of the ceiling hang "Grand Opening" banners. Half a dozen karate instructors, men and women wearing karate dress similar to Tony's, stand near the doorway, waiting. SHANE and MARY stand with Tony as 25 or 30 spectators watch.

> SHANE
>
> Let's get this show on the road. I know this is a newsworthy event and all, but this isn't the only news that's fit to print.

> TONY
>
> Okay. I think we're ready.

Tony bows to the karate instructors. They bow in return, then kneel in a straight row in front of the rest of the audience, watching Tony.

> TONY (Cont.)
>
> Ladies and gentlemen, thank you very much for coming today for the opening of my fifth studio. What we do here is both art and sport, dedicated to discipline, strength, and endurance.

4. Editing Cues

The last technical element on the script is the editing cue that is written at the end of a scene. Editing cues include "CUT TO," "DISSOLVE TO," and "FADE OUT." Again, such cues should be used sparingly and left to the film's director, director of photography, or editor. Occasionally, however, the editing cue will be necessary to explain the juxtaposition of scenes.

Editing cues should be in all capital letters, justified right, with a colon to indicate the jump to the next scene. It looks like this.

DISSOLVE TO:

These four elements highlight the mechanical requirements of the screenplay. The shooting script differs because it requires that scenes be numbered and that the pages indicate when a scene continues on the next page. There is no other magic to the mechanics of script writing. The writer simply needs tremendous literary and visual creativity, the ability to tell a story, and a strong, interesting point of view.

5. Additional Tricks and Techniques

In addition to the format of the screenplay, there are a number of even more minute details that make a script seem professional and mainstream. Since most investors and producers are looking for reasons not to get involved with a particular project, it is important to avoid small problems that give rise to such excuses. One of these issues is the method of binding a screenplay. Each script should be three-hole punched and held together with brass grommets. This is not the best way to keep a script in good condition, but it remains the proper etiquette. An even more sophisticated variation is to eliminate the center hole and grommet, binding the script with two grommets only.

Another point of etiquette is the cover page. The cover should be the same white bond paper as the rest of the script. The title should be in normal 12-point type, centered on the upper third of the page. The phrase "screenplay by" and the name of the author can be centered under the title. Etiquette is giving way to desktop publishing on the matter of title size. While larger titles are not considered proper form, they are no longer considered distasteful and, since the large type size attracts attention, many scripts are beginning to use larger titles.

Finally, know the difference between a preliminary draft and a shooting draft of the script. The shooting draft includes scene numbers, camera information, and certain other details that do not belong in a script until much further into the production process. Do not write the script in shooting draft format until it is prepared for principal photography.

Copyright Forms and Circulars

Circular 45 (Excerpts)—Motion Pictures Including Videotapes

GENERAL INFORMATION

Statutory Definition

Motion pictures are audiovisual works consisting of a series of related images that, when shown in succession, impart an impression of motion, together with any accompanying sounds. They are typically embodied in film, videotape, or videodisk.

How Copyright Is Secured

Copyright in a motion picture is automatically secured when the work is created and "fixed" in a copy. The Copyright Office registers claims to copyright and issues certificates of registration but does not "grant" or "issue" copyrights.

Only the expression (camera work, dialogue, sounds, etc.) fixed in a motion picture is protectible under copyright. Copyright does not cover the idea or concept behind the work or any characters portrayed in the work. Works that do not constitute a fixation of a motion picture include:

- a live telecast that is not fixed in a copy
- a screenplay or treatment of a future motion picture

Publication

Publication of a motion picture takes place when one or more copies are distributed to the public by sale, rental, lease or lending, or when **an offering** is made to distribute copies to a group of persons (wholesalers, retailers, broadcasters, motion picture distributors, and the like) for purposes of further distribution or public performance. Offering to distribute a copy of a motion picture for exhibition during a film festival may be considered publication of that work.

For an offering to constitute publication, copies must be made and be ready for distribution. The **performance** itself of a motion picture (for example, showing it in a theater, on television, or in a school room) **does not** constitute publication. Publication of a motion picture publishes all the components embodied in it including the music, the script, and the sounds. Thus, if a motion picture made from a screenplay is published, the screenplay is published to the extent it is contained in the published work.

COPYRIGHT NOTICE

Before March 1, 1989, the use of copyright notice was mandatory on all published works, and any work first published before that date should have carried a notice. For works first published on and after March 1, 1989, use of the copyright notice is optional. For more information about copyright notice, see Circular 3, "Copyright Notice." NOTE: The notice requirements for works first published before 1978 are governed by the previous copyright law. See page 6 for such works. The status of certain foreign works was affected by amendments to the Copyright Act pursuant to enactment of the Uruguay Round Agreements Act (URAA). See page 7 for more information.

COPYRIGHT REGISTRATION

Advantages of zzz

Registration in the Copyright Office establishes a public record of the copyright claim. Before an infringement suit may be filed in court, registration is necessary for works of U.S. origin and for foreign works not originating in a Berne Union Country. Timely registration may also provide a broader range of remedies in an infringement suit. See Circular 1, "Copyright Basics," for more information on the benefits of registration.

How to Apply for Registration

To register either a published or unpublished motion picture, send the following to the Copyright Office:

1. **A signed application** on Form PA

2. **One complete copy** of the motion picture being registered (see page 5 for specific requirements)

3. **A separate written description** of the contents of the motion picture

4. **A nonrefundable filing fee** of $30* for each application in the form of a draft (that is, a check, money order, or bank draft) payable to: Register of Copyrights. Do not send cash.

DEPOSIT REQUIREMENTS FOR REGISTRATION

In addition to the application and fee, you must send a copy and a description of the work being registered. The nature of the copy and description may vary, depending upon the factors indicated below:

For All Published Motion Pictures:

1. A separate description of the nature and general content of the work, for example, a shooting script, a synopsis, or a pressbook.

2. One complete copy of the work. A copy is complete if it is undamaged and free of splices and defects that would interfere with viewing the work.

For motion pictures first published in the United States:

One complete copy of the best edition. Where two or more editions are published in the United States, the best edition is the one preferred by the Library of Congress.

Currently, the Library accepts in descending order of preference:

A. Film

1. Preprint material with special arrangement

2. 35mm positive prints

   3. 16mm positive prints

B. Videotape formats

   1. 1-inch open reel tape

   2. Betacam SP

   3. D-2

   4. Betacam

   5. Videodisk

   6. ¾-inch cassette

   7. ½-inch VHS cassette

For motion pictures first published abroad:

One complete copy as first published or one copy of the best edition.

For Unpublished Motion Pictures

   1. **a separate description** of the work

   2. **a copy of the work** containing all the visual and aural elements covered by the registration. An alternative deposit option is available for unpublished motion pictures. For information, contact the Motion Picture Team in the Copyright Office Examining Division at (202) 707-8182.

Requirements for Motion Pictures That Cannot Be Viewed by the Copyright Office Staff

The Examining Division does not have equipment to view motion pictures in certain formats, including 1-inch open reel videotapes, Betacam and Betacam SP videocassettes, D-2 and other digital videocassettes, and 8mm videocassettes. If you send one of these formats, please include the credits in the separate written description. If the work was first published before March 1, 1989, the Copyright Office must examine the work for the required copyright notice. In this case, please send the best edition copy and a copy that the Examining Division can view, for example, a ½-inch VHS videocassette.

NOTE: For the deposit requirement for works published before Jan. 1, 1978, see page 7.

EXCEPTIONS TO THE NORMAL DEPOSIT REQUIREMENT

Special Relief

Where it is unusually difficult or impossible to comply with the deposit requirement for a particular motion picture, you may submit a written request for special relief from the normal requirement. The request, addressed to the **Chief of the Examining Division**, must state why you cannot provide the required copy and describe the nature of the substitute copy being deposited. This letter should be included with the registration material. The decision to grant or deny special relief is based on the acquisitions policies and archival considerations of the Library of Congress and the examining requirements of the Copyright Office.

Motion Picture Agreement

The Motion Picture Agreement establishes several alternative deposit procedures for published motion pictures. How well it serves a particular applicant depends on a number of factors, including the frequency of filing registrations. For detailed information, call the Motion Picture, Broadcasting, and Recorded Sound Division (MBRS) at (202) 707-5604, or write to:

> Library of Congress
> MBRS
> Attn: Reference Assistant
> 101 Independence Avenue SE
> Washington, D.C. 20540-4805

MANDATORY DEPOSIT FOR WORKS PUBLISHED IN THE UNITED STATES

Requirement Under Mandatory Deposit

The owner of copyright or the owner of the exclusive right of publication of a motion picture published in the United States has a legal obligation to deposit in the Copyright Office within three months of publication in the United States one complete copy of the best edition and a description of the work. Failure to deposit this copy after the Copyright Office demands it can result in fines and other penalties.

Satisfying Mandatory Deposit Through Registration

Depositing the required copy with an application and fee for copyright registration simultaneously satisfies any mandatory deposit requirement for the motion picture. Satisfying the mandatory deposit requirement alone does not provide the benefits of copyright registration.

THE MOTION PICTURE COLLECTION AT THE LIBRARY OF CONGRESS

The Library of Congress is the nation's central collection of books, recordings, photographs, maps, audiovisual works, and other research materials. Many of the Library's acquisitions are obtained through copyright deposits. The material acquired by this means is critical to the Library's recognized success in maintaining superior and comprehensive collections.

Motion pictures form an essential part of the Library's holdings. As feature films, television programs, videos, and other audiovisual media become increasingly popular as a means of communication, education, and entertainment in our society, they also form a greater part of our historical record. The preservation facilities and bibliographic control provided by the Library ensure that many of these works will be available to future generations.

MOTION PICTURES FIRST PUBLISHED BEFORE 1978

The current copyright status of motion pictures first published before 1978 depends in part on the provisions of the 1909 Copyright Act. These provisions governed the past application of the notice requirement, the deposit requirement, and certain information in the registration record.

Copyright Notice

For a work first published before 1978, copyright was secured if all published copies bore a copyright notice in the proper form and position. The elements of the notice generally are 1) the symbol © (the letter C in a circle), the word "copyright," or the abbreviation "Copr."; 2) the year in which copyright was secured; and 3) the name of the owner of copyright at the time of publication. If published copies did not bear the required notice, copyright was lost and could not be restored. The absence of a year date in the notice for motion pictures published before 1978 would not result in the loss of copyright. If a year date is included, however, it should be correct.

Under a 1994 amendment to the U.S. copyright law pursuant to enactment of the Uruguay Round Agreements Act (URAA), copyright in certain foreign works that had previously been in the public domain (including those that had entered the public domain because of publication without the required notice) was restored as of January 1, 1996. Works whose copyright has been restored may be registered on Form GATT. See Circular 38b, "Highlights of Copyright Amendments Contained in the Uruguay Round Agreements Act," for more information.

Term of Copyright

Works first published with notice before 1978 had a 28-year initial term of copyright and a 67-year renewal term. Legislation enacted in 1992 made renewal of the second term automatic for works copyrighted between January 1, 1964, and December 31, 1977. However, there are benefits that derive from making a renewal registration during the 28th year of the original term. See Circular 15, "Renewal of Copyright," for more information.

Deposit Requirement

To register a claim in a motion picture first published before 1978, you should deposit **one copy of the work as first published**, that is, one of the first prints or tapes made from the master and distributed. If it is impossible to send such a copy, you may request special relief from the requirement (see the previous section on **"Special Relief"**). In this case, you should include with the substitute copy a letter confirming that the copy is identical to the copies as first published, **including the copyright notice**. In considering a special relief request, the Copyright Office may require more information about the facts of first publication.

Registration Record

The application for a work first published before 1978 must name as claimant the person or organization that was the owner of copyright **at the time of first publication**. This name should agree with the name that appears in the copyright notice.

EFFECTIVE DATE OF REGISTRATION

A copyright registration is effective on the date the Copyright Office receives all the required elements in acceptable form, regardless of how long it then takes to process the application and mail the certificate of registration. The time the Copyright Office requires to process an application varies, depending on the amount of material the Office is receiving and the personnel available. Additionally, it may take several days for mailed material to reach the Copyright Office and for the certificate of registration to reach the recipient. If you apply for copyright registration, you will **not** receive an acknowledgment that your application has been received (the Office receives more than 600,000 applications annually), but you can expect:

- a letter or telephone call from a Copyright Office staff member if further information is needed
- a certificate of registration to indicate the work has been registered
- if registration cannot be made, a letter explaining why it has been refused

If you want to know when the Copyright Office receives your material, send it by registered or certified mail and request a return receipt from the post office.

Allow 4-6 weeks for the return of your receipt.

Circular 22 (Excerpts)—How to Search the Copyright Office

Methods of Approaching a Copyright Investigation

There are several ways to investigate whether a work is under copyright protection and, if so, the facts of the copyright. These are the main ones:

1. Examine a copy of the work for such elements as a copyright notice, place and date of publication, author, and publisher. If the work is a sound recording, examine the disk, tape cartridge, or cassette in which the recorded sound is fixed, or the album cover, sleeve, or container in which the recording is sold.

2. Make a search of the Copyright Office catalogs and other records.

3. Have the Copyright Office make a search for you.

A Few Words of Caution About Copyright Investigations

Copyright investigations often involve more than one of these methods. Even if you follow all three approaches, the results may not be conclusive. Moreover, as explained in this circular, the changes brought about under the Copyright Act of 1976, the Berne Convention Implementation Act of 1988, the Copyright Renewal Act of 1992, and the Sonny Bono Copyright Term Extension Act of 1998 must be considered when investigating the copyright status of a work.

This circular offers some practical guidance on what to look for if you are making a copyright investigation. It is important to realize, however, that this circular contains only general information and that there are a number of exceptions to the principles outlined here. In many cases it is important to consult with a copyright attorney before reaching any conclusions regarding the copyright status of a work.

How to Search Copyright Office Catalogs and Records

Catalog of Copyright Entries

The Copyright Office published the *Catalog of Copyright Entries* (CCE) in printed format from 1891 through 1978. From 1979 through 1982 the CCE was issued in microfiche format. The catalog was divided into parts according to the classes of works registered. Each CCE segment covered all registrations made during a particular period of time. Renewal registrations made from 1979 through 1982 are found in Section 8 of the catalog. Renewals prior to that time were generally listed at the end of the volume containing the class of work to which they pertained.

A number of libraries throughout the United States maintain copies of the CCE, and this may provide a good starting point if you wish to make a search yourself. There are some cases, however, in which a search of the CCE alone will not be sufficient to provide the needed information. For example:

- Because the CCE does not include entries for assignments or other recorded documents, it cannot be used for searches involving the ownership of rights.
- The CCE entry contains the essential facts concerning a registration, but it is not a verbatim transcript of the registration record. It does not contain the address of the copyright claimant.

Effective with registrations made since 1982 when the CCE was discontinued, the only method of searching outside the Library of Congress is by using the Internet to access the automated catalog. The automated catalog contains entries from 1978 to the present. Information for accessing the catalog via the Internet is provided below.

Individual Searches of Copyright Records

The Copyright Office is located in the Library of Congress James Madison Memorial Building, 101 Independence Avenue SE, Washington, D.C. 20559-6000.

Most Copyright Office records are open to public inspection and searching from 8:30 A.M. to 5 P.M., Eastern time, Monday through Friday, except federal holidays. The various records freely available to the public include an extensive card catalog, an automated catalog containing records from 1978 forward, record books, and microfilm records of assignments and related documents. Other records, including correspondence files and deposit copies, are not open to the public for searching. However, they may be inspected upon request and payment of a $80 per hour search fee.

If you wish to do your own searching in the Copyright Office files open to the public, you will be given assistance in locating the records you need and in learning procedures for searching. If the Copyright Office staff actually makes the search for you, a search fee must be charged. The search will not be done while you wait.

In addition, the following files dating from 1978 forward are now available over the Internet: COHM, which includes all material except serials and documents; COHD, which includes documents; and COHS, which includes serials.

The Internet site addresses for the Copyright Office files are:

World Wide Web: www.loc.gov/copyright

Telnet: locis.loc.gov

Access to LOCIS requires Telnet support. If your online service provider supports Telnet, you can connect to LOCIS through the World Wide Web or directly by using Telnet.

The Copyright Office does not offer search assistance to users on the Internet.

Searching by the Copyright Office

In General

Upon request, the Copyright Office staff will search its records at the statutory rate of $65 for each hour or fraction of an hour consumed. Based on the information you furnish, we will provide an estimate of the total search fee. If you decide to have the Office staff conduct the search, you should send the estimated amount with your request. The Office will then proceed with the search and send you a typewritten report or, if you prefer, an oral report by telephone. If you request an oral report, please provide a telephone number where you can be reached from 8:30 A.M. to 5 P.M., Eastern time.

Search reports can be certified on request for an extra fee of $65 per hour. Certified searches are most frequently requested to meet the evidentiary requirements of litigation.

Your request and any other correspondence should be addressed to:

> Library of Congress
> Copyright Office
> Reference and Bibliography Section, LM-451
> 101 Independence Avenue SE
> Washington, D.C. 20559-6000
> (202) 707-6850
> Fax: (202) 707-6859
> TTY: (202) 707-6737

What the Fee Does Not Cover

The search fee does **not** include the cost of additional certificates, photocopies of deposits, or copies of other Office records. For information concerning these services, request Circular 6, "Obtaining Access to and Copies of Copyright Office Records and Deposits."

Information Needed

The more detailed information you can furnish with your request, the less expensive the search will be. Please provide as much of the following information as possible:

- The title of the work, with any possible variants
- The names of the authors, including possible pseudonyms

- The name of the probable copyright owner, which may be the publisher or producer
- The approximate year when the work was published or registered
- The type of work involved (book, play, musical composition, sound recording, photograph, etc.)
- For a work originally published as a part of a periodical or collection, the title of that publication and any other information, such as the volume or issue number, to help identify it
- The registration number or any other copyright data

Motion pictures are often based on other works such as books or serialized contributions to periodicals or other composite works. **If you desire a search for an underlying work or for music from a motion picture, you must specifically request such a search. You must also identify the underlying works and music and furnish the specific titles, authors, and approximate dates of these works.**

Searches Involving Assignments and Other Documents Affecting Copyright Ownership

For the standard hourly search fee, the Copyright Office staff will search its indexes covering the records of assignments and other recorded documents concerning ownership of copyrights. The reports of searches in these cases will state the facts shown in the Office's indexes of the recorded documents but will offer no interpretation of the content of the documents or their legal effect.

Limitations on Searches

In determining whether or not to have a search made, you should keep the following points in mind:

No Special Lists

The Copyright Office does not maintain any listings of works by subject or any lists of works that are in the public domain.

Contributions Not Listed Separately in Copyright Office Records

Individual works such as stories, poems, articles, or musical compositions that were published as contributions to a copyrighted periodical or collection are usually not listed separately by title in our records.

No Comparisons

The Copyright Office does not search or compare copies of works to determine questions of possible infringement or to determine how much two or more versions of a work have in common.

Titles and Names Not Copyrightable

Copyright does not protect names and titles, and our records list many different works identified by the same or similar titles. Some brand names, trade names, slogans, and phrases may be entitled to protection under the general rules of law relating to unfair competition. They may also be entitled to registration under the provisions of the trademark laws. Questions about the trademark laws should be addressed to the Commissioner of Patents and Trademarks, Washington, D.C. 20231. Possible protection of names and titles under common law principles of unfair competition is a question of state law.

No Legal Advice

The Copyright Office cannot express any opinion as to the legal significance or effect of the facts included in a search report.

Some Words of Caution

Searches Not Always Conclusive

Searches of the Copyright Office catalogs and records are useful in helping to determine the copyright status of a work, but they cannot be regarded as conclusive in all cases. The complete absence of any information about a work in the Office records does not mean that the work is unprotected. The following are examples of cases in which information about a particular work may be incomplete or lacking entirely in the Copyright Office:

- Before 1978, unpublished works were entitled to protection under common law without the need of registration.
- Works published with notice prior to 1978 may be registered at any time within the first 28-year term.
- Works copyrighted between January 1, 1964, and December 31, 1977, are affected by the Copyright Renewal Act of 1992, which automatically extends the copyright term and makes renewal registrations optional.

- For works under copyright protection on or after January 1, 1978, registration may be made at any time during the term of protection. Although registration is not required as a condition of copyright protection, there are certain definite advantages to registration. For further information, request Circular 1, "Copyright Basics."

- Since searches are ordinarily limited to registrations that have already been cataloged, a search report may not cover recent registrations for which catalog records are not yet available.

- The information in the search request may not have been complete or specific enough to identify the work.

- The work may have been registered under a different title or as part of a larger work.

Protection in Foreign Countries

Even if you conclude that a work is in the public domain in the United States, this does not necessarily mean that you are free to use it in other countries. Every nation has its own laws governing the length and scope of copyright protection, and these are applicable to uses of the work within that nation's borders. Thus, the expiration or loss of copyright protection in the United States may still leave the work fully protected against unauthorized use in other countries.

WGA Registration Instructions (with photographs removed)

The Writers Guild's Registration Service (or Intellectual Property Registry) registers over 30,000 pieces of literary material each year, and is available to members and nonmembers alike.

Writers are invited to submit material to be archived by the Writers Guild to protect their work. For more information on this service, contact the Registration department at (323) 782-4500.

PURPOSE AND COVERAGE

The WGA Registration Service has been set up to assist writers in establishing the completion dates of particular pieces of their literary property written for the fields of radio, theatrical and television motion pictures, video cassettes/disks and interactive media.

Registration provides a dated record of the writer's claim to authorship of a particular literary material. If necessary a WGA employee may produce the material as evidence if legal or official Guild action is initiated.

The Registration Office does not make comparisons of registration deposits, nor does it give legal opinions, advice or confer any statutory protections.

Registration with the Guild does not protect titles.

PROCEDURE FOR DEPOSIT

- Materials may be submitted for registration in person or by mail.
- The Registration Office must receive:
  1. One (1) unbound, loose-leaf copy of material on standard $8\frac{1}{2}$" × 11" paper.
  2. Cover sheet with title of material and all writers' full legal names.
  3. Social security number (or foreign equivalent), return address and phone numbers of authors.
  4. Registration fee: WGAw and WGAe members, $10. Non-members, $20.
- When the material is received, it is sealed in an envelope and the date and time are recorded. **A numbered receipt is returned serving as the official documentation of registration and should be kept in a safe place.**
- Notice of registration shall consist of the following wording: REGISTERED WGAw No.＿＿ and be applied upon the title page.
- Member Stamp

At the time of registration, WGAw members may request that a maximum of two (2) copies of the material being registered be stamped with the legend "MEMBER WGAw." The stamp indicates only that one or more of the writers listed as an author on the title page was a WGAw member at the time the material was registered with the title page bearing the stamp. There is no additional fee for use of the stamp.

REGISTRABLE MATERIAL

- Registrable material includes scripts, treatments, synopses, outlines, written ideas specifically intended for radio, television and theatrical motion pictures, video cassettes/disks, and interactive media.

- The WGA Registration Office also accepts stageplays, novels and other books, short stories, poems, commercials, lyrics and drawings.

DURATION AND EXPIRATION

- Registration is valid for a term of five (5) years and may be renewed for an additional five (5) years at the current registration rate. Renewals will be accepted up to three months prior to the expiration of the original registration. A grace period will be extended allowing renewals as late as three months following the expiration of the original registration.

- **At the time of registration, or renewal, you authorize the WGA to destroy the material without further notice to you on the expiration of the first term of registration or any renewal period.**

ACCESS TO REGISTRATION INFORMATION

- Only the writers listed on the registration receipt may request confirmation of registration, the registration number, date of deposit, or any other information.

- The WGA will honor such written requests from writers regarding the registration of their own work(s) only if accompanied by photo identification. All verification or confirmation requests from a writer should contain as much specific information as possible, such as registration number, title of material, effective date, and social security number of writer, and may be submitted by facsimile, mail, or in person. The fax number for the Registration Service is (323) 782-4803.

ACCESS TO COPIES OF DEPOSITED MATERIAL

- Because the deposited material cannot be returned to the writer without defeating the purpose of registration, registered material may not be withdrawn. It is therefore important to always retain a separate copy of the material being registered.

- If a writer finds it necessary to obtain a copy of deposited material, duplicates may be purchased for the price of registration upon written request by one or more of the listed authors, identified by photo identification. In the event an author is deceased, proof of death and consent of the representative of the heirs and/or estate must be presented in order to obtain a copy of the material.

- Requests for duplication of deposited material must be submitted by 5 P.M. Thursday of any week. Duplicates will be available Tuesday of the following week.

- In no event, except under these provisions, shall any deposited material, copies of deposited material, or information regarding deposited material be provided unless an official guild action, court order, or other legal process has been served.

FREQUENTLY ASKED QUESTIONS

- **Does registration take the place of copyright?**

No. Any questions regarding copyright should be directed to the U.S. Copyright Office in Washington, D.C. at (800) 688-9889 or to an attorney specializing in that area of law. Copyright application forms are available to walk-in customers only.

- **Does registration with the Writers Guild protect titles?**

No.

- **Does registration help a writer become a member?**

No. Questions concerning the rules for admission to membership in the guild should be referred to the WGA's Membership department at (323) 782-4532.

- **Does registration help in determining writing credits?**

Generally, no. If there is a dispute as to authorship or sequencing of material by date, then registration may be relevant. Questions concerning the WGA credit determination procedures should be directed to the Credits department at (323) 782-4528.

REGISTRATION HOURS

9:30 A.M. to 5:30 P.M., Monday through Friday

WGAw, Registration Department

7000 West Third St.

Los Angeles, CA 90048

Information: (323) 782-4500

FAX: (323) 782-4803

WGA Home Page: www.wga.org

WGA Writing Credit Definitions

Excerpted from *Screen Credits Manual* (January 1999)

III. Guild Policy on Credits

A. DEFINITIONS

1. Writer

The term "writer" is defined in the Minimum Basic Agreement. In general, the term "writer" means a person employed by a Company to write literary material or a person from whom a Company purchased literary material who at the time of purchase was a "professional writer," as defined in the Minimum Basic Agreement.

For purposes of credit, a team of writers, as defined in the Screen Credits Manual Section I.B., is considered as one writer.

If literary material covered under the Minimum Basic Agreement is written by one member of a team, separate and apart from the work of the team, such literary material shall be considered separate from the literary material by the team for purposes of assessing contributions to the final shooting script. Therefore, such individual is eligible to receive writing credit as an individual writer and/or as a member of a team.

2. Literary Material

Literary material is written material and shall include stories, adaptations, treatments, original treatments, scenarios, continuities, teleplays, screenplays, dialogue, scripts, sketches, plots, outlines, narrative synopses, routines, and narrations, and, for use in the production of television film, formats.

3. Source Material

Source material is all material, other than story as hereinafter defined, upon which the story and/or screenplay is based.

This means that source material is material assigned to the writer which was previously published or exploited and upon which the writer's work is to be based (e.g., a novel, a produced play or series of published articles), or any other material written outside of the Guild's jurisdiction (e.g., literary material purchased from a non-professional writer). Illustrative examples of source material credits are: "From a Play by", "From a Novel by", "Based upon a Story by", "From a series of articles by", "Based upon a Screenplay by" or other appropriate wording indicating the form in which such source material is acquired. Research material is not considered source material.

4. Story

The term "story" means all writing covered by the provisions of the Minimum Basic Agreement representing a contribution "distinct from screenplay and consisting of basic narrative, idea, theme or outline indicating character development and action."

It is appropriate to award a "Story by" credit when: 1) the story was written under employment under Guild jurisdiction; 2) the story was purchased by a signatory company from a professional writer, as defined in the Minimum Basic Agreement; or 3) when the screenplay is based upon a sequel story written under the Guild's jurisdiction. If the story is based upon source material of a story nature, see "screen story" below.

5. Screen Story

Credit for story authorship in the form "Screen Story by" is appropriate when the screenplay is based upon source material and a story, as those terms are defined above, and the story is substantially new or different from the source material.

6. Screenplay

A screenplay consists of individual scenes and full dialogue, together with such prior treatment, basic adaptation, continuity, scenario and dialogue as shall be used in, and represent substantial contributions to the final script.

A "Screenplay by" credit is appropriate when there is source material of a story nature (with or without a "Screen Story" credit) or when the writer(s) entitled to "Story by" credit is different than the writer(s) entitled to "Screenplay by" credit.

7. "Written by"

The term "Written by" is used when the writer(s) is entitled to both the "Story by" credit and the "Screenplay by" credit.

This credit shall not be granted where there is source material of a story nature. However, biographical, newspaper and other factual sources may not necessarily deprive the writer of such credit.

8. "Narration Written by"

"Narration Written by" credit is appropriate where the major writing contribution to a motion picture is in the form of narration. The term "narration" means material (typically off-camera) to explain or relate sequence or action (excluding promos or trailers).

9. "Based on Characters Created by"

"Based on Characters Created by" is a writing credit given to the writer(s) entitled to separated rights in a theatrical or television motion picture on each theatrical sequel to such theatrical or television motion picture.

Where there are no separated rights, "Based on Characters Created by" may be accorded to the author of source material upon which a sequel is based.

10. "Adaptation by"

This credit is appropriate in certain unusual cases where a writer shapes the direction of screenplay construction without qualifying for "Screenplay by" credit. In those special cases, and only as a result of arbitration, the "Adaptation by" credit may be used.

B. RULES FOR DETERMINING CREDIT

In determining relative contribution, the relevant factors shall be what material was actually used, not the Arbitration Committee's personal preference of one script over another.

. . .

Screen credit for screenplay will not be shared by more than two writers, except that in unusual cases, and solely as the result of arbitration, the names of three writers or the names of writers constituting two writing teams may be used. The limitation on the number of writers applies to all feature length photoplays except episodic pictures and revues.

. . .

C. PRODUCTION EXECUTIVES

The term "production executives" includes individuals who receive credit as the director or in any producer capacity. The following rules govern writing credits of production executives who also perform writing services when there are other writers involved on the same project.

1. Automatic Arbitration Provisions
Schedule A of the Minimum Basic Agreement provides:

"Unless the story and/or screenplay writing is done entirely without any other writer, no designation of tentative story or screenplay credit to a production executive shall become final or effective unless approved by a credit arbitration as herein provided, in accordance with the Guild rules for determination of such credit."

2. Notice Requirements
If a production executive intends to claim credit as a team on any literary material with a writer(s) who is not a production executive, he/she must, at the time when such team writing begins, have signified such claim in writing to the Guild and to the writer(s) with whom he/she claims to have worked as a team. Failure to comply with the above will preclude such production executive from claiming co-authorship of the literary material in question, and such literary material shall be attributed to the other writer.

. . .

D. REMAKES

In the case of remakes, any writer who has received writing credit under the Guild's jurisdiction in connection with a prior version of the motion picture is a participating writer on the remake. As such, those prior writers are entitled to participate in the credit determination process and are eligible to receive writing credit pursuant to the rules for determining writing credits. The final shooting script written by a prior writer(s) shall be considered literary material.

If under the "Rules for Determining Writing Credits" (Section III.B.) the Arbitration Committee determines that such prior writer(s) is not entitled to receive writing credit, the Arbitration Committee may, within its discretion, accord such prior writer(s) a credit in the nature of a source material credit, such as "Based on a Screenplay by. . . ."

However, the rules do not preclude a prior writer(s) from receiving both writing credit and a credit in the nature of a source material credit at the discretion of the Arbitration Committee.

Remakes shall be considered non-original screenplays under Section III.B.4.b.(2) of this Manual.

E. WITHDRAWAL FROM CREDIT

Prior to the time a credit question has been submitted to arbitration, a writer may withdraw from screen writing credit for personal cause, such as violation of his/her principles or mutilation of material he/she has written. If the other writer-contributors do not agree, the question shall be referred to arbitration. The Arbitration Committee in such cases shall base its determination on whether there is such personal cause.

After screen credits have been determined by arbitration, a writer may not withdraw his/her name from screenplay credit. He/she may, however, by notification to the Guild, withdraw from any other form of credit.

Withdrawal from writing credit will result in loss of any and all rights accruing from receipt of writing credit. Use of a pseudonym rather than withdrawing from credit will not result in such a forfeiture. . . .

Sample Contract

Filmmaker's contract to hire a producer: The following agreement provides a general outline to the types of issues that a filmmaker should address in a contract with any of the primary participants in the production company. The contract is written between the production company and the producer, but it is explicitly stated that the production company is owned by the filmmaker who plans to serve as both writer and director on the project. The contract provides a sample for the types of credit, control, and compensation issues that need to be addressed between the filmmaker and every one of the professional elements that go into the making of the film.

PRODUCER AGREEMENT

THIS AGREEMENT is made and entered into as of the date first ascribed below, by and between XYZ Film Company, LLC, 1234 Main Street, Hollywood, California 90210 ("Company") and John Doe, an individual, 5678 W. 46th St., New York, NY 10021 ("Producer"), with reference to the following facts:

Company is a wholly-owned limited liability company owned by Jane Roe ("Writer/Director").

Company has or will acquire rights to a screenplay to be written and directed by Writer/Director and desires to make such screenplay into a motion picture (the "Picture"); and

Producer has extensive professional experiences as a line producer and producer of feature motion pictures.

NOW THEREFORE, In consideration of the mutual covenants, conditions and undertakings hereinafter set forth, the parties hereto agree as follows:

1. **Services Provided.** Company hereby employs the services of Producer, and Producer hereby accepts such employment, for the purpose of serving as producer and line producer of the Picture, for the period of [three] weeks of pre-production, [five] weeks of principal photography on an exclusive basis, and such post production as is reasonably necessary for completion of the Picture on a non-exclusive, but first-priority basis. Each week shall include six working days. The Producer will provide such services as are generally performed by producers including his service coordinating the creative, financial, technological and administrative process throughout the term of this agreement, subject to the direction and control of Company and such other contracts as Company shall enter with other parties.

2. **Term.** The term of this Agreement shall commence on the date hereof and shall continue thereafter until Producer has fully completed all services required hereunder, unless sooner terminated in accordance with the provisions of this Agreement.

3. **Credit.** Provided Producer completes all services required hereunder and the Picture is completed by Company, then Producer shall receive credit on the screen, in motion picture trailers, and in paid print advertising issued by Company and under Company's control which is at least 10 inches or larger. The credit shall be "Produced by John Doe." On the screen such credit shall be displayed above or before the title of the Picture in a size of type not less than *fifty percent (50%)* of the size of type used to display the title of the Picture. At its sole discretion, Company may assign "Produced by" credit to one or more additional persons in addition to Producer in the event Company determines such other person or persons provided substantial producer services in addition to Producer. No casual or inadvertent failure to comply with the provisions of this clause shall be deemed to be a breach of this Agreement by Company. Producer shall notify Company of any breach of this paragraph, after which Company shall take reasonable steps to correct all new prints, copies and advertising on a prospective basis, but Company shall not be required to recall or alter any prints, copies or advertisements in production or dis-

tribution. No monetary damages are available for breach of Company's duties under this paragraph.

4. Consideration. In consideration for Producer's services hereunder and provided Producer is not in default hereunder, Company shall pay Producer as follows:

(a) Fixed Consideration. Producer shall receive a stipend of [\$100.00] per day actually worked during pre-production and principal photography, not to exceed [Forty-Eight Hundred (\$4,800.00)] Dollars. The payment shall be paid on a weekly basis.

(b) Net Profits. If Company produces the Picture, Producer shall receive an amount equal to [ten percent (10%)] of one hundred percent (100%) of Net Profits in the Gross Receipts of the Company in the Picture or [One Hundred Thousand (\$100,000)] Dollars, whichever is lower.

(i) Gross Receipts means all income, if any, actually received by Company from the sale, exhibition, or distribution of the Picture in theatres, video/DVD or similar format, broadcast television, satellite, cable exhibition, or any other method of exhibition, display or performance now known or hereafter created. Gross Receipts does not include income from any other source related to the Picture, including without limitation, income derived from sale of sequel, prequel, or remake rights, publishing interests such as novelizations, comic books, etc., sales of the screenplay, "making of" or other related projects, or any other spin-offs or related Company projects or activities.

(ii) The term Net Profits shall mean the Gross Receipts, less the deductions of all Company expenses of every kind related to the Picture. Without limiting the foregoing, the deductions shall include all costs, charges and expenses paid or incurred in connection with the preparation, production, completion and delivery of the Picture, deferred compensation, charges for any services, union or trade obligations, interest expenses, obligations to any completion guarantor, legal and accounting charges, the cost of all material, services, facilities, labor, insurance, taxes (other than income, franchise and like taxes), copyright royalties attributable to the Picture for music, artwork, script or other, judgments, marketing and promotional expenses, distribution fees, recoveries, settlements, losses, costs and expenses, including reasonable attorney's fees, sustained or incurred by Company in connection with the Picture or anything used therein and in connection with the production thereof. Company shall pay Producer twice annually all amounts due hereunder for all monies accrued during the proceeding six-month period, not later than forty-five (45) days following the end of each such period.

(c) Reimbursements. Producer shall be reimbursed for all reasonable advances or expenses incurred in the production of the Picture, such as for location scouting, equipment rental and the like, provided such expenses have been approved by Company in advance and Producer provides adequate documentation and receipts of the expense.

5. **Authority.** Company shall coordinate with Producer throughout the production to the greatest extent practicable throughout production; provided however, Company reserves final approval of all essential production elements including without limitation, script, budget, casting, locations, and film editing. Subject to direction of Company, Producer shall comply with all contractual and union and guild obligations and Company requirements.

6. **Termination.**

(a) This Agreement may be terminated by Company at any time, with or without cause. If Company elects to terminate this Agreement and Producer is not in default hereunder, Company shall pay Producer his accrued fixed compensation and a pro rata proportion of the contingent compensation. (By way of example, if Producer is terminated after twelve days, he will receive 12/48 of his contingent compensation, equal to 25% of 10%, meaning 2.5% of the Net Profits.) The costs of additional producer(s) shall be added to the cost of production. In the event Company determines Producer has materially breached his obligations hereunder, no contingent compensation shall be paid.

(b) This Agreement may be terminated by Producer upon seven days' advanced written notice. Unless otherwise agreed in writing by the parties, in the event Producer terminates this Agreement, he shall receive only his accrued fixed compensation, but shall not be eligible for any contingent compensation.

7. **Work Made for Hire.** Company shall own the copyright in the Picture without any claim by Producer. Producer is employed as on a work made for hire as a specially commissioned audiovisual or motion picture work and acknowledges that the copyright in the Picture shall vest exclusively in Company as author.

(a) The Picture shall be registered for copyright in Production Company's name both in the United States and elsewhere.

(b) To the extent Producer has created any copyrighted elements incorporated into the Picture and such work made for hire provision is not recognized by the jurisdiction, Producer hereby assigns all rights or the maximum rights allowed under that jurisdiction's laws to Company, including without limitation Rental Lending Rights if recognized, rights to enforce any claim of attribution and integrity, or rights to exploit any interest in the Picture in any media now known or hereafter developed.

8. Unique Services. It is hereby agreed and understood that Producer's services to be furnished hereunder are special, extraordinary, unique, and not replaceable, and that there is no adequate remedy at law for breach of this contract by Producer.

(a) Company shall be entitled to both legal and equitable remedies as may be available, including both injunctive relief and damages. Company may elect not to submit to arbitration for the purpose of seeking emergency, preliminary or temporary injunctive relief.

(b) Producer's services shall be in such time, place, and manner as Company may reasonably direct in accordance with customary motion picture industry practice. Such services shall be rendered in an artistic, conscientious, efficient and punctual manner to the best of Producer's ability to adhere to the budget and shooting schedule.

(c) Producer grants to Company the perpetual non-exclusive right to use and license others to use Producer's name, biography and reproductions of Producer's physical likeness and voice in connection with the production, exhibition, advertising, promotion or other exploitation of the Picture and all subsidiary and ancillary rights therein and thereto; provided, however, Company shall not use or authorize the use of Producer's name or likeness as a direct endorsement of any product or service without Producer's prior consent.

9. Resolution of Disputes. ANY AND ALL DISPUTES HEREUNDER SHALL BE RESOLVED BY ARBITRATION OR REFERENCE. ANY PARTY HERETO ELECTING TO COMMENCE AN ACTION SHALL GIVE WRITTEN NOTICE TO THE OTHER PARTY HERETO. THEREUPON, IF ARBITRATION IS SELECTED BY THE PARTY COMMENCING THE ACTION, THE CLAIM ("ARBITRATION MATTER") SHALL BE SETTLED BY ARBITRATION IN ACCORDANCE WITH THE THEN RULES OF THE AMERICAN ARBITRATION ASSOCIATION ("AAA"). The arbitrator or the referee shall diligently pursue determination of any Arbitration under consideration and shall render a decision within one hundred twenty (120) days after the arbitrator or referee is selected. The determination of the arbitrator on all matters referred to it hereunder shall be final and binding on the parties hereto. The award of such arbitrator may be confirmed or enforced in any court of competent jurisdiction. The referee, arbitrator or its designee shall have full access to such records and physical facilities of the parties hereto as may be required. The costs and expenses of the referee or arbitrator, and the attorneys' fees and costs of each of the parties incurred in such, shall be apportioned between the parties by such arbitrator, as the case may be, based upon such arbitrator's determination of the merits of their respective positions.

10. **Confidentiality.** Publicity. Company shall have the exclusive right to issue and to license others to issue advertising and publicity with respect to the Picture, and Producer shall not circulate, publish or otherwise disseminate any such advertising or publicity without Company's prior written consent.

11. **Assignment.** Producer agrees that Company shall have the right to assign, license, delegate, lend or otherwise transfer all or any part of its rights or duties under this Agreement at any time to any person. Producer acknowledges that the personal services to be rendered by Producer hereunder are of the essence of this Agreement and agrees that he shall not assign this Agreement, in whole of in part, to any person, and that any purported assignment or delegation of duties by Producer shall be null and void and of no force and effect whatsoever. This Agreement shall inure to the benefit of Company's successors, assigns, licensees, grantees and associated, affiliated and subsidiary companies.

12. **No Obligation.** Company agrees to uses all reasonable efforts to cause the Picture to be produced, however, the parties recognize that the production of an independent motion picture is an inherently difficult undertaking. Company is under no obligation to produce the Picture hereunder. In the event Company abandons production of the Picture hereunder, Producer is entitled to such fixed compensation as had previously accrued and is not entitled to any additional compensation, damage or loss as a result of such failure to undertake or complete the Picture.

13. **Assurances.** Each party shall execute all documents and certificates and perform all acts deemed appropriate by the Company or required by this Agreement in connection with this Agreement and the production of the Picture.

14. **Complete Agreement.** This Agreement constitutes the complete and exclusive statement of the agreement among the parties with respect to the matters discussed herein and therein and it supersedes all prior written or oral statements among the parties, including any prior statement, warranty, or representation.

15. **Section Headings.** The section headings which appear throughout this Agreement are provided for convenience only and are not intended to define or limit the scope of this Agreement or the intent or subject matter of its provisions.

16. **Attorneys' Fees.** In the event any action or arbitration proceeding be instituted by a party to enforce any of the terms or conditions contained herein, the prevailing party in such action shall be entitled to such reasonable attorneys' fees, costs and expenses as may be fixed by the court or arbitrator.

17. **Applicable Law.** Each party agrees that all disputes arising under or in connection with this Agreement and any transactions contemplated by this Agreement shall be governed by the internal law, and not the law of conflicts, of the State of New Hampshire.

18. **Notices.** Any notice or other writing to be served upon either party in connection with this Agreement shall be in writing and shall be deemed completed when delivered to the address listed above.

19. **Amendments.** Any amendments, modifications, or alterations to this Agreement must be in writing and signed by all of the parties hereto.

20. **Severability.** Each provision of this Agreement is severable from the other provisions. If, for any reason, any provision of this Agreement is declared invalid or contrary to existing law, the inoperability of that provision shall have no effect on the remaining provisions of the Agreement which shall continue in full force and effect.

21. **Counterparts.** This Agreement may be executed in counterparts, each of which shall be deemed an original and all of which shall, when taken together, constitute a single document.

Dated _____

"Company"   "Producer"
XYZ Film Company, LLC   John Doe

By: _____   By: _____

Title: _____   John Doe

Contact Listings

Unions and Associations

The Producers Guild of America
6363 Sunset Blvd., 9th Floor
Hollywood, CA 90028
(323) 960-2590
E-mail: membership@producers
   guild.org
www.producersguild.org

Writers Guild of America, West
7000 W. Third St.
Los Angeles, CA 90048
(323) 951-4000
(800) 548-4532
www.wga.org

Directors Guild of America
7920 Sunset Blvd.
Los Angeles, CA 90046
www.dga.org

Screen Actors Guild
5757 Wilshire Blvd., 8th Floor
Los Angeles, CA 90036
(323) 549-6828
www.sag.org

**International Alliance of
   Theatrical Stage Employees
   (IATSE)**
1515 Broadway, Suite 601
New York, NY 10036
(212) 730-1770
www.iatse.lm.com

Breakdown Services

Breakdown Services, Ltd.
1120 S. Robertson Blvd.
Los Angeles, CA 90035
(310) 276-9166
New York: (212) 869-2003
Vancouver: (604) 943-7100
www.breakdownservices.com

Music Clearance Resources

**National Music Publishers'
    Association, Inc. (NMPA)**
475 Park Avenue South, 29th Floor
New York, NY 10016-6901
(646) 742-1651
FAX: (646) 742-1779

The Harry Fox Agency
711 Third Ave.
New York, NY 10017
(212) 370-5330
FAX: (212) 953-2384
Los Angeles: (323) 466-3861
Nashville: (615) 242-4173
www.nmpa.org

Clearing House, Ltd.
849 S. Broadway
Los Angeles, CA 90014
(213) 624-3947
FAX: (213) 624-3827

BZ Rights and Permissions, Inc.
125 W. 72nd St.
New York, NY 10023
(212) 580-0615
FAX: (212) 769-9224

The Music Report
Adam W. Wolf
1120 S. Robertson Blvd.
Los Angeles, CA 90035
(310) 276-9166
E-mail: adamw@breakdownservices.
    com

Film Commissions

California Film Commission
7080 Hollywood Blvd., Suite 900
Hollywood, CA 90028
(800) 858-4749
(323) 860-2960
FAX: (323) 860-2972
E-mail: filmca@commerce.ca.gov
commerce.ca.gov/film

EIDC—LA Film Office
7083 Hollywood Blvd., 5th floor
Hollywood, CA 90028
(323) 957-1000
FAX: (323) 463-0613
Permit FAX: (323) 962-4966
www.eidc.com

The Mayor's Office of Film,
   Theatre and Broadcasting
1697 Broadway, #602
New York, NY 10019
(212) 489-6710
(212) 307-6237
www.ci.nyc.ny.us/html/filmcom/
   home.html#

British Film Office (LA Office)
11766 Wilshire Blvd., Suite 440
Los Angeles, CA 90025
(310) 996-3027
FAX: (310) 481-2965
E-mail: film@britfilmusa.com
www.britfilmusa.com

Financial Services

Lewis Horwitz Organization
1840 Century Park East, Suite 1000
Los Angeles, CA 90067
(310) 275-7171
FAX: (310) 275-8055
E-mail: horwitz@lewishorwitz.com

Comerica Entertainment Industries
9920 S. La Cienega Blvd., Suite 1010
Inglewood, CA 90301
(310) 417-5449
FAX: (310) 417-5644

American Film Marketing
   Association
10850 Wilshire Blvd., 9th Floor
Los Angeles, CA 90024-4321
(310) 446-1000
FAX: (310) 446-1600
E-mail: info@afma.com
www.afma.com

Association for Independent
   Video and Filmmakers
(Foundation for Independent Video
   and Film)
304 Hudson St., 6th floor
New York, NY 10013
(212) 807-1400
FAX: (212) 463-8519
www.aivf.org

Completion Bond

Motion Picture Bond Company
1801 Avenue of the Stars, Suite 1010
Los Angeles, CA, 90067
(310) 551-0371

Other Trade Associations

Bookstores

Film and Theatrical Bookstores
Drama Book Shops
723 7th Ave.
New York, NY 10019
(212) 944-0595

Samuel French Theatre and Film Book Shops
7623 W. Sunset Blvd.
Los Angeles, CA 90046
(213) 876-0570

Samuel French Bookstore
11963 Ventura Blvd.
Studio City, CA 91604
(818) 762-0535

Larry Edmunds Bookstore
6644 Hollywood Blvd.
Hollywood, CA 90028
(213) 463-3273

Motion Picture Association of America (MPAA)
15503 Ventura Blvd.
Encino, CA 91436
(818) 995-6600

AIVF Guide to Int'l Film and Video Festivals
625 Broadway, 9th Floor
New York, NY 10012
(212) 473-3400

Motion Picture Distributors— The Majors

Universal Studios
10 Universal City Plaza, Suite 3200
Universal City, CA 91608
www.universalpictures.com

Warner Bros.
4000 Warner Blvd.
Burbank, CA 91522
www.movies.warnerbros.com

Paramount Pictures Corporation
5555 Melrose Ave.
Los Angeles, CA 90038
(323) 956-5000
www.paramount.com/motion
  pictures/index.html

Twentieth Century Fox Film Corp
10201 W. Pico Blvd.
Los Angeles, CA 90064
(310) 369-1000
www.foxmovies.com

Sony Pictures Entertainment
10202 W. Washington Blvd.
Culver City, CA 90232
(310) 244-6926
www.spe.sony.com/movies

Walt Disney Company
500 S. Buena Vista St.
Burbank, CA 91521
disney.go.com

MGM United Artists
2450 Broad Way
Santa Monica, CA 90401
(310) 449-3000
www.mgmua.com

Significant Independent Producers

Artisan Pictures, Inc.
2700 Colorado Ave.
Santa Monica, CA 90404
(310) 449-9200
www.artisanent.com

HBO Enterprises
1100 Avenue of the Americas
New York, NY 10036
(212) 512-1000

Lions Gate Films International
4553 Glencoe Ave., Suite 200
Marina del Rey, CA 90292
(310) 314-2000

Overseas Filmgroup
Division of First Look Media
8800 Sunset Blvd., Suite 302
Los Angeles, CA 90069
(310) 855-1199

Pathe International
Kent House, Market Place
London, W1N 8AR
United Kingdom
44-207-323-5151
FAX: 44-207-631-3568
www.pathe.com

Village Roadshow Pictures, Ltd.
3400 Riverside Dr., Suite 900
Burbank CA 91505
(818) 260 6070
FAX: (818) 260 6041
E-mail: mlake@vrpe.com
www.village.com.au

Selected Bibliography

THE TEXT INCLUDES a good deal of discussion regarding contract provisions, however, it does not contain actual form contracts. The number of contracts necessary would fill an entire second volume, and such forms are often used without properly consulting an attorney regarding the correct use of their content. For attorneys and others looking for examples of contracts, the following books should provide ample information.

Contracts and Form Agreements

Entertainment Industry Contracts (New York: Matthew Bender and Company, Inc., Looseleaf)

Kohn, Al, and Bob Kohn. *Kohn on Music Licensing*, 2nd ed. (New York: Aspen Law and Business, 1999)

Lindey, Alexander. *Lindey on Entertainment, Publishing, and the Arts: Agreements and the Law* (Deerfield, IL: Clark Boardman Co., Looseleaf)

Litwak, Mark. *Contracts for the Film and Television Industry* (Los Angeles: Silman-James Press, 1998)

Simensky, Melvin, and Thomas D. Selz. *Entertainment, Document Supplement* (New York: Matthew Bender, 1998)

Other Law Related Books of Interest

Baumgarten, Paul A., Donald Farber, and Mark Fleischer. *Producing, Financing, and Distributing Film: A Comprehensive Legal and Business Guide* (New York: Limelight Editions, 1992)

Donaldson, Michael. *Clearance and Copyright* (Los Angeles: Silman-James Press, 1996)

Goodell, Gregory. *Independent Feature Film Production* (New York: St. Martins Press, 1982) (This is a wonderfully thoughtful text and, though out of print, well worth utilizing as a solid reference.)

Moore, Schuyler M. *The Biz: The Basic Business, Legal and Financial Aspects of the Film Industry* (Los Angeles: Silman-James Press, 2000)

Samuels, Edward. *The Illustrated Story of Copyright* (New York: St. Martins Press, 2000)

Nonlegal Reference Books

Collier, Maxie. *The iFilm Digital Video Filmmaker's Handbook* (Los Angeles: Lone Eagle Publishing, 2001)

Langer, Adam. *The Film Festival Guide* (Chicago, IL: Chicago Review Press, 2000)

Long, Ben, and Sonja Schenk. *The Digital Filmmaking Handbook* (Hingham, MA: Charles River Media, 2000)

Maier, Robert. *Location Scouting and Management Handbook* (Wodburn, MA: Focal Press, 1994)

Rosen, David. *Off Hollywood—The Making and Marketing of American Specialty Films.* (New York: Independent Feature Project and Sundance Institute, 1987)

Sales, John. *Thinking in Pictures* (Boston: Houghton Mifflin, 1987)

End Notes

Introduction

1 www.live-at.com provides a useful point to begin searching online independent film services.

Part 1 Making A Film Company To Make A Movie

1. The Film Concept

1 *Night on Earth* written and directed by Jim Jarmusch.

2 "Rights" is a generic term for an interest, ownership, or control in the material. Copyright is known as a "bundle of rights" because the rights to perform, publish, sell, or modify are all separate rights and may be held by different people. As is described below, to get permission to use material, the permission must come from the person who owns such a right.

3 17 U.S.C. § 101 et. seq. (2000).

4 17 U.S.C.A. § 106 (2000). In the case of sound recordings, copyright holders also have the exclusive right to perform the work publicly by means of a digital audio transmission. Id.

5 Id. at § 101.

6 *Stewart v. Abend*, 495 U.S. 207 (1990).

7 *Russell v. Price*, 612 F.2d 1123, 1128 (9th Cir. 1979).

8 17 U.S.C.A. at § 204.

9 The 1976 Copyright Act extended many existing copyrights to a period of 75 years from the date of original creation. 17 U.S.C. § 304(b). But note that works whose copyright had expired before 1976 remain in the public domain. The rules for each piece of material may vary greatly, so it is vital that the copyright of an older work be reviewed before it is assumed that the work is in the public domain.

10 See *Russel v. Price*, 612 F.2d 1123, 1124 (9th Cir. 1979). Even here, however, the possibility exists that copyright protection still exists in some parts of Europe because Germany had provided a longer copyright term than other European nations. Under the rules of the European Commission, the greatest protection in any European Commission country must be extended to the citizens of every other member. As a result, it may be that works that had been in the public domain in England now have additional copyright protection.

11 This may not include sound recordings in piano rolls or records. Federal copyright protection did not exist for these works until 1972, and as a result, the sound recordings may not yet have lost their protection.

12 17 U.S.C. § 102. (2000). There are listed eight categories of works subject to copyright protection.

    (1) literary works;
    (2) musical works, including any accompanying words;
    (3) dramatic works, including accompanying music;
    (4) pantomimes and choreographic works;
    (5) pictorial, graphic, and sculptural works;
    (6) motion pictures and other audiovisual works;
    (7) sound recordings; and
    (8) architectural works.

13 This may not be true of published works that were first published prior to January 1, 1978. The filmmaker must be careful, however, not to assume that a work is no longer protected by copyright. The lack of a copyright symbol is not adequate to suggest that even a work published before 1978 is free to be used.

14 Id. at § 102(b) ("In no case does copyright protection for an original work of authorship extend to any idea, procedure, process, system, method of operation, concept, principle, or discovery, regardless of the form in which it is described, explained, illustrated, or embodied in such work.").

15 *Hoehling v. Universal City Studios, Inc.*, 618 F.2d 972 (2nd Cir. 1980), cert. denied, 449 U.S. 841 (1980).

16 See *Davies v. Krasna*, 54 Cal. Rptr. 37 (Cal. Ct. App. 1966), superceded on other grounds, 14 Cal. 3d 502 (1975).

17 Restatement (Second) Torts § 559 (1977). Under California law, "libel is a false and unprivileged publication by writing . . . which exposes any person to hatred, contempt, ridicule, or obloquy, or which causes him to be shunned or avoided, or which has a tendency to injure him in his occupation." Cal. Civ. Code § 45 (West 1999).

18 *New York Times Co. v. Sullivan*, 376 U.S. 254, 279–80 (1964).

19 *Gertz v. Robert Welch, Inc.*, 418 U.S. 323, 344, (1974).

20 *Davis v. Costa-Gavras*, 654 F. Supp. 653, 655 (S.D.N.Y. 1987).

21 *James v. San Jose Mercury News, Inc.*, 17 Cal. App. 4th 1, 10 (Cal. App. 6th Dist. 1993), quoting *Moseian v. McClatchy Newspapers*, 205 Cal. App. 3d 597, 608–09 (Cal. App. 5th Dist. 1988), cert. denied 490 U.S. 1066 (1989).

22 *Moseian v. McClatchy Newspapers*, 205 Cal. App. 3d 597, 608-09 (Cal. App. 5th Dist. 1988), cert. denied 490 U.S. 1066 (1989).

23 *Masson v. New Yorker Magazine*, 501 U.S. 496, 522 (1991).

24 *Springer v. Viking Press*, 90 A.D.2d 315, 457 N.Y.S.2nd 246 (1st Dept. 1982) aff'd, 60 N.Y.2nd 916, 470 N.Y.S.2d 579 (1983).

25 Restatement (Second) Torts, § 652E (1977).

26 *Gertz v. Robert Welch, Inc.*, 418 U.S. 323 (1974).

27 See Prosser, *Law of Torts*, pp. 802–804 (1971). "The right to withdraw from the public gaze at such times as a person may see fit, when his presence in public is not demanded by any rule of law is also embraced within the right of personal liberty." *Pavesich v. New England Life Ins. Co*, 122 Ga. 190, 196, 50 S.E. 68, 70 (1905).

28 Restatement (Second) Torts § 625B (1977) ("One who intentionally intrudes, physically or otherwise, upon the solitude or seclusion of another or his private affairs or concerns, is subject to liability to the other for invasion of his privacy, if the intrusion would be highly offensive to a reasonable person.")

29 *Price v. Hal Roach Studios, Inc.*, 400 F.Supp. 836, 843 (S.D.N.Y. 1975).

30 *Zacchini v. Scripps-Howard Broadcasting Co.*, 433 U.S. 562 (1977). In this case, Zacchini—the human cannonball—was taped doing his entire 15-second act at the local fair. He successfully sued the television company that broadcast his act without paying him.

31 Cal. Civ. Code § 3344(a) (Deering 1999). The statute also provides for $750 in statutory fees and injunctive relief.

32 Similarly, the popcorn manufacturer would also be unable to stop the newspaper from using the photograph of Webster eating the popcorn.

33 *KNB Enters. v. Matthews*, 78 Cal. App. 4th 362, 368, 92 Cal. Rptr. 2d 713, 718 (2nd Dist. 2000) (holding use of models' photographs on subscription Web site constituted actionable violation of Cal. Civ. Code § 3344, not preempted by federal copyright laws).

34 Id.

35 U.S. Copyright Office, Circular 22 "How to Investigate the Copyright Status of a Work," www.loc.gov/copyright/circs/circ22.html.

36 The term generally used would be "exploit." Exploit has the correct connotation, because the filmmaker can do anything to the material the contract allows and the contract should be drafted to allow almost everything as well as nothing. Be careful not to treat the guerrilla film as if it can be made in a "kinder and gentler" fashion. The film project may be sold prior to filming and the filmmaker should have enough control over the material to satisfy a studio if one decided to buy out the project.

37 See *Desney v. Wilder*, 299 P.2d 257, 265 (Cal. 1966); *Buchwald v. Paramount Pictures*, 13 U.S.P.Q.3d 1497 (Cal. Super. Ct. 1990).

38 This book cannot begin to explain how to write or develop a quality screenplay. There are a number of successful books on screenplay format and content including *How to Write a Screenplay* by Sid Field and many others.

39 FL19, Dramatic Works: Scripts, Pantomimes and Choreography, www.loc.gov/copyright/fls/fl119.pdf.

40 Thomson & Thomson, Inc. available at www.thomson-thomson.com.

2. The Film Company

1 See 26 CFR 301.7701–3 (2001) (Classification of certain business entities.)

2 26 CFR 301.7701–3(a) (2001).

3 I.R.C. § 351 (2001).

3. Duties Of The Film Company

1 FSA 53. See also, *The Biz . . .* for a brief introduction to the application of the GAAP principles.

2 This story is captured in *Hearts of Darkness, a Filmmaker's Apocalypse* by Eleanor Coppola. A new, extended version of the film, *Apocalypse Now Redux*, has been released which restores the so-called "French Plantation Scene" to the film.

4. Financing The Film Project

1 One specific breakdown is as follows: 20 percent paid weekly during preproduction; 60 percent paid weekly during principal photography; 10 percent paid upon delivery of the rough cut; and 10 percent paid upon delivery of the completed picture. Baumgarten, Farber, and Fleischer, *Producing, Financing and Distributing Film*, 76 Limelight Editions (2nd ed. 1992).

2 The Association of Independent Video and Filmmakers provides an updated list of potential funding resources. It is available at www.aivf.org/info_services/funder_faq.html.

3 Contrast this with a home purchase money mortgage that may be nonrecourse against the buyers of the property in some states. If the loan was a second mortgage or line of credit, anti-deficiency laws will not apply.

4 *TSC Industries, Inc. v. Northway, Inc.*, 426 U.S. 438, 449 (1976); *Basic, Inc. v. Levinson*, 108 S. Ct. 978 (1988).

5 This is not apocryphal—copyright lasts seventy years past the life of the author, so management of the work must include some planning for the period after the lifespan of the author.

6 Proportional or pro rata payments would mean that each dollar earned is split by each group in proportion to the amount that person or group is entitled to receive. In the example above, $40 in income would be paid $15 to the investor and $25 to the group of parties entitled to deferred compensation.

7 Securities Act of 1933 § 4 (2), 15 U.S.C. § 77d(2) (2001).

8 Securities Act of 1933 § 3(a)(11), 15 U.S.C. § 77c(a)(11) (2001).

9 But § 10(b) of the Securities Exchange Act of 1934 would apply regarding any fraud or misrepresentation so long as an instrumentality of interstate commerce were used—something like a telephone, e-mail, or U.S. post.

10 Reg. D. § 501.

11 Treas. Reg. § 301.7701-2(c)(2)(i).

12 Treas. Reg. § 1.721-1(b)(1), the income should be based on the value of the service at the time provided.

13 See Rev. Proc. 93-27, 1993-2 C.B. 343, providing nontax treatment for profit participation or partnerships. Louis A. Mezzullo, Qualified Plans, Professional Organizations, Health Care, and Welfare Benefits, ALI-ABA COURSE OF STUDY MATERIALS, Vol. I (February 13–15, 1997).

14 See, I.R.C. § 721(a) and 707(a)(2).

Part 2 Filming The Movie—preproduction And Production

7. Assembling The Production Team

1 Available at www.wga.org/members_index.html.

2 Above the line participants are the stars and key personnel who are separately identified individually in the production budget. See Chapter 5, Section C, for a complete definition.

3 Available at sag.org/filmmakers.html.

4 For example, these services may be available from Entertainment Partners Home Page, www.ep-services.com, Media Services, www.media-services.com, and Web-Movie.com: Payroll_Services, www.webmovie.com.

5 D.R. Reiff and Associates, a New York based entertainment insurance company, provides a 20 percent discount for IFP members. Availble at www.reiffinsurance.com.

8. The Key Members Of The Independent Film Company

1 Producers Guild of America, *So you want to be a producer*, www.producersguild.org/want/. A detailed list of tasks is available at www.producersguild.org/want/.

2 One technique to salvage comic moments is to note where the cast laughs at the script during the first live reading. Often, the repetition that comes from working and reworking a scene can drain any humor out of the material. Reminders about where the humor once existed may help to keep the material fresh.

3 Public domain works are those that were once protected by copyright but have had their copyright expire. Works published before 1923 are in the public domain in the United States. Because films are distributed internationally, the copyright status must be determined under both U.S. law and the laws of other nations where the source work has been published.

4 DGA Basic Agreement § 7-101 available at www.dga.org/index2.php3.

5 DGA explanation of the Directors Guild of America Low-budget Agreements available at www.dga.org/index2.php3?chg=.

6 Encyclopedia Britannica, online at www.britannica.com.

7 www.breakdownservices.com.

8 Castnet.com, www.castnet.com/castdocs/castnetcastingdirectors.html. ("If you are an independent filmmaker or writer/director who is doing your own casting for a low-budget or student film, . . . Castnet offer[s] many other services that can help you cast your project, including electronic casting notices to actors and third-party talent searches.") Star Caster Network, a former competitor to both Breakdown Services, Ltd. and Castnet.com, has partnered with Breakdown Services, Ltd. and no longer operates independently.

9 www.backstage.com/backstage/index.jsp.

9. Equipment And Locations

1 Massachusetts Film Office, Film Production Guide, available at www.state.ma. us/film/Pguide/pg-wp.htm. Additional information available at the Firearms Records Bureau, Massachusetts Department of Public Safety, 200 Arlington St., Ste. 2200, Chelsea, MA 02150, 617-660-4780, Fax 617-660-4613.

2 The EIDC publishes an excellent guide for location issues. Entertainment Industry Development Corporation, *Introduction to Location Filming Introduction to Location Filming: Your Property a Star—A "How to" Guide from EIDC* available at eidc.com/Property.pdf.

Part 3 Selling The Movie—postproduction, Distribution, And Marketing

11. Music And Sound

1 See 15 U.S.C. § 115 (2001) (providing a statutory rate presently starting at $0.055 per song for each recording manufactured).

2 See Al Kohn and Bob Kohn, *Kohn on Music Licensing* 2nd ed., 1999. For the non-music lawyer, this is perhaps the most comprehensive and clear single volume available. The forms included in the book are explained fully and readily usable for the film licensing.

12. Postproduction

1 X is not an MPAA rating. It is a self-selected designation, typically associated with pornographic materials, but was intended originally to simply show that the material was not appropriate for minors.

13. Theatrical Distribution

1 See Adam Langer, *The Film Festival Guide* (Chicago Review Press, 2000). The Guide provides comprehensive information on festivals throughout the world, not just those in North America.